SHAKER FURNITURE MAKERS

Jerry V. Grant and Douglas R. Allen

PUBLISHED FOR HANCOCK SHAKER VILLAGE, INC., PITTSFIELD, MASSACHUSETTS

BY UNIVERSITY PRESS OF NEW ENGLAND, HANOVER AND LONDON

University Press of New England

Brandeis University	Clark University	Dartmouth College	University of Rhode Island	University of Vermont
Brown University	University of Connecticut	University of New Hampshire	Tufts University	

Printed in Japan

∞

Library of Congress Cataloging-in-Publication Data

Grant, Jerry V.
    Shaker furniture makers / Jerry V. Grant and Douglas R. Allen.
        p.   cm.
    Bibliography: p.
    Includes index.
    ISBN 0-87451-488-6
      1. Cabinetmakers, Shaker. 2. Cabinetmakers—United States—
Biography. 3. Furniture, Shaker. 4. Furniture—United States—
History—19th century. I. Allen, Douglas R. II. Hancock Shaker
Village. III. Title.   NK2407.G68   1989   749.214—dc19
[B]   89-5263
                                CIP

Published with the assistance of the Getty Grant Program

5 4 3 2 1

Contents

Foreword

The idea for this book came from Carl A. Weyerhaeuser, to whom it is lovingly dedicated. His interest in all things Shaker and the history of this sect, which he shared with his mother, Maud Moon Weyerhaeuser Sanborn, goes back to the mid-1940s and is carried on by his son Charles.

It is rare that three generations in a family are so committed to the same enduring interest. This devotion was manifest in Maud Sanborn's having the Shaker Meeting House in Shirley, Massachusetts, moved to Hancock in 1962, and in Carl and Charles's serving as trustees of Hancock Shaker Village for over twenty-five years, during which time they supported it with their interest and substance.

In 1972, the idea for this book was born when Carl Weyerhaeuser, admiring the sheen, color, and construction of a particularly interesting chair, said, "I wish I knew more about the Shaker craftsmen who made the furniture." The subject of Shaker furniture previously has not been treated solely from the point of view of its makers, and thus the challenge here has been to compose an intricate and original portrait of the human beings involved. This book will enrich our knowledge of the Shaker craftsmen who worked in twelve of the nineteen known Shaker communities.

This study has been a relentless labor of love by many people over a period of fifteen years. In acknowledging first our thanks to Carl, who thought of it and subsidized it, we also thank in his name the following people who contributed their scholarship, time, and effort to make the story complete:

Aviva Baal-Teshuva
Sister Mildred Barker
Tim Bookout
Priscilla J. Brewer
Mary Lou Conlin
Robert P. Emlen
Dorothy Filley
Katherine Finklepearl
Peter Hammell
Theodore Johnson
John Kassay
Robert F. W. Meader
Charles E. Muller
Julia Neal
Edward Nickels
John Harlow Ott
E. Ray Pearson
Elaine Piraino-Holevoet
Timothy D. Rieman
Paul J. Rocheleau

John Scherer
June Sprigg
Marjorie Steele
Richard Steinert
James C. Thomas
Helen Upton

It seems appropriate to quote Elisha Myrick, an Elder at the Harvard, Massachusetts, Shaker community: "As in material, so in the spiritual, what we sow, we shall reap. The quantity and quality depend on industry and cultivation."

Carl Weyerhaeuser's desire to have a more intimate knowledge of Shaker craftsmen has enriched the history of this revered sect and brings to us a deeper understanding of and empathy for an uncommonly industrious, practical, and gifted people.

Hancock Shaker Village, Inc.
September 1988

Amy Bess Miller

Preface: On Seeing Shaker Furniture

Admirers of Shaker furniture view it from different perspectives. Some acclaim its usefulness and praise its fine workmanship. Some take aesthetic pleasure in its distinctive shapes and proportions, in the tones and hues of its stained or painted finish or in the natural textures and colors of the wood itself. Others perceive the best examples of the furniture as prayerfully crafted expressions of the Shakers' religious faith. As we see it in our different lights, our personal responses to specific pieces vary, as do our responses to, say, individual paintings. One person admires with excitement a candlestand or desk, whereas a companion finds the same pieces only mildly interesting.

People also see Shaker furniture in a variety of settings. Visitors to Shaker communities have seen the furniture as it was being used in dining rooms, retiring rooms, or the kitchen of a dwelling house, or in a schoolroom, office, or workshop—perhaps after being shown around by a Shaker sister or brother. Their recollections of the furniture are enhanced by personal images—a Shaker sister, perhaps, kneading dough on a baker's table or knitting a child's sweater while sitting and talking in a rocking chair. One may also view the furniture in a museum collection, where, even though it may be housed in what was once a Shaker setting, it is now at an aesthetic distance from the living environment of a Shaker village. Gallery exhibits and books of photographs provide us with still different frames of reference; and regarding a piece of Shaker furniture in a private home or antique shop, amid a visual mix of "worldly" furniture and other artifacts,

provides another kind of experience. We find in each instance that the setting of the furniture in some measure shapes our reactions to it.

Our appreciation of the Shakers' furniture is affected by the context in which it is presented, but not all of the influences come directly from the physical setting. Photographs, for example, which for many of us provide an introduction to Shaker furniture, represent a physical environment, but at the same time may enhance certain aspects of the furniture—for instance, its form, line, and texture—while excluding another, such as color. The photographer-as-artist evokes new ways of seeing the furniture. An observer now sees it to a certain degree with the nuances of shadow and light, of form and feeling that were part of the photographer's vision.

In a similar way, researchers, writers, and curators also have enhanced our appreciation of Shaker furniture by placing it in an historical, social, or religious context. In the course of doing the research for this book we discovered that just as our impressions of the furniture had different resonances and meanings depending on whether we saw it in a museum or in a private home, in a photograph or in a Shaker community, so our appreciation of the furniture was influenced by the information we had about Shaker society. Our perception of the furniture was influenced as much by seeing it in the context of new information as by seeing it in a specific physical environment. Seeing the personalities of the furniture makers emerge during the writing of this book had this sort of influence, and we found ourselves drawn into an intensified understanding of their world and their work. We wanted to present Shaker furniture in a new context through our biographical portraits of prominent furniture makers—as part of the personal lives of the master craftsmen whose hands gave it beauty and purpose. We also wanted to learn more about how the furniture itself was made, and we were rewarded with striking new insights. We found detailed information about the woods they used and step-by-step descriptions of their joinery and finishing techniques scattered through private diaries and Shaker family journals. (When quoting from these sources we have, with very few exceptions, preserved the original spelling and punctuation and have not disrupted the flow of the text through the use of *Sic*.) This information was mixed in with notes about everything from spiritual matters to changes in the weather and the comings and goings of visitors, with the result that we began to see the furniture making as an integral part of the everyday lives of the craftsmen. Not only was the furniture illuminated from different perspectives, but other aspects of the Shaker culture were vivified in new ways.

Pieces of furniture that we formerly regarded as favorites were now challenged by other pieces that became more interesting in light of new biographical associations. Knowing why a certain piece was made, or for whom and under what circumstances, had the effect in some cases of making it more appealing than another piece that may have been superior from a design or construction standpoint but for which we had no real-life connection. It is our hope that seeing the work of the craftsmen in this light will also add a new imaginative depth to the readers' perspective, enhancing their appreciation of Shaker furniture.

Although previous studies have given us a detailed knowledge of Shaker communal life and crafts, intriguing questions about the furniture makers have long been unanswered. What personal experiences made them laugh or cry? What moved them spiritually? How did they come to join the Shakers? What distinguished their lives in that society? If they eventually chose to leave, why did they make that choice, and what became of them afterward?

In 1937, Faith and Edward Deming Andrews published their pioneering book, *Shaker Furniture: The Craftsmanship of An American Communal Sect.* Although they noted in that book that certain Shaker furniture makers had signed and dated some pieces of their work, their conclusion regarding Shaker joiners was that "their personalities are lost in the depth of the cause they served, their occupations seldom recorded." This became the prevailing opinion among writers on the subject for nearly fifty years. Despite the fact that since 1937 the Shaker way of life has been chronicled in detail and much new information about Shaker furniture revealed, little about the furniture makers themselves has been discovered and published.

The personalities of the craftsmen remained enigmatic because the information that would have illuminated their lives was either lost or destroyed or buried in documents preserved in widely scattered archives. The furniture seemed destined to remain anonymous, in a category of artifacts that people could imagine mystically emerging from the spiritual fabric of the Society itself. The names of some Shaker craftsmen were known, but not the details of their lives or how their individual circumstances related to the furniture they created. The fact that their work was an inspired part of a long-lived utopian adventure made it all the more lamentable that their life stories were untold.

In the archives, however, lay a hidden treasure. The research for this book, built on the foundation established by Faith and Edward Deming Andrews and others, has made it possible to trace the mazy, often-broken threads in a tangled skein of information, to sketch the lives of individual joiners, and to identify many specific pieces of furniture that they made. For some Shaker joiners we found detailed descriptions of a variety of their work in the pages of their own diaries or in family journals, whereas there were other craftsmen whose work was unknown save for a single piece of boldly signed furniture. As more notes were made and the furniture makers began to emerge as real characters, some appeared as people to whom we were drawn as to a new friend who is fresh and appealing. There were others whose personalities did not exude such warmth, and these we approached more cautiously, with little expectation of establishing a close personal rapport.

We sought known examples of furniture attributable to each of these men, and enough biographical information to enable us to present them as somewhat rounded characters for at least a portion of their lives. Using as many reliable facts as could be found, we tried to integrate the exact pieces of furniture they made with the stories of who they were as flesh-and-blood Shaker brothers. Even so, in order to include representatives from all of the Bishoprics, we had to treat some furniture makers about whom we still know relatively little, whose personalities at this point are mere outlines rather than full portraits of their lives. There are of course many other Shaker joiners for whom attributable pieces of furniture are known, yet for whom biographical information is too limited at this time to make their inclusion in this book possible.

Even though the Shaker craftsmen worked for the good of the community more than for personal advancement, they were in many cases very strong individuals. Many were saintly in their devotion; some had strong fleshly appetites for things of the world. The stronger the individual, the more "laboring" was necessary for him to put his personal concerns aside in order to concentrate on the advancement of the faith. As will be seen from the portraits, some of their intense personal efforts, even with the counseling of others, were in vain. Some of the master craftsmen left the Society, while others remained Shakers for life.

Although they worked from common aspirations and beliefs, and in fact pooled their labor and ideas as they traveled from community to community, the Shaker craftsmen also worked from their unique knowledge and experience as individual furniture makers. As individuals they contributed intriguing variations to what is often thought of as a homogeneous style of furniture, and we found an even greater and more interesting variety in their lives.

We offer the portraits as a tribute to these Shaker brothers, whose achievements as craftsmen illustrate the balance between the temporal and the eternal that was also their aim and often their achievement in life.

September 1988   J.G. and D.A.

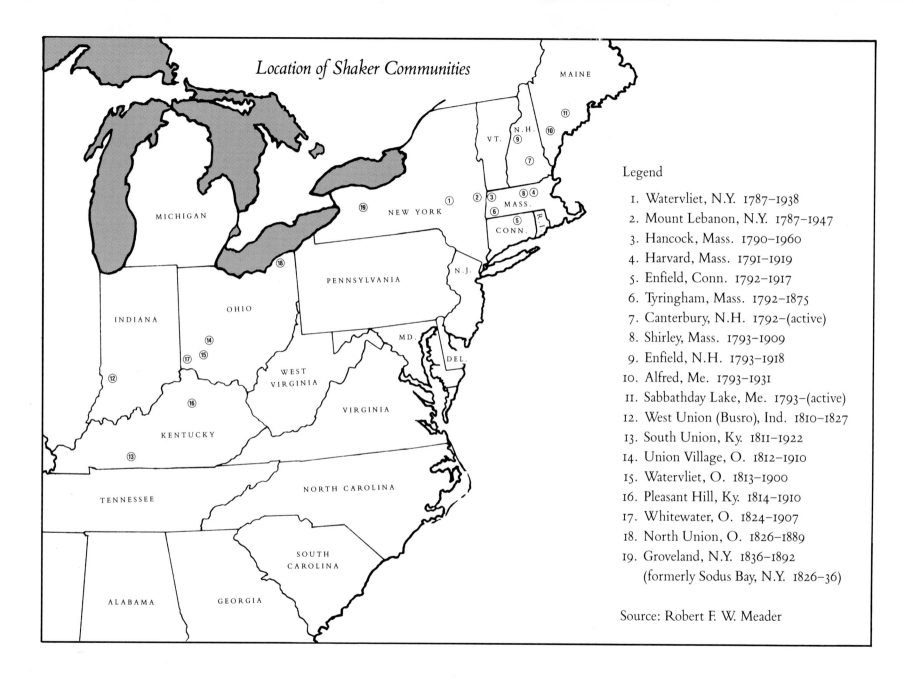

Location of Shaker Communities

Legend

1. Watervliet, N.Y. 1787–1938
2. Mount Lebanon, N.Y. 1787–1947
3. Hancock, Mass. 1790–1960
4. Harvard, Mass. 1791–1919
5. Enfield, Conn. 1792–1917
6. Tyringham, Mass. 1792–1875
7. Canterbury, N.H. 1792–(active)
8. Shirley, Mass. 1793–1909
9. Enfield, N.H. 1793–1918
10. Alfred, Me. 1793–1931
11. Sabbathday Lake, Me. 1793–(active)
12. West Union (Busro), Ind. 1810–1827
13. South Union, Ky. 1811–1922
14. Union Village, O. 1812–1910
15. Watervliet, O. 1813–1900
16. Pleasant Hill, Ky. 1814–1910
17. Whitewater, O. 1824–1907
18. North Union, O. 1826–1889
19. Groveland, N.Y. 1836–1892
   (formerly Sodus Bay, N.Y. 1826–36)

Source: Robert F. W. Meader

Introduction: Furniture in a World Apart

Of the Shakers at New Lebanon, New York, the first community to be formally gathered into gospel order, it has been written that "on Christmas Day, 1787, all for the first time sat down together at the table."[1] The newly gathered sisters and brothers were not, however, sitting on low-backed dining chairs and celebrating at the great communal trestle tables now associated with Shaker meals. Living in a frontier region in the early stage of their religious and social experiment, the Shakers were exposed to considerable risks and hardships and had little time in which to build any but the most essential pieces of furniture. Their most immediate challenge was to provide food and shelter for converts and livestock.

Calvin Green, a young boy at New Lebanon during this time, recalled the privations they endured. "We labored hard, lived poor and had crowded poor accommodations for shelter," he wrote. "The children . . . worked hard and were not overfed. I was hungry all the time." Their inspired toil had its effect, however, as can be seen in two Shaker sisters' later description of the labors of those first years. According to Anna White and Leila Taylor, "Gradually, the rough misshapen mass took to itself form and comeliness; the various parts of the spiritual body began to cleave atom to atom, and law, order and union of component parts was secured as the life principle permeated the whole."[2]

The Shakers enjoyed a material success—their reward for nurturing their spiritual body—that was soon evident to the outside world.

In 1793, Peter Whitney wrote of the Shakers at Harvard, who had formed their community just two years before: "Such is their agricultural skill and perseverance, that they have reduced the most rugged and indomitable part of Harvard to a state resembling that of a garden. . . . They are neat in their apparel and furniture. Their houses which they have erected in this town, are large and commodious and approaching something like elegance."[3]

Many of the first Shaker converts brought personal property into the community with them. Their belongings often included furniture, and existing inventories show the variety of pieces that were consecrated to the church. Abigail Hawkins, for example, noted that she brought with her to New Lebanon on February 6, 1789: "One oldish bedstead, two feather beds and beding mixed feathers, 2 oldish chairs, 1 little oldish chair, one Low Case Draw[er]s 13 years old, one midling sized ovel Table 13 years old, and one small looking glass."[4]

During the early stage of development in the Pleasant Hill, Kentucky, community, an inventory of Samuel Banta's estate included the following items when he joined in the spring of 1807:

6 Feather beds bedsteads & furniture worth $300.00
1 Desk & book Case   2 Chests & trunks worth $45.00
1 Corner Cupboard & earthenware worth $30.00
1 Candlestand   2 Candlesticks worth $3.00[5]

In the early days, the Shakers used furniture from the outside world simply because it was all they had. It is likely that the brethren spent time making some pieces of furniture suited to their new communal lifestyle—for example, dining tables, tailoring counters, kitchen furniture, large storage chests, and chairs—but dated examples of early pieces known to be the products of consecrated Shaker hands are at present largely unknown. Only later, when the Shakers had more time in which to replace worldly furniture with furniture of their own design, did Shaker furniture as we know it become plentiful.

Responding to the demand for chairs in different locations—in retiring rooms, offices, and workshops—the Shakers soon began to produce them in large quantities. Chair making for their communities was a notable success, and by 1789, chairs were being manufactured at New Lebanon for sale. For many years, however, benches rather than chairs were made for use in meeting rooms, kitchens, and dining rooms, which indicates that there were higher priorities than mere physical comfort well into the 1800s. Not until 1847 could the following entry be made in a Union Village, Ohio, journal: "Low chairs obtain'd to set on at the dining table instead of benches which had formerly been us'd—an advance in comfort and convenience."[6]

The furniture that had been brought in from the outside world was gradually replaced by furniture of Shaker design and manufacture. Some of the old furniture was taken to the "Poor Office" in the community to be given away, together with clothing and other provisions, to people in need. On December 14, 1819, for example, the *Albany Daily Advertiser* reported the Shakers' response to a disastrous fire: "It gives us peculiar pleasure to mention, that some day last week, eight large wagons loaded with provisions, household furniture, clothes, and clothing, all the very best kind and quality, arrived in the city of Schenectady, a donation from the Shakers Societies at New Lebanon and Niskeuna, for the unfortunate and distressed inhabitants of that city."[7]

New arrivals to Shaker communities during the 1820s continued to bring some furniture with them, although by then the Shakers were producing a greater quantity of their own furniture. At New Lebanon, for example, Nathan and Betsy Haskins—the parents of Orren Haskins—brought furniture with them when they united with the Shakers in January 1822. These items, listed with their estimated values, were: one desk, $5.50; one case of drawers, $8.00; one table, $1.50; one chest, $1.50; eight chairs, $2.00; and their most valuable possessions, two beds and bedsteads, $37.50.[8]

Other furniture was brought in from the "world" as later converts came to the communities. Another New Lebanon journal noted on March 14, 1838, that "A quantity of furniture, owned by Permilla Bradley, [was] bro't here for her two little daughters. Bed & bedding—table, trunk &c. &c."[9] In later years some of this furniture was sold to hirelings who came to work for the Shakers, and the remaining pieces probably continued to be used by Shaker families in the outer circle, that is, the novitiate families who were held to less strict standards of separation from things of the world than was the church family, the family at the center of the spiritual circle.

The need for new furniture in the late eighteenth century was reduced somewhat by a slowdown in the number of converts to Shakerism from 1785 until the beginning of the Kentucky revival in 1805. One writer, speaking about the New Lebanon Shakers in a 1791 magazine article, observed that "the sect seems rather to be diminishing, as the natural means of increase are cut off: few proselytes are gained: and the severity and constancy of their fatiguing exercises carry them off in a few years."[10] Writing in the *Testimonies of Christ's Second Appearing,* the Shakers themselves offered another and more reasonable explanation, which was that they were working to solidify the gains made during Mother Ann's missionary journey through New England. "The testimony was withdrawn from the world about the year 1785," they noted, "and was rarely opened to any until about the year 1798;

after which, there were a few small openings, in different places, to such as were in a special manner awakened; but nothing very remarkable appeared in the order of providence, to open the way for the spreading of the Gospel, until about the beginning of the present [i.e., nineteenth] century."[11] However, the first several decades of the nineteenth century saw a great increase in converts to the Shaker faith, and this in turn created a need for more furniture.

Many of the earliest Shaker cabinetmakers entered their communities with woodworking skills acquired in the outside world. For example, David Rowley learned the cabinetmaking trade by apprenticing himself to a cabinetmaker from his hometown in Connecticut ten years before he joined the Shakers at New Lebanon. It seems likely that Gideon Turner had also worked as a cabinetmaker before entering the same community, for in 1788, on becoming a Shaker, he "consecrated to the use of the church 1 Set Carpenter tools & 1 Set Joiners Tools valued at eight pounds."[12] When Benjamin Goodrich left the New Lebanon Shakers in 1796, the inventory of his personal property included tools that were most commonly used in making furniture or finishing interior woodwork in a building: "1 hand, one pannel, one fine and 2 Small fine Saws 5 in.; 1 Pannil plain—1 Plow [plane] with 3 Irons; 3 Sash plains; 1 pair Sash plains—1 Large and 1 Small Bead; 2 Rabit plains—3 Quarter Rounds $^1/_2$—$^3/_8$ & $^1/_4$ inch; 1 pair Inch hollows and Rounds." The inventory also included tools that were more commonly used by housewrights: "3 Screw Augers 1$^1/_2$--1$^1/_4$ & 1 inch in Size and 1 two inch do [and] 1 pair framing Chizzels."[13] Both the Turner and the Goodrich inventories illustrate something that was usually the case with brothers who were woodworkers—they were house carpenters as well as furniture makers.

Records are scarce of the occupations practiced by brothers before they joined the Shakers. At Union Village, Ohio, however, a journal[14] was kept of those persons who had come to the community inquiring about the faith; and this journal, which notes whether or not they

united with the Shakers, also records their previous occupation. On this list are the names of several brothers who had worked in an interesting variety of woodworking professions. Andrew Howard, for example, "formerly from New Hampshire came for a privilege, having once lived at Canterbury—he is a Carpenter by trade & is 53 years of age."

William Leech, William Collis, Lorenzo Dow Littleton, and William Stevens all united with the Shakers during the 1850s and also had been carpenters. John West, Louis Wilke, and James Morris were listed as having been cabinetmakers before joining. Other men practicing related professions who joined the Union Village community during the 1850s included Charles Forbes, "a wood turner by trade," Peter Edward, "occupation tea tray maker a native of Lancashire England," Adolphus St. Dennis, "occupation Piano Fort[e] Maker," and James Reed, "by trade a finisher of Cabinet Ware."

There are few references in early Shaker journals to specific pieces of furniture. One of the earliest is found in a letter written by the New Lebanon Ministry on March 2, 1807, thanking a brother for sending a gift of some lumber from Ohio to New Lebanon. "Beloved brother Peter," the letter reads, "we would inform you that we had a very nice table made of those black walnut boards which you sent by John Wright. We ate upon it the last Monday morning in Novr for the first time."[15]

One of the earliest known dated pieces of furniture, a case of drawers now at Hancock Shaker Village (ill. 1 and 2), has the date "1806" written on the back in both paint and pencil. Because this piece is recognizably Shaker, it seems safe to assume that during the previous decade and a half Shaker craftsmen had been making enough furniture for the community so that by 1806 the plain, clean lines of Shaker style had clearly evolved.

One of the earliest pieces of furniture to include initials or a name with a date is a pine case of drawers (ill. 3) from New Lebanon,

1. This tall case of drawers, dated "1806," suggests that a particular design aesthetic had developed quite early among Shaker cabinetmakers. Pieces of furniture of this size appear as monuments to a communal life-style and raise questions about the mechanics of living in a Shaker community. Was a piece such as this shared by six roommates, each having the use of one small and one large drawer?

Source: Hancock Shaker Village, Inc., Pittsfield, Mass.

2. The date "1806" is painted on the back of this case of drawers.
Source: Hancock Shaker Village, Inc., Pittsfield, Mass.

3. In *Shaker Furniture,* Faith and Edward Deming Andrews attribute this piece to Amos Bishop of the New Lebanon community. However, there is little information in Shaker records to suggest that Amos Bishop was a cabinet-maker. It seems more likely that this case of drawers was the work of Anthony Brewster, a Shaker brother from the same community whose cabinetmaking activities are frequently documented in the Shaker records of this time.

Source: Photograph by courtesy of *The Magazine ANTIQUES*

inscribed, "Made by A.B. 1817." It was probably made by Anthony Brewster, although, as the Andrewses have suggested, it could also have been made by Amos Bishop.[16]

It took Shaker furniture makers some time in the eighteenth century to free themselves from worldly styles, and their own distinctive style emerged gradually. Then in the later years of the nineteenth century Shaker cabinetmakers once again seemed to have been influenced by worldly styles, as can be seen in such aberrations as the decorative bric-a-brac on furniture attributed to Henry Green of Alfred, Maine, and the worldly forms of furniture copied by Thomas Fisher at Enfield, Connecticut.

Shaker furniture from the years of expansion and prosperity in the middle of the nineteenth century, however, is in a class by itself. One factor contributing to the stylistic purity of the furniture made from the 1820s through the late 1860s was that many of the cabinetmakers active during this period came into the Shaker families as children or young adults. In various New York communities, for example, we find that Freegift Wells joined the society at age eighteen, Isaac Youngs[17] and Amos Stewart at nine, Orren Haskins at five, Giles Avery at six, Samuel Turner at thirteen, Henry Hollister at three, and Elisha Blakeman at eleven.

Whereas their mentors had been trained in cabinetmaking in the outside world and thus had been influenced by worldly styles, the craftsmen of this "second generation" had their roots firmly planted in the Shaker tradition. They were steeped in a Shaker style that was relatively uncontaminated by worldly influences because they had been taught by craftsmen who had already labored to put aside worldly superfluities in their own work. For instance, the older men, who in earlier years may have admired and perhaps carved "ball and claw" feet on table legs, never taught the practice to their own apprentices. They did not instruct the apprentices in decorating furniture with rope turnings or acanthus-leaf carvings, or book-matched veneering or other worldly embellishments that were in vogue as the younger men came of age. Therefore the young men perhaps found it easier to resist the temptation to use such techniques. In addition, these second-generation brothers were making furniture at a time when there was little doubt that their sect would continue its prosperous growth, and it seems appropriate that this buoyant period is now viewed as the classic period of Shaker cabinetmaking.

The Shakers never seemed to have a labor force large enough to do all the work that needed to be done in their communities. They therefore often needed to hire outsiders—for instance, carpenters, masons, farm laborers, millers, and hatters—to do some of this work. More often than might be expected, local cabinetmakers were hired to make furniture or to finish off the cabinetry in new or renovated buildings when Shaker cabinetmakers were occupied by other projects, or when there were too few of them to accomplish the work in a timely manner. The 1845 revision of the "Millennial Laws of 1821" commented on the extent to which these worldly cabinetmakers should be employed: "It is advisable for the center families in each bishopric, to avoid hiring the world to make household furniture, except for the outer court."[18] However, even at the New Lebanon Church Family, the spiritual center of the Shaker faith during the eighteenth and nineteenth centuries, some of the community's furniture was not made by Shaker joiners. This was true even during the peak years of expansion, when skilled cabinetmakers were in good supply in the community.

There are also many examples of the Shakers having purchased ready-made furniture or having had furniture made for them by worldly cabinetmakers. Records at Union Village, Ohio, show that in 1812 two of the brothers went "to town for kitchen furniture & [that they ate] off the new table [the] same evening."[19] Two New Lebanon brothers went to Vermont in 1825 "in search of an easy chair."[20] From the late 1820s on, Thomas Bowman, Jr. and Sr., and various members of the Shumway family in the towns of New Lebanon and Lebanon Springs were employed by the Shakers to make furniture. Church Family account books show that in 1829, Thomas Bowman was paid $4 for "making 2 Bedsteads," and in 1830 he was paid $10 for "1 Case of Drawers." During this time Thomas Bowman took advantage of his relationship with the Shakers by buying "2 Steel Squares @ 20/- [20 shillings] & 6/ [6 shillings]," a "Brace & Bitts @ [$]8.50," and "1 Tool-Basket @ [$0].88." Several years later the accounts show that Thomas had been paid for "Making Tanners' Table 72/- [72 shillings] & one calfskin 4/ [4 shillings] [$]9.50."[21]

In April 1841, William Shumway was employed by the Upper Canaan Shakers after the family moved into their new dwelling "to finish the upper room, with the rest part of the garret,—make the drawers—cupboard doors & stair railing; to the amount of $70.00."[22] The North Family at New Lebanon engaged one of the Shumways in 1859 to make a case of drawers and cupboard for the Church Family residence, the Great House, as repayment for the work Brother George Wickersham had done in preparing the drafts for the North Family's great stone dairy barn.[23] In 1867, working for the Lower Canaan Family, "John Shumway made a case of drawers for the Elder Sisters['] room[,] the first new furniture brought into the house for quite a number of years,"[24] and in March 1875, William Shumway was hired to make a bookcase and secretary for Elder Thomas Smith at Canaan. The New Lebanon correspondent to the *Berkshire County Eagle* wrote of this desk, "It is made of bird's eye maple, butternut and chestnut and shows more fully what has always been known, that William is one of the best workmen, and the finest artists in this line we have in town. He has done many complicated jobs for the Shakers, and some of which they thought could not be beaten."[25]

Other communities also purchased furniture from the outside and hired worldly cabinetmakers. A journal entry at Groveland noted for December 12, 1839, that "Lucius goes to Danville and got some chairs for the Office. Noah goes to Mt. Mo[rris] to git a table for the Office," and for October 10, 1840, that "Lucius goes to Mt. Mo[rris] brings home a table."[26] A Union Village, Ohio, journalist recorded on July 3, 1841, "We had a Bureau made for the Office. We made two Corner Cupboards for dining room."[27] In addition, two dozen chairs were purchased by the Union Village community in Lebanon, Ohio, on March 30, 1846.[28]

The great fire of 1875 in the New Lebanon Church Family, which destroyed eight buildings, including the family's dwelling house, created a special need to purchase furniture. With a decrease in the number of brothers in the community, the Shakers apparently thought it impossible to replace all of the lost furnishings through their own labor. With the exception of chairs purchased from the South Family, most of the furniture to outfit the new dwelling was purchased from the world. Bedsteads, "as plain as the times will admitt," were bought in Albany; and "a thing composed of cupboard & drawers . . . one for each Brother," was made for them in Pittsfield. Settees with bent plywood seats decorated with perforations were purchased for the family's meeting room; and following a discussion, the family decided to purchase marble-topped dining tables (see ill. 4).[29] Marble-topped tables also found their way into the Union Village, Ohio, community, where, in December 1893, "Hewitt Horton strained his back by lifting a Marble Table in his room. He is nearly helpless with it."

A journal kept by the Shakers at Canterbury, New Hampshire, contains the following entry for July 1919: "Take out tables and chairs in the Family Dining Room. Have 7 tables 7 ft. x 3 ft. with Opal glass tops made for us at a cost of $315.00. Also 56 Brown Leather Seat Oak dining chairs costing $168.00 to take their places. These bought of Hoitt and Co." With the nineteenth-century dining-room furniture gone, including the chairs made by Micajah Tucker in 1834, the new furniture considerably changed the appearance of this room, as can be seen in illustrations 5a and 5b.[30]

4. These marble-topped trestle tables were purchased by the Church Family at New Lebanon to replace the tables destroyed by the 1875 fire that devastated the dwelling house and nearly all of its contents. The dining chairs were purchased as well, even though the Shakers' own chair factory was flourishing during the mid–1870s.

Source: Historic American Building Survey, National Park Service

5. These two views of the Church Family dining room at Canterbury show a change from Shaker-made (**a**) to non-Shaker-made (**b**) dining furniture. The new tables, with their "Opal glass" tops and the oak chairs with "Brown Leather" seats, were purchased in 1919 from Hoitt and Co. The chairs cost $3 each.

Sources: (**a**) Hancock Shaker Village, Inc., Pittsfield, Mass.; (**b**) Anne R. Whipple

In later years the focus of cabinetmaking changed. As the number of Shakers decreased, communities were left with rooms full of unused beds, tables, and chairs; and they found that the need for new furniture had evaporated. They also had less need for massive pieces, such as eighteen-drawer chests, that had been uniquely suited to crowded communal living arrangements.

Building new sorts of pieces for particular uses became necessary. For example, when the Shakers began using sewing machines in the 1850s, sewing machine counters (ill. 6) had to be made to accommodate them. Giles Avery, working at the Watervliet community in 1873, noted in his journal that he had been "cutting up stuff in the Shop for a sewing machine counter for Eldress Polly."[31] And at Canterbury in June 1926, the brothers built a "Record Cabinet" for the Meeting

6. This counter, which once housed a sewing machine, was the logical output of Shaker cabinet shops in the last four decades of the nineteenth century. As membership declined there was little need to continue producing furniture in the same quantity as had been required in the previous seventy years. Occasionally there was a special need for a piece of furniture to accommodate changes in the Shakers' life-style, work habits, and technology.
Source: The Shaker Museum, Old Chatham, N.Y.

Room to house the records purchased for the family's new gramaphone.[32]

Repair work was also a focus for the cabinetmakers during the second half of the nineteenth century and on into the twentieth. Much of the furniture that had been used for fifty or seventy-five years was in need of attention. At New Lebanon, for example, in May 1870, the

"Dining room tables [were] taken to the wash house to be planed and painted."[33] When buildings fell into disuse and were dismantled, built-in cupboards and cases of drawers were often reduced in size by eliminating some of the drawers or shelves or by making them into two smaller pieces. Also, double beds, in which two sisters or two brothers had slept during the first half of the nineteenth century, were cut down to make single beds. As more information comes to light, the history of Shaker furniture becomes more obviously entwined with the larger history of the Shaker movement. The evolution of beds, for example, parallels changes in the Shaker society itself, for changes in the kinds of beds the Shakers made and bought for their use can be seen as a reflection of important social and demographic changes within their society.

Although beds were probably among the first pieces of furniture to which Shaker cabinetmakers turned their hands in the fledgling communities, many of the early Shakers slept on plain straw ticks, and those beds that were available had been brought in from the world. As more converts arrived, double beds became the rule—two brothers to one bed, two sisters to another in their respective rooms of the dwelling, and at least two and sometimes more boys or girls to a bed in the children's orders. The trundle bed came into widespread use in retiring rooms at the zenith of the Society's expansion in the 1830s and 1840s, and in the early 1850s Elisha Blakeman created what might be considered the acme of space-efficient beds, one that slept eight boys and that took up "much less room than 4 bedsteads."[34]

By the 1860s, however, there was a widespread decline in the Shaker population. As the number of brothers or sisters in each retiring room decreased, the Shakers took advantage of the extra space by introducing single beds. At Mount Lebanon, Elisha Blakeman had helped make single beds for nearly all of the brothers by 1868, and within another year and a half he had made single beds for nearly all of the boys by narrowing their old double beds. Similar renovations were made to beds used by the sisters, and the same kind of change was probably occurring in all the communities during this period. As a sister from Union Village, Ohio, noted in 1863, "We change our high bed for a narrow one, [and] we like it much beter."[35]

Through the remainder of the century and into the 1900s, changes were made to beds that reflected a desire to make them more comfortable and convenient than the old feather beds had been. When one of the Shumways was hired by the South Family at Mount Lebanon to "cut down 6 beds[,] they were to[o] high," it is likely that the Shakers were adapting the beds to accommodate springs and mattresses.[36] Putting new springs and mattresses on the old high-legged Shaker bed frames would have made the beds difficult to get into and out of because they would have been much too high off the floor, especially at a time when a greater number of Shakers than ever before were approaching old age.

In other instances, beds were sold to and purchased from the outside world. At Canterbury, New Hampshire, the Church Family journalist recorded in 1910 that "it was this year that Webster & Rosenthal bought the old feather beds, clocks & misce[llaneous] things."[37] And in May 1919 the same journalist included this entry: "Buy of Chas. A. Hoitt Co. Manchester, N.H., Two complete bed room sets. Each set consisting of two beds with #50 National Springs, dresser, 3 rocking chairs, 1 straight backed chair, and 1 small writing desk. Also 2 extra Golden Oak beds and springs and a Chiffonier for the Bath Room. Cost Complete $209.00."[38]

At Hancock, Massachusetts, many of the old beds had been stored in the attic of the Church Family dwelling. In an effort to get rid of clutter, the sisters were instructed to remove the beds from the attic by way of the fourth floor window. In a quaintly utilitarian move, some of the old headboards and footboards were then made into lawn benches, as in illustration 7, and placed around the grounds for the convenience of the sisters.[39]

Estimates of the exact number of Shakers vary, but well over five

7. Sr. Olive Hayden Austin is seated on a lawn bench made from the head and foot boards of a bed no longer needed by the Church Family at Hancock. Sr. Olive recalled the day when the sisters, being charged with emptying the attic of many old beds, cleverly dropped them from the windows. Sad about the loss of these fine examples of the brothers' workmanship, the sisters were delighted to find that some of the frames had been put to a new use.
Source: A. Hayward Benning Collection

thousand members were living in the communities at any given time during the years of peak membership, from the 1830s to the 1850s. Pieces of furniture were needed for daily use and on special occasions during every season of the year in retiring rooms, kitchens, dining rooms, workshops, meeting houses, schoolrooms, and infirmaries. An attempt to estimate the total amount of furniture would be futile, but it is intriguing to consider where all of it is now.

Some pieces are still in use at the two active Shaker communities, Sabbathday Lake, Maine, and Canterbury, New Hampshire. The remainder of the surviving furniture is found in museums, private collections, and antique shops, or is as yet undiscovered or unidentified in garages, barns, and attics, or even in use in the living rooms of people who may have no idea about a piece's Shaker origin.

When the Tyringham, Massachusetts, settlement closed in 1875, it marked the beginning of a series of formal closings of Shaker communities that ended when Hancock, Massachusetts, closed in 1960. The Shaker furniture in those communities took a variety of circuitous routes to arrive at the places where it is today. When a community closed, the Shakers who were living there moved to other settlements, often taking along favorite pieces of furniture that had become as much a part of their home as the buildings and grounds they were forced to leave. Although some furniture was moved at the request of individuals, on other occasions the church leadership sent large quantities of furniture to communities that still had need of it. After the closing of the Harvard community in 1918, five truckloads of pieces chosen by certain sisters were taken to their new home at the New Lebanon North Family, but two train carloads were sent to Sabbathday Lake for the use of the Shakers there.

Similar transfers of large quantities of furniture from Ohio to New Hampshire occurred in 1919 and 1920. A journal from Canterbury noted for July 1919: "Have a carload of furniture come from Union Village, Ohio. It reaches Eastside, N.H. July 2nd and is brought home the next day. . . . This furniture is some that was not needed out there, owing to the people moving into smaller quarters."[40] The same journal recorded the following for July of the next year: "Have a carload of furniture from Union Village, Ohio. It reaches Eastside to-day."

The movement of furniture from one community to another makes it very risky indeed to assign a provenance to a piece based solely on where it was found or acquired. In 1892, for example, most of the Groveland Shakers moved east to Watervliet and took much of the community's furniture with them. Some of these pieces were taken to New Lebanon when Watervliet closed, and it is possible that when New Lebanon closed in 1947, some of this same furniture was moved to Hancock.

Pieces of furniture that were left in Shaker buildings when the villages were sold met different fates. An article written twelve years after the closing of the community at Tyringham gives an account of the disposition of some of the furniture that remained. A correspondent for the *New York Evening Post* wrote: "This whole estate [that is, the Church Family property] passed some years ago into the ownership of Dr. Joseph Jones a Pennsylvanian, curiously enough of Quaker stock. Dr. Jones has allowed the Lenox people to gratify their fancy for antique furniture, and many treasures have been removed hence, but enough remains to preserve the character of the place."[41] The reference to Shaker furniture as a category of antiques at this early date is intriguing and seems to foreshadow things to come, but it must be assumed that many of the people who bought it at this time were merely looking for sturdy, attractive, and useful furniture for their country houses.

Just as Dr. Jones kept and used some of the furniture at Tyringham, furniture left by the Shakers in other communities was also sometimes used by the new owners. The collection of Hancock Shaker Village, for example, includes three trestle tables once used in the Shirley dining room. They were purchased from the Commonwealth of Massachusetts and had remained in service at the state-operated

Shirley Industrial School for many years following the Shakers' disposal of the Shirley property.

Sometimes the furniture was lost. For instance, some of the furniture left at Tyringham was destroyed when buildings were later razed, and much of the furniture that remained at Enfield, Connecticut, when it was closed in 1917 was lost over the years. After the Enfield property was acquired by the State of Connecticut to be used as a prison, some of the furniture was destroyed by inmates, and other pieces, considered unneeded, were burned by prison authorities.

Besides providing partial lists of specific pieces of furniture that were being sold, announcements of public sales of Shaker furniture give a sense of what was happening in the communities as they closed. An announcement of a sale at the Enfield, New Hampshire, community in 1918, for example, comes nearly five years before Enfield finally closed, for the last members didn't move to Canterbury until 1923.

The Church Family Shakers have for some weeks been having a sale of furniture and other household goods, chairs, tables, chests and drawers of various sizes and quality. They have still many things to dispose of as they contemplate selling the place later on. They have some large pieces like cases of drawers 6 or 8 feet tall, one good roll top desk good as new, two or three tall old style desks or secretaries. Most of these articles were made on the place when there was lumber of a value which we do not have today. Several old clocks quite valuable to one who values old things, and a few more modern clocks. If interested in buying please come and look it over as we shall close the house as the weather gets colder.[42]

The broadside reproduced in illustration 8 advertised a list of Shaker furniture pieces to be sold at auction in Kentucky in 1922 and clearly hints at a value already being placed on this furniture as a part of American history. In addition, it further illustrates the dismantling of the Shaker communities.

Partial List of Articles to be Sold at Shaker Village, near Harrodsburg, Ky.,
JULY 12th, 1922

Beginning at 11 o'clock.

ABOUT 27 BEDS
SIX CHILDREN'S BEDS
ABOUT 40 CHERRY CHESTS
ABOUT 10 CHESTS OF DRAWERS
A NUMBER OF CHAIRS
A NUMBER OF TABLES AN CANDLE STANDS
SEVERAL STOVES
A NUMBER OF SPINNING AND FLAX WHEELS
A NUMBER OF RUGS
TWO CORNER CUPBOARDS
SEVERAL CLOCKS
A NUMBER OF OTHER SMALL ARTICLES
MANUFACTURED AND USED BY THE SHAKERS.

This collection is the best specimen of early settler's furniture extant. It was all manufactured by the Shakers in the early part of the last century, or earlier, and has never been out of their possession.

The sale will be without reserve.

Shaker Village lies seven miles Northeast of Harrodsburg on the Lexington pike.

A good lunch can be secured on the grounds.

E. H. GAITHER, Executor of
W. F. Pennebaker.

8. This broadside advertised the 1922 auction of household furnishings once used by the Pleasant Hill Shakers.
Source: Courtesy of Shakertown at Pleasant Hill Kentucky, Inc.

During the 1920s, Faith and Edward Deming Andrews, two people who nurtured an appreciation of Shaker furniture, began to acquire pieces from the communities at Hancock, New Lebanon, Watervliet, Canterbury, and Sabbathday Lake. Sr. Sadie Neale was a deaconess at New Lebanon and at times oversaw the selling of furniture at the community during those years. On occasion she mentioned the Andrewses in her diary. For instance, she wrote on March 26, 1929, "Mr. and Mrs. Andrews come to look over old furniture in afternoon. I use some time going around with them," and on August 27, 1929, "Andrews couple come in afternoon. Select two or three old pieces and use considerable of my time."[43] The crotchety tone of her last remark notwithstanding, Sr. Sadie established a close and enduring friendship with Faith and Edward Deming Andrews, a relationship which they later recalled with great fondness in their memoirs.[44] Sr. Sadie and her natural sister Emma presided over the dissolution of the New Lebanon community as the property was being sold, family by family, and they provided a personal connection to Shaker history for the Andrewses and other visitors to the community during those years.

Br. Ricardo Belden, an Enfield, Connecticut, brother who moved to Hancock, played a role similar to that of the Neale sisters. A Shaker craftsman noted for his repair of old clocks, Br. Ricardo had personal contacts with interested buyers. In a letter concerning a piece of furniture eventually purchased by Hancock Shaker Village, Sidney S. Alberts provides some insight into how Br. Ricardo performed this duty: "It could very well be that my Shaker cabinet may have come from Watervliet when they closed. . . . I had a farm in Old Chatham then, and visited Brother Ricardo quite frequently. Every so often he would tell me that such and such a piece was declared 'surplus' and as such was for sale and was I interested. Usually I was. As to this particular piece, I remember his saying that it had just come up as 'surplus' and did I want to buy it. I did."[45]

Jennie Wells was a Shaker sister who had entered the Groveland community when she was four years old. She moved to Watervliet

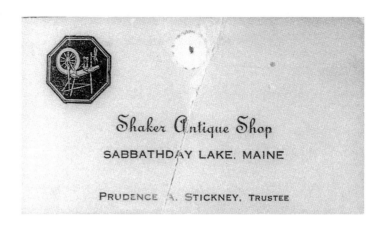

9. This business card was used by Sr. Prudence Stickney at the Shaker Antique Shop at Sabbathday Lake, Maine. Several Shaker communities sold some of their belongings through gift or antique shops.
Source: Alice Schwertfeger

when Groveland closed in 1892, and moved to Mount Lebanon when the Watervliet community was dissolved in 1938. Sr. Jennie was one of the last Shakers living at the Mount Lebanon North Family at the time of its closing in 1947. She was interviewed just before the closing by Berton Roueche, a writer for *The New Yorker*. After having watched Shaker furniture being sold off for many years, Sr. Jennie offered these comments:

Most of our visitors these days are antique collectors, and all they're interested in is buying up what little fine old handmade Shaker furniture we have left. Why, those people would grab the chairs right out from under us if we'd let them. Our furniture is very fashionable all of a sudden, you know. . . . We're always being told how beautiful our things are. I don't say they aren't but that isn't what they were meant to be. . . . All our furniture was ever meant to be was strong, light, and, above all, practical. It is, too, as you'll see when we go inside.[46]

The Portraits

The following portraits show that much of the furniture used by the Shakers was produced not by professional cabinetmakers but by Shaker brothers who made furniture in addition to their other regular duties. They were carpenters, coopers, wheelwrights, and mechanics; or makers of spinning wheels, reels, oval boxes, sieves, measures, clocks, and so on. But they had the skills to make an occasional piece of furniture as one was needed. Others, who were more sophisticated cabinetmakers and were employed primarily in that trade, likewise spent much of their time serving the community in different roles. They were church leaders, teachers, orchardists, teamsters, farmers, gardeners, caretakers of the boys, scribes, peddlers, trustees, and deacons.

The furniture they produced mirrors the variety of their backgrounds. For some, woodworking held a much more important place in their lives than it did for others, and some pieces exhibit a much higher quality of design and execution than do others.

There are several ways of attributing pieces of furniture to these individual makers. Each of these methods is valid, but to a different degree of certainty. An individual piece can be attributed to a certain maker by the presence of that maker's signature on the piece. This method is most positive when the signature appears together with a statement indicating that the name on the piece is that of the maker rather than of an owner or user of the piece. This is true, for example, of the case of drawers with a cupboard shown later in illustrations 33 and 34, which is signed "Made Feb 1831 Amos Stewart." The discovery of a Shaker sister's name on a piece of furniture does not suggest that she was the maker of the piece. Likewise, without knowing that a brother whose name is found on a piece of furniture was skilled in woodworking, it would be premature to conclude that he was the maker. Additional information, either evidence that this brother was a cabinetmaker or a statement accompanying the signature indicating that the name belongs to the maker, is needed in order to make an accurate attribution. The stronger this statement is about who made the piece, the better for purposes of attribution.

A few pieces of Shaker furniture are attributed to a specific cabinetmaker based on oral history or inscriptions added later by Shaker brothers and sisters who remembered a piece having been made by a certain brother. Nearly all of the furniture made by Emmory Brooks at Groveland is known to have been his work because of information supplied by members of the communities in which he lived. For the most part this is also the case with pieces made by Thomas Fisher of Enfield, Connecticut, Freegift Wells of Watervliet, New York, and Henry Green of Alfred, Maine.

An attribution can be enhanced if the provenance of a piece of furniture shows that it originated in the same community where the person to whom it is attributed lived. If this person is also well documented in Shaker records as an active cabinetmaker during the time he lived there, the attribution is further improved.

Once a positive attribution has been made for one piece, it is then possible in some cases—for example, with Abner Allen of Enfield, Connecticut, and Grove Wright of Hancock, Massachusetts—to attribute additional pieces to the same maker through a careful comparison of distinctive techniques used by that cabinetmaker in the construction of his furniture. Choices of materials and elements of design give additional support to this type of attribution. This method, as illustrated and discussed in detail in the portraits of Abner Allen and Grove Wright, previously has not been applied to the study and attribution of Shaker furniture.

The craftsmen are featured in order of the earliest dates for which there is good evidence that they were making furniture for a Shaker community. This arrangement illustrates the history of Shaker furniture as it evolved from the late eighteenth century into the first half of the twentieth century. Although the chronology is affected by gaps in the historical record, it is nonetheless accurate enough to help illuminate important aspects in the development of Shaker furniture and parallel stages in the evolution of Shaker society as a whole.

Written records make it clear that David Rowley, whose portrait appears first in this book, was a cabinetmaker who conducted business with the New Lebanon community even before he became a Shaker during 1809 or 1810. But in other instances, furniture attributable to individual craftsmen does not appear until long after they joined the Shakers. Samuel Turner, for example, entered the New Lebanon community in 1788, but the earliest documented piece of his furniture is dated 1836. Judging from the sophistication of his work by this later period, we can be reasonably certain that he learned and practiced the craft of cabinetmaking during the years between 1806 and 1836, while he was a member of the Pleasant Hill community in Kentucky. However, since we cannot prove this assumption, his portrait is placed according to the pieces we know he made during the 1830s. In the 1790s, Grove Wright joined the Shakers at Hancock, Massachusetts, and Abner Allen joined at Enfield, Connecticut. As with Samuel Turner, the quality of the workmanship of these two cabinetmakers makes it clear that both were active in the trade long before the appearance, in the 1830s, of the first pieces of their furniture bearing dates.

The lives of many Shaker furniture makers remain sketchy, and tantalizingly so. More details about the lives of some brothers discussed in this collection may eventually emerge from artifacts and written records, but for others, what little is known today is all that ever will be known. Even the briefest portraits, though, provide some historical continuity, show connections in both craftsmanship and spiritual values between brothers in geographically distant communities, and add personality and color to the larger story of Shaker cabinetmakers.

David Rowley

(1779–1855) New Lebanon, New York

David Rowley was born in Sharon, Connecticut, on September 16, 1779, and lived there on his family's farm until he was twenty-one years old. David was a spirited and energetic young man who loved the outdoors; but he was only 4 feet 10³/₈ inches tall, and the long days and seasons of strenuous farmwork would eventually take their toll on his small frame. "I concluded," he wrote in his journal, "that farming was too heavy [a] business for my physical endurance. Had it not been so, I think I should have always followed that occupation."[1]

Friends and family counseled him to study law or medicine, but David did not follow their advice. He later explained:

No mental calling promised me that active exercise which my very nature demanded & was likely to demand thro life. . . . [Moreover], life and active motion was so completely my boyhood heaven that I had neglected to improve my opportunity of gaining that degree of knowledge which is an important requisite to a profession in any of the higher sciences. . . . Consequently I fixed upon the Cabinet business as being a way of making a sufficient living & at the same time light active work, such as seemed best suited to my stature and ability. Accordingly I made a conditional bargain with Daniel Gay, a cabinetmaker living in my native town, & went to work for him.

David had found his worldly career in cabinetmaking but was increasingly frustrated in his search for spiritual fulfillment. He had been brought up as a Presbyterian and recalled his father as a man who "earnestly endeavored to instill in my mind in early life the peculiar doctrines of that sect—but without effecting a belief in me, that this denomination were the true Church; for I discovered in this sect such a lack of Christian piety & rectitude as conscientiously forbid such a belief."

During the years he worked for Daniel Gay, 1800 to 1806, David was in emotional turmoil as he searched for a faith and church to call his own. He eventually was "brought under the deep conviction of the lost fallen state of man," and occasionally had remarkable visionary experiences, some directly related to woodworking.

While plaining at my bench, [he wrote of one such experience,] my whole soul was enshrouded with a mantle of tribulation; but I kept on at my plaining, & soon it appeared to me that my plain began to go with less physical force or exertion on my part than usual. It moved more & more easily until it seemed that I had to hold on to the tool, in order to keep it from moving itself. I thought perhaps it did not take hold of the wood, & so I watched to see if it thru out shavings. I observed it did, but as it still moved without my aid as it were, I questioned the cause, & turned it over to see if it had not caught some little chip or splinter as plains sometimes do, & thus move without cutting; but to my surprise it was all clear. I then concluded it must be driven by some unseen foreign agency or power.

David's spiritual life remained troubled, but he "decided to settle

in life after the common course of the world." He traveled by chance to New Lebanon, New York, with an uncle who resided there, thought it a good place to settle, and purchased a piece of land and buildings in Lebanon Hollow. He returned home to Sharon and in 1807 married Sally Hamlin, the daughter of a Presbyterian deacon from his hometown. That year David and Sally moved onto his new property, where David "commenced business at cabinet work" as an independent journeyman.

Soon after he settled in Lebanon Hollow, David wrote, "I became acquainted with the people called Shakers, nearby. The more I became aquainted with them, the more plainly I saw that they were both by precept & example, the true followers of Christ." Within a few years, convinced that he had finally discovered a faith with which he could unite, David joined the Young Believers Order at the North House in the New Lebanon community. David occasionally had attended Shaker meeting, and the Shakers knew of him and his business as a cabinetmaker, as in a January 5, 1809, journal reference, which notes that "Benjamin B. goes up Roullys after some small pieces of mahogany for C[arding] M[achine]."[2] Calvin Green, in his "Biographic Memoir," now in the Western Reserve Historical Society Library, recounts that when he and Elder Daniel Goodrich saw David at meeting, they "felt a gift to speak to him . . . & told him that he had faith in the Gospel & ought to obey it—and powerfully called

upon him to come out from the world, take up his cross & follow Christ in the regeneration." Between Christmas and the new year, David declared "that the Shakers were his people—& their God should be his God." After several months of settling his wordly affairs, he made the transition from a worldly to a Shaker cabinetmaker.

Sally and their eighteen-month-old son, Hiram, stayed in the world and eventually returned to Connecticut. Although Sally may have visited her husband and brought Hiram with her on occasion, the only journal reference to Br. David's seeing his family again came roughly thirty-two years after he joined, when Sally and two of her brothers visited him at New Lebanon in 1842.[3]

Br. David lived at the North Family for twenty years, and although there are few accounts of that family during this time, it is certain that he was making furniture while he was there. For example, a Watervliet journal entry for May 11, 1814, stated that Deacon David (Miller) "returned from Lebanon about 8 o'clock this evening & brought home a desk that David Rowley has made for him, and also a few apples."[4]

It is likely that Br. David contributed much of the labor and many of the skills required to build and furnish the North Family residences and shops while he lived there— that is, if the first twenty years of his Shaker cabinetmaking life were as productive as the last twenty years, for which we do have records. On June 10, 1830, Br. David moved to the Church Family, where he continued cabinetmaking and sash making and occasionally helped to frame buildings and tend the orchard. Church Family journals provide a partial record of his work as a cabinetmaker:

In January 1837, "David Rowley has undertaken to make a quantity of cherry tables, to furnish the great house, in the various rooms—has begun 20 tables."[5]

On February 24 of the next year, "Two new dining tables were put into our dining room . . . lately made by David Rowley."[6]

10. This lithograph, titled "Shakers near Lebanon state of N York, their mode of Worship," is noted as having been "Drawn from Life." Although there are several obvious inaccuracies in the drawing, it is interesting to consider the possibility that the short Shaker brother is David Rowley. The drawing represents a public worship service (note the presence of the "worldly woman" and the artist himself) at which Br. David, as a member of the North Family in 1830, would almost certainly have been present. This version of this scene was probably produced by the Kellogg brothers in 1850 or 1851.

Source: Hancock Shaker Village, Inc., Pittsfield, Mass.

In the summer of 1840, David Rowley removed the superfluous brass pulls on drawers and replaced them with wooden ones, which were deemed, through spiritual communication, to be more appropriate to Shaker life.[7]

On March 9, 1843, "A new case of drawers & cupboards was bro't into No. 16 . . . made by David Rowley in the course of a few weeks, for that room."[8]

In February of 1849, David finished "a case of drawers for the Deaconesses"; in January of 1850, "he made a case of drawers this month for the physician sisters"; and in July of 1852, he completed "a case of drawers for the Office folks."[9]

This same journal recorded for November of 1854 that "David Rowley has been making a counter and drawers for the deaconesses a few weeks, and it was carried and up in their shop on the 28th inst." Also during 1854, Br. David produced the wooden parts of eighteen foot stools, made for sale, which the sisters covered.[10]

In addition to his cabinetmaking during this period, David built some machinery, made a loom for the sisters to use in weaving palm-leaf,[11] and in May of 1837 worked with Henry DeWitt to hew out enough "plain stock timber" for 100 planes.[12] These planes may have been made for Henry DeWitt, for Br. David himself, or for sale. Eleven cabinetmaker's planes, two marking gauges, a saw, and a pair of sawhorses at the Shaker Museum in Old Chatham, New York, were collected from the Church Family workshop and bear the impressed initials "D.R." (see ill. 11). Many of the planes also bear the stamp "Stothert, Bath," the mark of an English plane manufacturer; and so although these planes are not among the ones David helped Henry make, it is likely that they were his planes and were used by him at the Church Family.

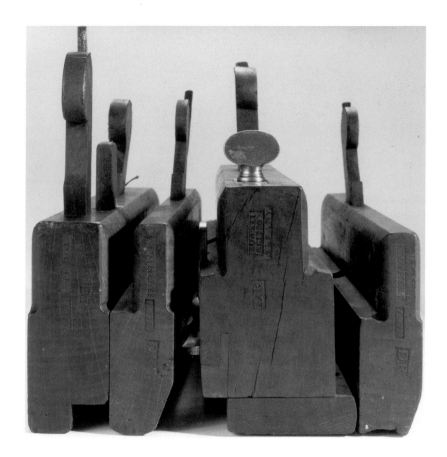

11. These planes are from the New Lebanon Church Family's workshop, where for almost twenty-five years David Rowley was the cabinetmaker. The planes are stamped with the initials "D.R." and with the imprint of their maker, "Stothert, Bath." George Stothert and his heirs manufactured planes in Bath, England, from 1785 until 1857. Eleven planes and two marking gauges in the collection of the Shaker Museum in Old Chatham, New York, are marked with the "D.R." stamp.

Source: The Shaker Museum, Old Chatham, N.Y.

As a portrait of David Rowley emerges from the journals and diaries, other facets of his role as a Shaker cabinetmaker become discernible. For example, since David had been a master joiner prior to the arrival of other New Lebanon cabinetmakers, he was in a position to have a mentor's influence on some of these other craftsmen. From journals, we know that when fifteen-year-old Elisha Blakeman came to New Lebanon in 1834, he went "to the Brick Shop to work at joinering with David Rowley,"[13] as David's apprentice. Although this is the only mention of Br. David in the role of teacher, it is certain that others saw his work as an example to be followed. For instance, when Orren Haskins began making furniture at the community in 1833, Br. David had been a cabinetmaker for thirty-three years, and although the only historical reference to their working together involved a coffin they made in October 1848, Orren undoubtedly learned lessons in cabinet-making from David Rowley over the years.

Inferences about his influence on others are not based solely on Br. David's greater age and experience but also on the length of time he was in the joiners' shop. While entries in journals show other cabinet-makers moving from shop to shop over the years and being assigned other significant responsibilities, the records show David Rowley as a singularly stable presence in charge of the Church Family joiners' shop for more than twenty years, until his death in 1855, at which point Orren Haskins took over that shop. Another distinction in David's position as a cabinetmaker is shown in how Isaac Youngs recorded Br. David's occupation in the list of the names, heights, weights, ages, and occupations he prepared for the Church Family every five years between 1840 and 1860. Although he identified several brothers as "joiners," "carpenters," and "woodworkers," Br. Isaac referred to David Rowley alone over the years as having the occupation of "cabinetmaker." Coming from a man who chose his words carefully and who was a furniture maker himself, this designation sets David Rowley apart, indicating perhaps that he was looked upon as the first among equals.

Comments made about Br. David after his death on November 14, 1855, reveal the true stature of the diminutive cabinetmaker. In a letter to the Canterbury Ministry describing an epidemic of influenza that struck the New Lebanon community in the autumn of 1855, the New Lebanon Ministry wrote that "the disease has not proved fatal to any-one excepting our good little Brother David Rowley who deceased very suddenly with an inflamation of the lungs, aged 76 years. David was a zealous soul in spiritual devotion and very useful and handy in temporal business, having universal love and respect of all his Brethren and Sisters who had a severe cross to part with him."[14]

Freegift Wells

(1785–1871) Watervliet, New York

"I started out for the Land of Promise on May 6th 1803, and arrived (I think), on the 17th. I was kindly received, & made welcome to a residence in the Ark of Safety."[1] This was Freegift Wells's recollection much later in his life of traveling from his family home on Long Island to Watervliet, where he joined the Shaker community.[2] On May 20, 1803, Freegift was eighteen years old, and this trip was the beginning of his personal odyssey as a Shaker—a lifelong journey that lasted for sixty-eight years. It was also part of an ongoing family migration that over the years became a Shaker saga.

The Wells family lived in Southold, New York, on the remote northern fork of Long Island. Freegift's grandfather had the same first name, and a family genealogy notes that the grandfather's name was "bestowed on him by his mother because he was the youngest [and probably the least expected] of her fourteen children."[3] It is fitting that his name was passed on when he died in 1785, the year his namesake was born, for the younger Freegift was the last of his mother and father's eleven children, the seventh of seven sons.

Freegift's oldest brother, Seth Youngs Wells, was a schoolteacher who became a Shaker at Niskayuna in 1798. He later returned to Southold and succeeded in converting his mother, sisters, and brothers to Shakerism. A history of Long Island published in 1845 describes what took place afterward:

> For a number of weeks, they kept up their dancing exercises, to the great amazement of the neighborhood, and annoyance of

all serious-minded people, without making any more proselytes, except a widow of a collateral branch of the family. The mother remained, till the death of her husband, which occurred several years afterwards. One or two of the sons, who had families, delayed a few years. But sooner or later, nineteen individuals of this single family have removed, and become incorporated with this dancing sect. This, however, is the beginning and end of Shakerism on Long Island.[4]

But it was just the beginning of the Wells family's long-lived association with the Society of Believers. Seth and Freegift Wells became prominent Shaker leaders, and because so many other members of the family lived to old age in the Society, their story inspired the *Berkshire County Eagle* to publish an article in 1863 entitled "Longevity Among the Shakers." "There are many individual members of the Society now living who have attained fourscore years," the article concluded, "but no instance, we believe, of so large a family growing up to old age together."[5]

The Wells family was related to another fruitful branch of the Shaker genealogical tree through Freegift's mother. Born Abigail Youngs, she was the sister of Isaac Newton Youngs, the clockmaker, scribe, and cabinetmaker at the New Lebanon community. Isaac Youngs was Freegift's uncle as well as a Shaker brother and fellow member of the fraternity of Shaker joiners, a relationship which we later see replicated when Thomas Wells, Freegift's nephew, joined the Shakers and became Freegift's apprentice in the 1830s.

The dissolution of natural family ties, however, was an essential element in becoming assimilated into the extended Shaker family. It was essential, certainly, for the most assiduously faithful converts, one of whom was Freegift Wells. This austere aspect of Shaker life was dramatically illustrated at the end of December 1861, when Freegift's brother Luther Wells invited him to join their brothers Stephen and Jesse and their sister Hannah for a dinner. It would have been a reunion of all the living natural children of Thomas and Abigail Wells, all of them members of the Watervliet community, and all in their eighties at the time, except Freegift, who was seventy-six. But Freegift declined the invitation. During all his years as a Shaker, he explained, he had guarded against the temptation to build up and support the relationship between natural kin, and he was fearful that such a dinner would be a bad example for other Shakers. He felt that it would encourage others to honor and cultivate the natural affections between family members, and this he thought would be detrimental to the common good.[6] Remaining true to his own strict belief over the years, Br. Freegift perhaps transformed the energies from whatever natural affections he had and channeled them into work.

Throughout his life as a Shaker, Br. Freegift kept his hands continually at work. Although he held positions of responsibility as Family Elder and later as Ministry Elder, he was also a schoolteacher and a skilled craftsman who worked as a mechanic, a wood turner, and a cabinetmaker. As a mechanic he made a variety of tools and machinery, including planes, cutting chisels, wash mills, simple lathes and "pattern lathes," wood drills, pile drivers, and augers for drilling wells; and at the age of seventy-five, he built a "dadoing machine" for himself. As noted in a recently published book, he was also a well-known chairmaker.[7] An example of this work is shown in illustrations 12 and 13.

Br. Freegift kept a work journal for much of his life, and his records date back to December 1812, at which time his woodworking tasks included both turning and carpentry. In the first entry, Freegift noted that he had been making staves for a tub wheel; and during the next year he made a bread bench and box, a work bench, and cheese hoops. After he made some bowls, he began applying himself to the wood-turning craft in earnest. He turned hundreds of dipper handles, first going after the timber and splitting out the wood for the handles.

During the years that followed, Br. Freegift turned a great variety of wood products: chairs for which all pieces except the back slats and seats were made on a lathe, bedposts, table legs, bowls, curtain rods, screw clamps, pen handles (wooden handles for silver writing pens designed to be sold, which Freegift, like his uncle Isaac Youngs, made in great quantities), hat blocks, doorknobs for the dwelling houses, basket molds and "a mould to make an eel-pot on," newel posts, shafts for water wheels, and always pegs and more pegs for the omnipresent pegboards installed in Shaker rooms. Using a pattern lathe, Freegift was able to turn prodigious numbers of wood pieces; and his woodworking became a high-production industry in which he emphasized quantity as well as quality. On January 21, 1824, Br. Freegift wrote, "continued to turn chair rounds, turned 100 in 36½ minutes."[8]

Although there is not much mention of joinery in his journals between 1812 and 1834, Br. Freegift was developing and honing his skills as a cabinetmaker during those years. The growing diversity of his talents is reflected in journal entries from 1834 that list the series of steps he took in making a "library," a kind of hutch that was also called a "hymnal cupboard":

February 14th: F[reegift] has been buzing out some stuff for a
   Library & drawers.
February 15th: F[reegift] has been rough plaining stuff for the
   Library.

12. This armless rocker is an example of the chairs thought to have been made by Freegift Wells between the 1830s and the Civil War. The front post of this chair is marked with the initials "F.W."
Source: Gustave G. Nelson

13. A closer view of the chair in illustration 12 shows the stamped initials "F.W." on the top of the front post.
Source: Gustave G. Nelson

February 17th: F[reegift] has plained out the sides of the Library.

February 20th: F[reegift] has now worked one day & a half at the Library.

February 26th: F[reegift] has finishe'd the library except the doors & drawers &c.

February 27th: F[reegift] has put the two library doors together to-day.

March 1st: F[reegift] has hung the library doors & put the lock on &c.

March 5th: F[reegift] dovetail'd the 3 drawers together.

March 27th: F[reegift] turn'd some knobs this afternoon for the drawers of the library.

April 2nd: We have moved the library into the house, got the books into it &c.[9]

In January 1834, the Ministry had decided that all books except Bibles, books published by the Shakers, and such schoolbooks as arithmetic and grammar books and dictionaries, were to be examined by a selected group of leaders—which in this Bishopric included Seth Wells and Isaac Youngs—to determine their appropriateness for Believers. Those books deemed not suitable were to be put away or burned, and the rest of the books were to be housed in the library, "in order that all may have an equal chance to get useful knowledge."[10] It is likely that other hutchlike furniture from this period began life as a "library" similar to the one Freegift built that spring.

The year 1830 brought another wave of Wells family members into Shaker society. Freegift's brother Benjamin and his four children—George, Thomas, Eliza, and Nancy—came from Long Island to live in the community at Watervliet; and Thomas, the younger of the two sons, became an apprentice to Freegift in the carpentery, and joinery, trades.

During that year, Freegift mentioned some of the work Thomas had done, such as making a paneled door for the physician's shop and cupboard door frames. In 1836, Freegift wrote that on January 13, Thomas began "to make himself a vice &c." and that on January 26 he "has put up a vice bench at the south end of the joiners shop." Later that year, however, Br. Freegift left for Ohio; and in 1840, while he was still away, his nephew Thomas, then twenty-one years old, seceded from Shaker society, taking with him a supply of tools that indicated he had become a cabinetmaker in his own right.

When news came in the spring of 1836 that the community at Union Village, Ohio, was in a state of disarray and rebellion, the Ministry and Elders of Watervliet unanimously elected Freegift as the "most suitable person . . . for repairing to Union Village, in the State of Ohio, for the purpose of regulating and organizing the Society of Believers in that place . . . as soon as the opening of River Navigation." Subsequently, on April 12, 1836, Freegift Wells and Elder Matthew Houston "set out from Watervliet on a journey to Union Village, Ohio, via New York, Philadelphia, Pittsburg, Cincinnatti &c." They arrived in good health after a sixteen-day trip, and Freegift took his place in the meeting house as First Minister of the community.[11]

Br. Freegift remained in Ohio until 1843. Although his major responsibilities were administrative, he also performed many tasks as a turner, joiner, and mechanic in the wood shop. In his journal entry for March 14, 1837, Br. Freegift recorded that Daniel Boyd of Union Village had presented him with a new brace and set of bits. During his years at Union Village, Freegift made drawers and bedsteads; he turned pegs, chisel handles, chairs, and a hat block. He also made planes, a broom machine, a "jointing machine for making glue joints," and a "compass saw" for the community.

Having succeeded during his seven years there in improving both the material and spiritual conditions in the Union Village community, Br. Freegift asked to be released from his administrative duties. On July 10, 1843, three days before Br. Freegift began his return trip to Watervliet, a man named David Carey took a work bench and tools to Cincinnati, "to ship east for Elder Freegift."[12]

14. Shakers living at Watervliet, New York, in the 1930s identified large man in the hat in this photograph as Freegift Wells.
Source: New York State Museum, Albany, N.Y.

15. This case of drawers was given to the New York State Museum, Albany, New York, by the Shakers at Watervliet in 1930. At the time of the gift, the Shakers noted that it had been made by Freegift Wells around 1846.
Source: New York State Museum, Albany, N.Y.

Between 1843 and 1857, Freegift was an Elder in Watervliet, and he was also a schoolteacher from at least 1847 to 1855. It is likely that these responsibilities absorbed most of his time, and we know little about his woodworking activities during these years except that he was not as active in cabinetmaking or turning as he was before and after this period. According to information provided by Shakers from the Watervliet community, a case of drawers (ill. 15) that they gave to the New York State Museum was made by Freegift around 1846. When Br. Freegift was released from the duties of the Elder's Lot at his own request on May 2, 1857—after having officiated as either a Family or Ministry Elder for more than forty-two years—he took up cabinetmaking in earnest once again.

Br. Freegift spent most of May 1857 moving his "tools & the like to the chamber at the south end of the herb shop," the place that would be his permanent workshop from that time on. He began to fix up the shop by "casing the windows & performing many other necessary chores pertaining to shop conveniences &c." and by "fixing an accommodation on the front of my bench for holding boards & the like for jointing."[13]

In the remaining months of that year, Br. Freegift continued putting his shop in order. He partitioned off a small room for tools in the northwestern corner of the shop, where he "furnished places for chisels, bits, plough irons & the like," then built a vise for which he "plained out two pieces of tough hickory," and bought a small bench vise. After going to the Second and South families to see their turning lathes, he built a lathe bench and resurrected his own lathe, first "cleaning it up with the screws &c. which had been laying useless for several years and got some rusty." At one point Br. Freegift dropped his brace while he was fixing up his lathe, a mishap which he noted in his journal entry for October 22, 1857: "I let my brace fall from the top of a short ladder on to a step stone & broke it, which I would not have done for the first 5 dollars that I ever saw. It was given to me by Br. Daniel Boyd at Union Village. However, I shall try to mend it."[14]

Br. Freegift built and set up a writing table in the shop. On December 4, he wrote that he had filed up a screw augur, "which I made for cutting vice screws perhaps 35 years ago & I do not believe it has been filed up since till today." After that, he brought over his "little lathe from the Elder's shop," cleaned and repaired it, and made, among other parts, "a pitman rod, & top box, a roller for the tredle." On December 28, 1857, he announced in his journal, "My little lathe is now finished & ready for business," and noted the next day, "In the afternoon I turned some in my little lathe, & find it works much better than it ever did before with the old tredle."[15]

Besides the descriptions of setting up his shop, Br. Freegift's journal from this period of his life gives us glimpses into two aspects of Shaker furniture making rarely seen in a cabinetmaker's notes: an account of the relationship over a period of years between a joiner and his apprentice; and step-by-step descriptions of how certain pieces of furniture at Watervliet were built, similar to the notes on the series of steps he took in building the "library" in 1834, but in greater detail.

Br. Freegift recorded some of the desultory woodworking tasks he performed during the first few months of 1858—turning curtain pulleys, some pegs, sewing machine spools, and bedposts—but the most notable event of this period occurred on April 13, 1858, when he noted in his journal, "This morning the Elders give me little Thomas Almond for an apprentice, & a fine boy he is, too."

Br. Freegift, who was seventy-three, lost no time in introducing ten-year-old Thomas to his newly outfitted shop. On the same day that Thomas came to him, Freegift wrote in his journal, "I have made him a bench to stand on & set him to turning at my little lathe." Within two months, Thomas was rough-turning brush handles, and Freegift was "learning Thomas to make mortises & tenons &c." He taught him to make window screens, and on July 29, Freegift noted, "With my instructions, Thomas framed 4 sticks together which looked quite workmanlike."

Over the next several years, the journal is replete with references

to the different kinds of tasks that Thomas was learning to perform in the shop and to Freegift's getting different kinds of wood and tools for Thomas to use. In his "Memorandum of Events," Freegift listed the tools he had purchased for Thomas:

1 Two Inch Steel Square	$1.50
1 Pannel Saw	1.50
1 Pair of Spring Dividers	.75
1 Trying Square	.56
1 Two Foot Rule	.69
1 Glass Level	.31
1 Double plane Iron	.47
1 Single Do	.31

These are all the tools that have been bought for Thomas exclusive of 4 plain Irons which were bought some time ago, 3 single ones & one double one which cost pehaps or not to exceed 1.50.

Although the time they spent together almost always involved work, it was not quite all work. There were times when the aging

16. This sewing desk in the collection of the New York State Museum was attributed to Freegift Wells by the Watervliet Shakers. The design of this piece is related to two other known desks, illustrations 17 and 18. Although the design of these three pieces is similar, construction details vary among them. It is possible that this item was popular at Watervliet and was reproduced several times by a cabinetmaker who made slight adjustments to the design and construction over a period of years or that it was reproduced by several different cabinetmakers. This piece is made of cherry and maple, with pine being used as the secondary wood in the drawers. The upper drawers are nailed together whereas the lower drawers are dovetailed. The castors and porcelain pulls apparently are original to the piece.

Source: New York State Museum, Albany, N.Y.

cabinetmaker indulged the boy ever so slightly, and some fondness and wry humor are evident in the journal on August 16, 1858, the first summer Thomas was with Freegift. "Through the earnest solicitations of little Thomas," he wrote, "I picked a watermelon, & found as I expected, that it was entirely green." As time went by, there were other signs of a friendship growing along with a master-apprentice relationship. In November of the first year, for example, Freegift anticipated the coming of winter from a boy's point of view and made a sled for Thomas. But the counterbalance to this hint of play came on December 7, when Freegift wrote in his journal that he was working on a snow shovel for the boy.

During the first year of his apprenticeship, Thomas turned window screws, brush handles, rake teeth, and pins, as well as working at planing. On December 29, 1859, Freegift had "turned one pin for a sample for Thomas to turn for the Wash house," and on December 31 he wrote that he had "dressed out pin [peg] timber this forenoon for Thomas to turn, & he turned 40 from 9 o'clock to first bell time—2^1/$_2$ hours." Freegift seemed pleased with his apprentice's work. On January 10, 1860, another journal entry highlighted the progress Thomas was making: "Made me a new Leather apron," Freegift wrote simply, "& altered my old one for Thomas."

In journal entries between February 29 and March 9, 1860, Br. Freegift described the process he used in making a small one-drawer table with a drop leaf. Although the process he describes is not unique to Shaker cabinetmakers, it is uncommon for the cabinetmaking process to be described in detail in the Shakers' journals.

On the first day of work on his small table, Br. Freegift "Went to the mill . . . sawed up a couple of maple plank 3 inches thick for table legs, but did not buz them." In other words, Br. Freegift selected some appropriate wood, sawed it to about the proper length, and roughly sawed it into squares for the legs. On the second day he "Went to the mill this forenoon & buzed out the stuff that I hunted up yesterday. Afternoon tryed out the legs for the little table." This day he used the "buz saw," that is, a circular saw, to cut the maple to the size needed for the table. He probably would have sawed them to taper from near the top of the leg to the bottom. "Tryed out the legs" refers to using a trying plane to smooth off the uneven surface left by the saw and to square the corners. On the third day Br. Freegift "plained out the two leaves which is composed of 5 strips & glued 4 of them together. Also plained out the end pieces." Here, Br. Freegift is describing the table top. One leaf was made of four boards glued together to make one wide board. The remaining "strip" apparently was for the drop leaf. The "end pieces" Br. Freegift refers to are probably "bread-board ends" for the table top. These are narrow strips of wood that are applied to the ends of the top to keep it from warping. On the fourth through sixth days Br. Freegift wrote, "Set out my table frame & morticed the legs &c.," and "Got my table together excepting putting on the leaf." On these days Br. Freegift made the base of the table. He did this by connecting the four legs with an apron, held together by mortise and tenons. On the seventh day, Br. Freegift, "Hunted up some stuff for a drawer." Since the table was to have a drawer, one side of the apron would have been made with an opening into which the drawer would fit. On the eighth, ninth, and tenth days, Br. Freegift made the drawer. He "Plained out the stuff for a drawer & sawed the dovetails . . . dovetailed the draw[er]," and "plained out the stuff for the bottom of a draw[er] for C[larissa]. V[edder].'s table & put it in, plained off the draw[er] & fitted it in &c."

Described here is the common process used in making drawers. The front, back, and two sides of the drawer were sawed and planed, and the ends of these were marked out for dovetails. (Dovetails are tightly fitting exposed flaring mortise and tenon joints usually used to join at right angles the end grain of boards. These joints are often used to join the four boards used to make a drawer.) The dovetails were sawed and chiseled out, the lower edge of the front and sides were grooved to hold the bottom, and the parts were glued together. The "&c." that ends Br. Freegift's description of making this table included any necessary finishing work. With Br. Freegift's description of this project and some knowledge of cabinetmaking, it is possible (ignoring proportion and scale) to visualize the table that he was making.

Dovetailing was another skill that Freegift taught Thomas. When Thomas's mother, Sally Almond, came to the community to visit in April 1860, Freegift wrote that Thomas gave his mother "a dovetail box with a slide cover, which he made near a year ago."

The bench in the shop gradually became a bench for two craftsmen. In January 1861, Freegift noted that he was working at his own end of the bench "to finish my hold-fast to my bench . . . laid out 9 mortices on the front side of my bench, bored them and morticed out 5 . . . finished my mortices & made a dog, or hook to go in them . . . then worked at Thomas's bench vice." On January 25, Freegift noted, "Thomas has got a complete head screw to his end of the bench & began to use it this evening." Then he added, "He is 13 years & 6 months old today, & it is possible that he may make a first rate believer, at any rate I hope he will."

A chronological account of the construction of what Br. Freegift called his "great stool chair" (a "potty chair" or "close chair") provides more furniture-making details and also affords glimpses into other aspects of Br. Freegift's life. The story begins on January 28, 1861, when Br. Freegift went to the mill to get a cherry plank for "posts to a stool chair." Two days later, he "overhauled [his] pile of boards & selected stuff for [his] big chair; and also make a draught of it to work by."

At that point, he interrupted work on his chair for one day. He wrote on January 31, "I went to the cider house & brought over some

17. This sewing desk, which is similar to those shown in illustrations 16 and 18, was acquired from the Shakers at Watervliet, New York. At that time the Shakers indicated that the desk had been used by Eldress Anna Case.
Source: The Shaker Museum, Old Chatham, N.Y.

boards to make Eunice's coffin of as we do not know how soon she may finish off, being speechless, & blind & also deaf as far as we know. I plained out the bottom board & struck a center line upon it & laid it by till it is needed."

On February 1, Br. Freegift resumed work on his chair and worked at it for thirteen days that month. On that first day, he wrote that he had "been trying & plaining out stuff for my stool chair &c." and on February 4 that he had "plained out my chair posts." On February 6, he "helped to get the mortising machine from the mill to the shop, took it to pieces & cleaned it all up, & did some motising &c." On February 8, he "sawed & plained out some cherry stuff for the cover of the chair," and by February 11 had finished mortising his chair posts. He next "fitted the casings on to the chair & rounded them off &c"; "went to the mill again and turned out my chair posts . . . also pinned on end pieces to the cover of my chair & fitted it in to its place"; "dressed out the arms for the big chair & fitted them on"; and then "rounded off the arms & glued and screwed them in their place." "So now it may be said," Freegift wrote on February 16, 1861, "that the chair is finished."

This last statement was premature. Br. Freegift worked on his chair for four more days that month: he glued it together, finished the seat casing, made the seat, and fitted that into place. By the time he made the bottom on which the chamber pot would rest and fitted that into the chair on February 23, it must have seemed finished indeed, but it was not done quite yet.

Time went by. Br. Freegift worked at other projects, many of them with Thomas Almond, and he also spent two weeks on a visit to his family's former Long Island home—but the chair surfaced again in his journal at the end of the year. On December 28, 1861, he wrote, "Worked some at my great stool chair to get off the varnish which was nearly as sticky as tar."

More time passed, filled with other work, and Br. Freegift took another two-week trip to Long Island, in the summer of 1863, before he was able to write the concluding chapter on the chair. On August 19, 1863, he wrote: "Have been taking off the old sticky varnish from my stool chair which had been on two years without drying at all. I took it off with Sal Soda water [an ammonia sulfate mixture], which did the work nicely. . . . August 20: 21: I also varnished my chair the second time over & it has dried good. . . . August 22: Fitted on the two covers of my stool & screwed them fast & fixed a place for it in the N.E. Corner of the shop." Thus Br. Freegift's "great stool chair" finally took its place in his shop.

On April 9, 1863, Freegift, chronicling another change in his relationship with Thomas, noted that "Thomas was taken from the boys class today & stationed in our room to live with me." Freegift made changes in the room's furniture to accommodate Thomas, in the same way he had modified his shop to include him at his bench. On April 14 he wrote in his journal, "Fixed over Thomas's bedstead, changed the rollers so as to draw it out endways." Thomas was almost sixteen now and had been Freegift's apprentice for five years.

That autumn Freegift and Thomas collaborated in making a long cherry table for the sisters; and after finishing that project, the two of them began making new tops for three other large tables, two of them 10 feet long, and one 11 feet long and 3 feet 7 inches wide. At this point in his journal (December 1863), Freegift began to write that "we" did this and "we" did that, in the process of making "our" tables. And on February 4, 1864, when they finished the fourth and last dining table and carried it into the dining room, Freegift announced in his journal that "we are now rigged out with a full set of new cherry dining tables." Before this time, Freegift's journal references had taken the form of "I did such and such," and "I instructed Thomas in this or that." Thomas Almond had now been working with Freegift for five years and nearly ten months, and these journal entries confirm that he had become a journeyman cabinetmaker. The two men now shared

the bench and worked side by side on separate projects. For the rest of that February, Thomas worked independently on a new counter while Freegift worked by himself on a clock case and a spectacle case.

On February 29, 1864, Br. Freegift referred in his journal to severe bouts of "the Cholic," which had begun to diminish his strength. Although the illness was severe enough for him to conclude that his "hours in this life were very few," Br. Freegift, who was nearly eighty years old, not only survived but continued making furniture in between other bouts of illness.

Life in the joiners' shop went through yet another change. On March 4 of the following year, 1865, Freegift wrote:

> The care of the Saw mill is given up to Thomas T. Almond, a boy of 17 years & 8 months old, but he is a smart fellow & I hope he will always do well & honor his privilege by faithfully bearing his cross to the end of his days. If he does this my blessing will always remain with him & he will receive a rich reward for all his labors. Hush now—What have I been writing? Likely as not he will get a peep at it sometime, but surely I hope it will not do him any hurt.

The details of what happened from then on are not known, but a Watervliet journal entry from two years later brings some imaginative focus to the picture of Thomas Almond growing up:

> [February 23, 1867] Thomas Almond made up his mind to leave, this afternoon, and some of his friends or relations came after him. . . .

18. This third version of the sewing desk is from the collection of the Art Complex, Inc., at Duxbury, Massachusetts. Although this piece is said to have had its origin at Sabbathday Lake, Maine, its form is so similar to the other two sewing desks that it seems most likely that it too was made in the Watervliet community.
Source: The Art Complex, Inc., at Duxbury, Mass.

[March 1, 1867] Thomas Almond, who left this family on Saturday afternoon last past, being assisted off, with his goods & chattals, by two men with team & sleigh; came himself this afternoon to get his "gal," one Ada Woods. He was lounging & hanging about the Mill and barns until about 7 O'cl[oc]k in the evening, when he got word to Ada, that he was after her and she of course, eloped with him in a secret manner, or, only by the knowledge of an individual or two, who were privy to the case.[16]

Thomas was almost twenty years old by then. Freegift was eighty-two and in declining health. On December 31, 1865, more than a year before Thomas left, Freegift had described ailments that would continue to plague him during the rest of his life:

Had no Cholic since October, of much account—But an abundance of distress in my hands & arms, including pain-throbbing-twinging-itching, a prickly feeling like that experienced in the feet when asleep—and sometimes shocks like those received from an Electrick Machine. By means of these difficulties which opperate more powerfully in the night than in the day time, I am deprived of much sleep, & comfortable rest thro' the night. And many times thro' the day my fingers are so numb, & unnatural that I cannot hold a pen to write, or a tool to work with, and I should think, if it were not for their twinging that they felt more like wooden fingers than they do like common fingers, & it is sometimes very difficult to button my clothes with them.

Despite his physical aches and pains, Br. Freegift continued to work. As late as July 1867 he was making bedsteads, and in the summer of 1870 he turned pipes for discharging surplus water from watering tubs and made a kitchen table. That same summer, Br. Freegift described how he made "a handsome walking cane" for himself out of a piece of wood that had been presented to him at Pleasant Hill, Kentucky, in 1843 by Micajah Burnett, who got it especially for Br. Freegift during a trip up the Arkansas River. Nearly thirty years after having received it, Br. Freegift wrote, "I turned it very smooth & nice from end to end and turned a handsome head out of Turkey Box, and today I have commenced using it, in my 86th year. The name of the wood is Bodock, and it is nearly as yellow as Saffron flowers."[17]

January of 1871 found Br. Freegift still giving yeoman service to his craft. A journal record shows that on January 4, "Daniel took the door off from the Hinges & carried it to Freegift's shop for him to work on"; and on January 5, "Br. Freegift came and worked on the outside door all the afternoon & it was very cold. It is a great job for a man between 85 & 90 but no one can do it so nice."[18]

In 1865, Br. Freegift had written a testimony in which he talked about how in Mother Ann's day it had been found that recreation and self-enjoyment were detrimental to the "Spiritual protection" of Believers. "It was proved beyond a doubt," Br. Freegift averred, "that a diligent person had more power to resist temptation, than one who was slack in hand labor. . . . Mother said an idle soul tempted the Devil. And it is probable that this was the cause of making the following remark, viz. That she wanted her children to *wear out,* and not *rust out.*"[19] Taking this as his own credo, Br. Freegift personified Mother Ann's exhortation to be diligent to the very end. On April 10, 1871, a Watervliet journal recorded that "Brother Freegift worked out of doors Sat. on his Asparagus Bed, burnt it over got extremely warm & exposed himself so he is very sick and since dinner they got him over to the Sick House he does not realize it is thought to be his last sickness."[20] It was indeed. Br. Freegift died five days later, a month before his eighty-sixth birthday.

Samuel Calvin Ely

(1780–1816) Enfield, Connecticut

One of the earliest known Enfield joiners, Calvin Ely was listed in Shaker records as a chairmaker and carpenter at the Church Family at Enfield, Connecticut. In a journal that he kept from 1813 to the time of his death, Br. Calvin, as he was called, described some of his woodworking. In one case he went with two Shaker brothers "up to Williams Swamp after a walnut tree for chair rungs &c."[1] He turned rungs, and front and back posts for chairs, as well as broom handles. He also built a clock case and a sister's workbench, and worked with another brother to make cherry tables. Br. Calvin also built at least two "patent" looms and turned dogs for the South Family's cider mill; and he worked with a Br. William on other tasks, which included constructing buildings and making coffins.

In January 1815, Br. Calvin made some tools, "Jointers fore plains &c. &c."; and during the remainder of that winter he helped prepare beams for the "upbuilding" of the Church Family dwelling house (that is, either removing the roof and adding a story and then replacing the roof, or lifting the entire building one story off the ground and adding a story underneath, as was done with the Canterbury schoolhouse, thus avoiding having to rebuild the roof). In October 1815 he and Br. William began making doors for the new built-in dwelling house cabinets; and on March 2, 1816, Br. Calvin noted in his journal, "I finished all the cobbard doors in the boddy of the house. In number 57."[2]

A record of Br. Calvin's death was written by his mother, Beulah Ely. According to her account, "He was taken sick of a violent fever the third day of March 1816. The fever run through then he was taken with violent hickups which continued till the seventh day. After that he seemed to be gaining, but had a disagreeable feeling in his side. Then an ulcer gathered in his side which ended his life the Second day of April 1816. He died ten minutes before eleven o'clock at night. If he had lived till the Sixth of July he would [have] been thirty-six years old."[3]

Isaac Newton Youngs

(1793–1865) New Lebanon, New York

"His mechanical genius was remarkable. In him was combined, The Carpenter, Cabinetmaker, Clock and Watch-maker; which obligation he filled to the last. He many years did the Tayloring, and when needed, could turn Machinest, Mason, or anything that could promote the general good. Very many of our little conveniences which added so much to our domestic happiness owe their origin to B[rother] Isaac. . . . Thus, our Br[other] filled out a life of usefulness. And now that his mortal race is run, it is pleasant to reflect on his virtues."[1]

These were the words of Elisha D. Blakeman, a fellow New Lebanon cabinetmaker, in an impassioned eulogy written in September 1866 to the memory of Isaac Newton Youngs, the man he called his "friend and Father." Br. Elisha also noted that Br. Isaac had been a musician and a school teacher, but it seems that he admired above all Br. Isaac's efforts and accomplishments as a historian and a scribe.[2]

Br. Elisha specifically mentioned a history of the Church Family at New Lebanon, which Br. Isaac viewed as perhaps his most important work, and described how Br. Isaac recorded "many long and precious" spirit messages during the great revival of the 1830s and 1840s, when "the smallest song did not escape his vigilent eye, and his industrious pen." He then went on to praise the volumes of journals, letters, essays, and hymns that Isaac produced—a legacy of "invaluable intellectual lore" that, he declared, would "live to edify and benefit pos-

terity, and society, when our Brother shall have been forgotten, living only in song or story." In fact, it is for his work as a writer that Isaac is most celebrated today.

In July 1859, Br. Isaac briefly described his work: "I have written journals a good many years, beginning in the year 1815. I wrote 14 volumes of general & religious matters—also wrote the Domestic Family Journal since 1834—and more than a dozen various journals of my own labor, my journies, &c. &c. and perhaps this is enough."[3]

Although he was then sixty-six and in failing health, Br. Isaac continued to keep the Church Family journals, commenting that "there is no one [else] that can well do it." It is fortunate that he did, for without Br. Isaac's dedication, much of the most interesting and useful information about cabinetmaking and cabinetmakers at New Lebanon would have been lost. Today Isaac's observations and ideas, recorded over more than half a century, give life to the story of the Shakers at New Lebanon. His journals and other writings not only provide a detailed view of other Shakers in the community but also give us a record of his own work and an intimate self-portrait.

Br. Isaac's early journals depict a young man seeking to understand his belief in God. On the pages of these journals he wrestled with questions of good and evil, and he was often tortured by self-doubt as he tried to reconcile Shaker beliefs with the realities of his own human passions, especially desires of the flesh. As he struggled to achieve spiritual harmony, his efforts to set the elements of his own soul in order paralleled his efforts to create work with his hands that was precise and honest and true. Over the years he was as painstaking and meticulous in tending to the fine details of his work as a Shaker craftsman as he was persistent and particular in trying to understand his spiritual nature.

Br. Isaac never became a church leader, but he maintained an unswerving personal devotion to Shaker principles for fifty-eight years. He was unusually forthright in expressing the questioning bent of his mind on occasions when he felt his faith wavering, and this may be why he was not (or did not desire to be) appointed to a position of leadership within the Shaker hierarchy. Nonetheless, through his writing and his many other contributions to Shaker life, he became one of the most influential and respected figures among all of the Shaker craftsmen.

Isaac was born to Martha Farley and Seth Youngs, Jr., in Johnstown, New York, on July 4, 1793. Martha soon after deserted her husband and children, and while the rest of the family went to live with the Shakers at Watervliet, Isaac, who was six months old, went to stay with his Uncle Benjamin and Aunt Mary in nearby Schenectady. Here Isaac was introduced to a Youngs family tradition—clockmaking.[4]

Br. Isaac later recalled in a journal devoted to his clockmaking, "When I was a child, I lived with my uncle, who was a clockmaker— I used to be with him in his shop & watch his motions, learned the parts of a clock, & could put one together perhaps when 6 or 7, & knew the time of day before I could talk plain. I had a relish for clocks & liked to be among them and handle the tools, but as I left my uncle, the spring before I was 10 years old, I did not arrive to much understanding of the business. I went to where no such thing was carried on & clocks were scarce,"[5] that is, to the Shaker community at Water-

vliet. But the dearth of clocks among the Shakers was a condition that Isaac in time would help to change.

It was 1803 when Isaac went to Watervliet; and on February 7, 1804, he went to live with Seth Youngs Wells, who was his nephew and the oldest brother of the cabinetmaker Freegift Wells. Elder Seth, a church leader and a scholarly man who was twenty-six years older than Isaac, was the next man after Benjamin Youngs to have a major influence on Isaac's life.[6] Isaac stayed with Seth for four years at Watervliet; and on March 24, 1807, he was formally admitted to the Shaker Society. Later that year he moved to the New Lebanon community, forty miles to the east, where he went to live in the Church Family.

The first trade that fourteen-year-old Isaac learned at New Lebanon was tailoring, under the tutelage of Rufus Bishop, a man who was to become his close friend and later First Elder in the New Lebanon Ministry. Adept at working with his hands, Br. Isaac soon mastered the tailoring trade, a skill he put to great use for the Shakers throughout the rest of his life. However, in 1815, when Isaac was twenty-one, he was able to resume his childhood fascination with clocks. He was permitted to work with Amos Jewett, one of the early Shaker clockmakers,[7] and soon he was making "tolerable good ones" himself, working at something infinitely more exciting to him than tailoring.

In his "Clock Maker's Journal,"[8] Br. Isaac described clocks that he made, beginning with one for the Elders' Shop in 1815 ("it being the first I have made of course it must be called No. 1") and continuing to 1835, when he made No. 16. Early in this period, Anthony Brewster, another Shaker cabinetmaker at New Lebanon, worked with Isaac at making cases for some of the clocks; and remarks in two journals provide a glimpse of their collaboration. Br. Isaac's journal merely mentioned that between November 25 and the 30, he "Made two timepieces, No. 3 & No. 4. To have cases." It was Benjamin Lyons who recorded that on November 28, "Anthony goes to work with Isac Youngs, making a case for a timepeas;" and added that on December

2, "Anthony Bruster finishes the case for the timepeas and sets it up in the spinhous."[9]

The Great House, the main dwelling house of the Church Family at New Lebanon, was rebuilt and enlarged in the early 1830s, and in 1833 Br. Isaac undertook "to make a clock for the whole house." Although he made it during the time he kept his "clock journal," Br. Isaac did not record it there, but rather described it in a letter to Elder Benjamin Seth Youngs at South Union, Kentucky: "The main clock or principal machinery," Br. Isaac wrote in December 1833, "is to stand in the Second Loft, in the little notch in the corner of the partion marked c. & with this there is be a connexion to faces in each loft."[10]

In addition to noting the main clock's connection to hands on clock faces on other floors of the house, the letter "c" mentioned as identifying the location of the clock provides a clue to another of the "little conveniences" that Br. Isaac made for the family. He goes on to explain to Benjamin that "the rooms are all numbered, but not with any Showy sign or label—then we have large figures printed on paper about an inch in depth for which I made some types on purpos which we paste onto the furniture[,] chairs, brooms—store things &c. &c. that belong to the several apartments which helps much to keep things in their place."[11]

Br. Isaac's interest in this lettering system is another illustration of his desire to impose order on life around him. It seemed at times as if he wanted the world to run like clockwork, like the orderly, logical world of mechanical parts that he understood so well. This interest also gives us another example of his joinery. At the Shaker Museum in Old Chatham, New York, Br. Isaac's initials and the date December 1833 are found on a box with compartments holding paper letters and numbers he made for this lettering system (see ill. 19 and 20).

19. This box, presumably made by Br. Isaac, contains thirty-six compartments for keeping his paper labels in order. The inscription on the inside of lid reads, "December 10, 1833," and is signed "iny," surrounded by Isaac's distinctive flourishes. The box, made of pine and stained red on the outside, is dovetailed together. Although its size is similar to the Shakers' seed boxes, its construction is much finer.

Source: The Shaker Museum, Old Chatham, N.Y.

20. These labels were printed by Br. Isaac with type he cut especially for the purpose. The numbers are 1 inch high, and the letter about ³/₈ of an inch. They were printed in black ink on a variety of papers similar to those used for seed packages and herb labels, and were intended to help "much to keep things in their place."

Source: The Shaker Museum, Old Chatham, N.Y.

Br. Isaac's woodworking was not limited to clockworks and clock cases. In 1839 he made a kindling bin for the woodbox on the second loft of the "great house," and a "box with bail to put wood and shavings in."

During the same year he was involved in another woodworking project of an entirely different order. In September 1839 he bore most of the labor in framing the new schoolhouse, a building which he had planned with the pupils in mind. It was to be "sufficiently large & airy . . . for their comfort & accommodation—for the convenient arrangement of the classes, and for the movement and exercise of the scholars on all proper occasions."[12]

He had earlier written a letter to his natural brother, Elder Benjamin S. Youngs, at South Union, Kentucky, advising him on design options for a new schoolhouse (see ill. 22). In that letter, Isaac included a description and drawings of possible arrangements of the scholars' desks, as well as drawings of the desks that were being used in the New Lebanon Church Family School, a rare example of a Shaker craftsman discussing the design of a piece of furniture. Br. Isaac was concerned with all aspects of the plans for the new schoolhouse, and it is likely that he was involved in designing and building these desks, of which he wrote, "Our desks are 8 feet long, 20 inches wide, about 2 feet 1 inch high on the front. 4 inches deep on the front, 6½ on the back, without the lid & top: top flat, 7 inches—lid slants 2½. Back board projects a little above thus" (see ill. 23 and 25).

Apparently the design sent by Br. Isaac was found to be satisfactory by the Kentucky communities. The collection at Shakertown at Pleasant Hill includes a desk matching the style and dimensions given in his letter. The Kentucky desk conforms more closely to the drawings and description sent by Br. Isaac than it does to the original desk that he was describing in the letter (see ill. 24).

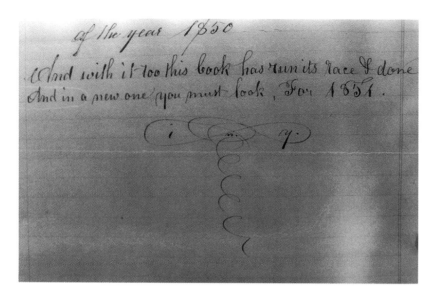

21. Isaac Newton Youngs used his initials, surrounded by this distinctive flourish, to sign his letters, diaries, and the account books he kept. The signature pictured is from an account book he kept for the Church Family and is nearly identical to the one he drew under the "1833" date on the inside of the lid of the box holding his paper labels.

Source: Hancock Shaker Village, Inc., Pittsfield, Mass.

22. These drawings were part of a letter from Isaac to Elder Benjamin S. Youngs at South Union, Kentucky, concerning the design of the students' and teacher's desks used at the New Lebanon Church Family's schoolhouse. The teacher's desk was designed to be used in conjunction with the raised platform in the front of the schoolroom. When the desk is closed, it is convenient to work at it standing up; but when the desk is open, it is convenient to work sitting in a chair on the platform.

Source: The Western Reserve Historical Society, Cleveland, Ohio

23. Two views of a students' or scholars' desk collected by Faith and Edward Deming Andrews from the attic of the 1839 schoolhouse in the New Lebanon Church Family. It is made of oak, cherry, and pine. Four scholars could sit at this desk.

Source: Hancock Shaker Village, Inc., Pittsfield, Mass.

24. A Shaker school desk from Kentucky. The design and dimensions are very similar to the school desks made at New Lebanon. It is interesting to note that the desk is actually more similar to Br. Isaac's drawings than it is to the original desks from which Br. Isaac made the drawings. For instance, it has square, tapered legs rather than turned ones. It is made of pine and is stained red.

Source: Shakertown at Pleasant Hill Kentucky, Inc.

25. This photograph shows Shaker girls sitting at a school desk similar to one pictured in illustration 23.

Source: Hancock Shaker Village, Inc., Pittsfield, Mass.

Br. Isaac's letter to Elder Benjamin also included details about the teacher's desk (ill. 22), of which he noted:

As to the teacher's desk, such a form as ours is perhaps as good as any. It is so calculated as to stand up, or sit down at it to write. It is 4 feet long & 20 inches wide & nearly 4 feet high on the back. It has two leav[e]s to fold or shut up, both so formed that when open they are right to set at in a chair, on a platform 8 inches high, & when shut, to stand at, on the floor, having a slant of about 3¹/₂ inches in 15. Below the bottom of the upper part of the desk there are drawers for papers, books, &c. The leaf contains an apartment to put in papers &c. In the inside, there are partitions, shelves &c. for various articles.

Another example of a desk that could be used either while standing or sitting, which is shown in illustration 26, indicates that this design was either previously in use or was copied from the desk described in Br. Isaac's letter.

In February 1840, Br. Isaac began work on what he called six "little timepieces." On February 8 he noted in his "clock journal" that he had spent a week "getting out stuff for the cases," and on the last day of the month he recorded that he had spent most of the month working on the clocks, with much time "taken up on fixing my tools to work with—making a crown wheel buz saw—fixing the engine for swedging out teeth to tin wheels &c. &c." By May 9, most of the clocks were finished, although he had some work left to do on one

26. Three views of a desk so remarkably similar in style to the teacher's desk drawn by Isaac Youngs that it is included here as a related piece. However, the dimensions of the desk pictured here and the one in the drawing differ considerably. This desk is made of pine and is painted apricot-orange.
Source: *The Book of Shaker Furniture* by John Kassay (Amherst: University of Massachusetts Press, 1980), copyright © 1980 by The University of Massachusetts Press

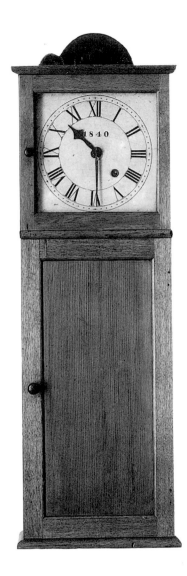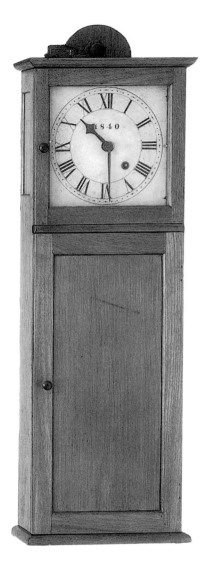

27. These wall clocks were made by Br. Isaac in 1840. Of the six clocks he made in this style, at least five of them still exist. These timepieces have wooden works and were made to run one day on a winding. Although all their faces appear to have been painted at the same time and bear the date 1840 on the front and similar poems about time written by Br. Isaac on the reverse, some of them apparently were not completed until a later date. He wrote that he finished No. 23 in 1847.

Source: Hancock Shaker Village, Inc., Pittsfield, Mass.

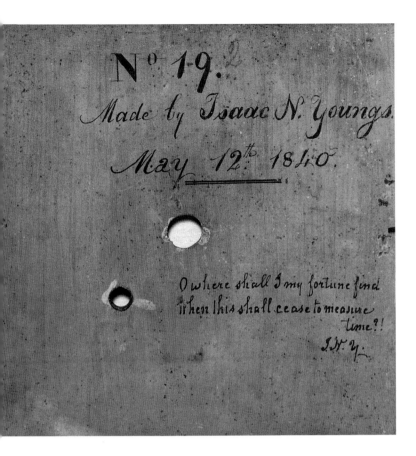

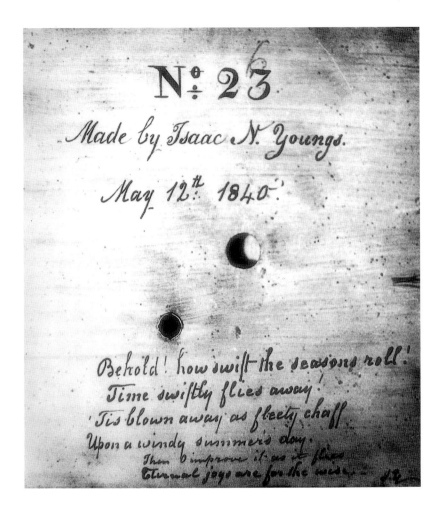

28. The backs of the faces of the clocks numbered 18, 19, 20 (unlocated), 21, 22, and 23 have all been examined. Clock No. 19 (ill. 28**a**) also has the number 2 on the back of its face; and clock No. 23 (ill. 28**b**) has the number 6. The 2 and 6 provide evidence that these were the second and last clocks in the series of six "little timepieces" that Br. Isaac began in February 1840.

Source: (**a**) Hancock Shaker Village, Inc., Pittsfield, Mass.; (**b**) James W. Gibbs

that was to include an alarm mechanism. On May 16 he finished that clock and took it to the Second House garret for John Meacham, and on May 28 he took three of the clocks to the Second Order. He tallied up the time it took him for this work thus: "It took me in making these 6 clocks & cases about 382 hours—nearly 64 hours apiece."[13]

He did not completely finish these clocks, however, until 1847, when he put the finishing touches on clock No. 23 (ill. 28a), a clock with one hand, which he made for the Second Order Barn. "It has one pointer," Br. Isaac commented, "but I think it more exemplary for a barn than a full made, first rate clock. It is rather a new idea to have clocks in barns, but they seem to be needful & admisable under suitable restraint."[14] Five of these clocks exist today, three in the collection at Hancock Shaker Village, one in a private collection, and one in the Time Museum in Rockford, Illinois.

Later in 1840, the year he embarked on making the six clocks, Br. Isaac was involved in other cabinetwork. In the middle of February 1841, Br. Isaac recorded that he "finished a job of work which he has been doing since the 7th of December for the tayloressess—viz. making two counters with drawers in them. Henry DeWitt helped about it & did about a fortnight's work—and also Benjamin Gates who worked about 10 days."[15]

Although he occasionally performed work such as framing the schoolhouse, Br. Isaac was primarily occupied by work that, like tailoring and clockmaking, required careful attention to detail. He was extremely precise in making and fitting together his wooden clock-works and their cases, and much of his other work also required a meticulous, sometimes delicate touch. Among his other tasks were making silver and steel writing pens, and pens for drawing a five-line music staff with a single stroke (ill. 29); cutting types for the special Shaker notation (using letters in place of round notes) in the books of

29. This pen and others like it were made by Br. Isaac to ease the task of drawing the music staff for those who recorded the many volumes of music written in Shaker communities. They have a brass nib fastened on a wooden handle.
Source: Hancock Shaker Village, Inc., Pittsfield, Mass.

music he printed in 1843; fabricating another kind of type or stamp for marking cheeses; and making a leveling instrument used in building construction. He also turned hundreds of dozens of buttons in the 1840s and 1850s, some made of coconut, some of bone. Even the hand-writing in his journals was meticulous, as neatly and carefully wrought as the work he described.

In the early 1840s, following guidance received in a vision, the Shakers set aside a special location called a "feast ground" within each community. These spaces were used for outdoor worship ceremonies, and at the center of each, the Shakers erected a marble "fountain stone" engraved with a spiritual message. In 1842, Br. Isaac was asked to engrave the sacred stone for the feast ground at New Lebanon. Not having had experience in this type of work, he set about learning how it was done. Br. Isaac first examined the lettering on various grave-stones in the Church Family burying ground and went to West Stockbridge "to see someone who understands lettering, or engraving on Stone," before he "began to Engrave the Word of the Lord, on a sacred stone" (ill. 30).[16] After he finished the job on July 23, 1842, he recorded that there were 645 letters on the stone and commented that he "could generally cut 50 letters in a day; & one day cut 100." He was always, it seemed, a man with an eye and memory for detail. In March 1843, Br. Isaac engraved another stone, this one for the community at Groveland. Joel Turner did the rougher work of cutting and polishing the marble, as he had done for the sacred stone at New Lebanon, and Isaac was again given the precision task of carving the letters.

Br. Isaac made a variety of other contributions to the Shakers as a mechanic and joiner. In 1840, in addition to the clockmaking and cabinetmaking already noted, he made a machine "for cutting screws to clothes pins," that is, for cutting threads on wall pins or pegs so that they could be screwed into the wall pegboard. And in August and September of that year he worked with Henry DeWitt to build a new lathe for the spinning-wheel business. Br. Isaac recorded that this amounted to four weeks of work for both of them, plus the blacksmithing time, making a total of fifty-six days of work for the project.[17]

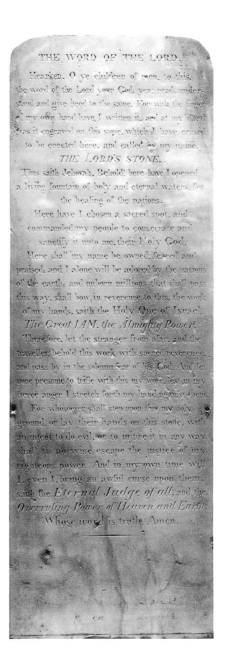

30. Fountain stones were erected in all Shaker communities during the early 1840s. Br. Isaac had the job of lettering the "Word of the Lord" on both the stone erected at New Lebanon and the one at Groveland. The Groveland stone is the only one still completely intact. It is signed below what would be ground level on the reverse side of the stone.
Source: New York State Museum, Albany, N.Y.

In 1853 he made frames for looking glasses, and in April 1854 he made a cupboard for sewing machine spools. Later in 1854 he made himself "a new slant, to write on, in the house." Also during that year, at the request of David Rowley, Isaac fixed the "screw tool machine" that was used for cutting 3/8″ threads on wooden screws.[18]

Br. Isaac continued to work as a maker and repairer of clocks, and he kept minutely detailed records of the weights and measurements and positionings of the clock parts. He was always interested in learning more about clockmaking, his first love. In October 1848 he went to Albany with a Shaker brother "to get some mechanical articles & to learn about spring clocks." He put this knowledge to work in January 1849, but with a sense of fatalism that was to reappear more and more frequently in his writing as he grew older. "I have done a little," he wrote, "may be 3 days work on a Spring time piece that I began in 1840. Hope to finish it some time before I die—but it is doubtful—I can get but little time to work at it." But characteristically, he persevered. He was able to work at it only sporadically during the winter, but he picked up the project again in May, and finally put the finishing touches on the clock in July 1849.

While on a trip to New York City in 1853 to see about buying sewing machines for the family, Isaac again sought to add to his knowledge of clockmaking. He made a visit to a clockmaker in the city and noted that while he was there, he had seen "a curious contrivance he was at work at—a head fixed so that the cap of hair ran up once in a few minutes, clear of the head! &c. & talked about compensation pendulums &c."[19]

Thanks in great measure to Br. Isaac's work over the years, clocks proliferated among the Shakers. In that place where once "clocks were scarce," as he had remarked in 1803, the pendulum had swung in the opposite direction; and in 1856 he was moved to comment:

Elizabeth Bates told me to day the Ministry bro't her a present of a clock from some body at Watervliet—It pleases her much—& I am glad for her merely as it respects her. But I fear for the effect it will have & the example—& the hard feelings some will have when they cannot have a clock as well as she—is it right?—will others admit it to be just? What are we coming to about clocks? How much I have felt my soul vexed at hearing folks say, "Others can have clocks to themselves—one in such a place—& such a place—why can't *I* have one."—I don't see as there is any stopping till we get a clock in every room & shop. . . . And watches come next. . . . Where in reason can we stop—till every man has a watch to carry with him—O how hard it is to please!![20]

However exasperated he may have been, Isaac continued his work, and in 1862 and 1863 he was still busy repairing clocks in spite of suffering from what was by then a chronic illness.

His work as a joiner had slowed considerably by 1857, when Br. Isaac offered some reflections on the carpenter's and joiner's trades as he had seen them develop during his time among the Shakers. In a historical memoir that he began that year, Isaac wrote:

There may be considered as one occupation, which has been followed from the first, in the construction of buildings, and in various jobs necessary for convenience, &c. . . . In the beginning, some individuals of Believers, who lived abroad, came and assisted in building. But for many years such work was all done within the Ch[urc]h. . . . Of late years, however, from necessity there has been much hiring in of the world, to do jobs of woodwork. . . . There were no essential improvements in this line, in a general sense for some years; the people were poor at first, inexperienced, & unable to put up costly & well built houses; their tools & conveniences for work were indifferent & inferior. But after the year 1813 there were some important improvements, particularly the buz saw was introduced, for streightening & slitting stuff—also matching works came in use; this greatly relieved the workmen of much hard labor. . . . Planing machines were introduced since the year 18——— [left blank] for planing

timber and boards, which have been of very great utility. . . .
Besides there has been a great increase in the number and quality
of tools, and various machines, &c. by which work can be done
easier, quicker and better.[21]

In 1840, when he was forty-seven years old, Br. Isaac listed his height
as 5 feet 8½ inches and noted that he wore a hair cap or wig, made for
him by some of the sisters. This bit of information and a traced outline
of his hand (ill. 31) are the only known indications of his physical
appearance. He was certainly a man of inner strength and resilience,
but over the years an extremely busy work life gradually took its toll
and played a part in his eventual physical and emotional deterioration.
As one of the most versatile of the skilled Shaker craftsmen, Isaac was
much in demand throughout his life to do work in one capacity or
another. In a long letter to a friend in August 1830, he showed signs of
overwork. "For I am that kind of folk," he wrote, "that is wanted in
several places at once & besides being needed in all general & important calls, in my leisure hours (if such a thing be possible) there are
many greedy wants, ready to swallow me alive."[22]

Br. Isaac's personal "Biography in Verse," written in 1837 when he
was forty-four, put his life into succinct perspective:

I'm overrun with work and chores
Upon the farm or within doors
Which ever way I turn my eyes;
Enough to fill me with surprise.

Of tayl'ring, Join'ring, farming too,
Almost all kinds that are to do,
Blacksmithing, Tinkering, mason work,
When could I find a time to shirk?

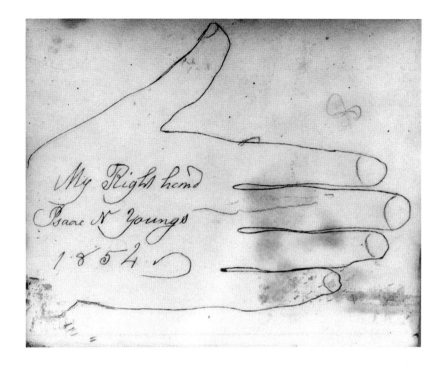

31. Br. Isaac traced his right and left hands onto the inside of the front and
back of a journal he kept between 1839 and 1858. It is so out of the ordinary to
find such a tracing in a Shaker manuscript that his willingness to commit such
an act in a way sets Br. Isaac apart from his brothers and sisters.
Source: The Western Reserve Historical Society, Cleveland, Ohio

Clock work, Jenny work, keeping school
Enough to puzzle any fool.
An endless list of chores and notions,
To keep me in perpetual motion.[23]

Br. Isaac's comments about his circumstances on June 2, 1855, sound
remarkably similar to his 1830 letter: "fixing some chairs, mending &
painting the bottoms—mending things, umbrella—injection pipes—

scissors—clocks—rule— . . . O my time is so filled up with little choars & jobs that I am almost out of patience—it seems almost as if I bro't nothing to pass, and can hardly tell what I have done—& still I feel in a hurry & sometimes in a worry I have so much to do, & cannot get time to do it—as soon as I get one chore done another is wanted."[24]

Though Br. Isaac's quotidian frustrations persisted, so did his desire for order. On July 4, 1855, he wrote: "I am 62 years old today—I feel myself approaching to the closing period of life. I want to be prepared for I know not when it will come. I feel very anxious that when I leave this world, all my concerns may be in order & my work properly done." Br. Isaac's desire to leave everything in order even extended to his selecting two hymns he wanted people to sing at his funeral, "Vain World" and "Happy Change." "Those who survive me," he commented, "may choose whatever they feel to in addition."[25]

Beginning in 1856, when he was sixty-three, Br. Isaac's references to his declining health became more and more frequent, but there were also moments of spiritual triumph. In August 1856 he reached a new level of confidence in his faith, which was apparent when he wrote, "I feel no doubt or discouragement in my own soul about the gospel. I feel it is my treasure, and I feel an assurance of future happiness—I feel I have gained much victory over evil, & especially over the great ruling passion lust, for I feel that is pretty much gone & dead—so far as I know."[26]

Although he worked at his record keeping after this time and continued to do occasional tailoring and clock repair work, his health was deteriorating. In 1859 he went to Saratoga, New York, to try the curative powers of the mineral springs. In 1860 he traveled East, again for his health, to Harvard and Shirley, Boston, Portland, and Gloucester; but those who knew Isaac saw the hopelessness of his finding a cure

during these trips. When his Elder, Daniel Crosman, wrote to the Harvard Ministry to ask permission for Br. Isaac to visit, he commented: "With Br[other] Isaac O dear me, it is a very hard case, can any thing be done to regulate the machinery & make it last a little longer, if some one can discover the defect, & cause the wheels to move with regularity again, they would perform a miracle in the latter days equal to former times. But we do not expect or look for any great extent, a little change may render temporary relief, & this is all that can reasonably be expected."[27]

Br. Isaac continued to be attracted to new ideas, and as in his clockmaking, music, and mechanics, he was challenged to find ways of putting them to work. In May of 1857, he and Elisha Blakeman built and put up a weather vane. After securing it to the top of the west barn, Br. Isaac commented that "anything like this, made on purpose, is a new article; it has been avoided I suppose, mostly for fear of being showy . . . [but] it seems to be admitted as convenient & proper, to readily know the course of the wind."[28]

In February 1864 he followed his experimental bent in looking for a way in which to improve his own well-being, about which he commented: "I begin about this time to make a trial of gymnastic exercise, for my health. William Calver & others have adopted the practice for some time to promote muscular strength; it is much recommended for this purpose. Let us see. There is much to be said about it; some ridicule, and others think it valuable to promote health and strength."[29]

Br. Isaac had good days and bad days. He would write about the wondrous things he might experience in the next twenty-five or fifty years but soon after would express grave doubts about living for even one more year. The passing of time, that inexorable fact of life that he had been acutely aware of since early childhood, had taken its toll on him, and in August 1864 he wrote that he was suffering from a severe depression: "I am very much out of health. I have very strange and wonderful experiences in the night—there seems to be two of me—I am rational and irrational! I am wide awake and fast asleep—and no mortal knows the sorrows and sufferings I undergo. —O could I know why all this is so: —some say it is all Hypo—who cares what name is attached, if it is really a disease; if it is really painful, if it be forced involuntarily on the patient—then it is a reality and the sufferer should be pitied and receive sympathy."[30]

His condition deteriorated so that by the next year he required constant supervision. In August 1865, when the person who was watching over him left the room, Br. Isaac fell to his death from his fourth story window.[31]

Much earlier, after Seth Wells died in 1847, Br. Isaac had written a eulogy about his mentor, in which he expressed regret that Seth had not left anything "in consequence in writing concerning himself."[32] Br. Isaac then revealed how important his own writing was to him. He said that he expected to follow Seth in a few years, "& bid adiew to time, & perhaps be shortly forgotten," but added:

I shall however leave a plain trace by my pen, which many will doubtless behold, & I hope with some satisfaction. . . . But whether or not, there be any trace left to my memory, or any solicitude be felt by those who follow me, whether I ever existed, or what I did—still to me, it is a matter of great concern that I be happy hereafter. For that reason, I spend much of my precious time, often out of my usual hours of sleep, writing to leave that which will shortly be of no use to me, but which I hope will edify those who follow after & be the means of encouraging them in the Gospel. If this be the case, when I am in Eternity, years & ages to come, I shall feel a happy reflection when I look thro the vail & see those on earth deriving a benefit from my labors; & when they come to join me in a blissful Eternity, our mutual happiness will be thereby increased.

Isaac N. Youngs

Years later, Alonzo G. Hollister added a fervent Amen: "Surely Bro. Isaac, thy labors are invaluable, & will do good to the end of time."

Benjamin Lyon

(1780–1870) New Lebanon, New York

Benjamin Lyon was born in Ashfield, Massachusetts, a town in Franklin County. He joined the New Lebanon community in 1806 and resided there until his death on July 14, 1870, his ninetieth birthday.

The earliest records of his cabinetmaking date from 1816 and are found in his work journals, which exhibit an interesting variety of phonetic spellings. Journal entries from June through December 1816 show Br. Benjamin making a cupboard for the bakeroom, a coffin, a cupboard for the shop, flooring for the office, the stair railing and "close pins" for a garret, "doars and drawers" for a cupboard, a case of drawers "for the brethrens' chamber," some "cupboard doars for the stoar hous & milkroom &c.," and, lastly, some wagon chests for the deacons.[1]

It is interesting that Br. Benjamin collaborated with another joiner on all of these woodworking projects, with the exception of the shop cupboard and the stair railing. At times Anthony Brewster worked with him, and at other times Jethro Turner.

In 1817, Br. Benjamin made a case of drawers with Anthony Brewster, then worked by himself to make some drawers for the shop. He also fixed up the "buz saw to saw dore stuff," and made a table. That November he and Elder Br. John William Porter finished "28 benches for ketchen use," and in December Br. Benjamin made "a copple of long ketching benches."[2]

In 1818 he made a long dining table, and in June 1819 a chest for the Deacons. Later that year he mentioned making "bedstid &c.," and

then there is a gap of fifteen years in his surviving journals. In January 1834, when the extant journals resume, he described himself working "at a bench for the sisters to work the dough with a lever to make crackers," and in May 1834 he labored to "repare a trundle bedsted &c."[3] In March 1836 he was "making a box out of hemlock boards to keep hats in," and in January 1837 he turned "goug handles & file handles" at the lathe.[4]

On April 11, 1837, he wrote, "I paint the Cupboard that I have made to go in the ketchen suller to put in Meet vitels to keep from the flies." And on April 27 he added, "Friday I finished the meet cupboard hang the doars and get the sisters to help cover it with a straner . . . and Permilla comes to finish it out for the first time that I recolect of her doing such a thing for nine years that is past we bring the cupboard and hang it in the Ketchen suller."[5]

Br. Benjamin worked at making wagons in the carpenters' shop, and after that, in the joiners' shop; but information about specific work that he did during the last thirty years of his life at New Lebanon has disappeared, along with any other journals that he may have kept in that period.

The only extant piece of furniture that is definitely attributable to Benjamin Lyon is a tailoring counter which was make in 1860 (see ill. 32). Br. Benjamin made this piece in partnership with Charles Weed, a Shaker brother who was born in Pittsfield, Massachusetts, in 1831, came into the Shakers at New Lebanon in 1838, and apostatized in

1862. This counter is especially interesting in that it is apparently the piece referred to in the "Farm Journal 1858–1867" kept by the Second Order of the Church Family. According to this record, on March 1, 1860, "Benjamin Lyon and Charles Weed are making a table with two rows of drawers for Hannah Train."[6]

32. The only known example of Benjamin Lyon's cabinetwork is this tailors' counter, which he made in partnership with Charles Weed. This piece is dated "1860" on the underside of a drawer. It is signed in pencil "Benjamin Lyon" in a large script, and "Charles Weed" is printed in a different hand.
Source: Mount Lebanon Shaker Village, Inc., New Lebanon, N.Y.

In 1821, six-year-old Giles Avery was placed by his parents in the Center Family at New Lebanon, and Benjamin Lyon was appointed to be his guardian. Br. Benjamin, thirty-one years old at the time, was an established furniture maker, and it is very likely that he introduced Giles to woodworking. In fact, it seems likely that Br. Benjamin was one of the early furniture makers at New Lebanon who were responsible for training some of the young Shaker brothers in woodworking, and these brothers in turn became the "second generation" of Shaker cabinetmakers.

In one of his last known journal entries, the importance Br. Benjamin placed on his craft is apparent, along with a hint of poignancy. He wrote on February 16, 1839: "Saturday . . . finely clean my self up go to Meeting have a presant from the spirituell world of a Transparent rule one foot long Hanah Blake gave the gift & said a song to be given."[7]

Anthony Brewster

(1794–1838) New Lebanon, New York

Anthony Brewster, born in Pittsford, Vermont, joined the New Lebanon community in 1807 at age thirteen and spent at least twenty-one years as a Shaker woodworker. Journal references to his making furniture cover only six months, but the quantity and variety of his work during that period indicate that he was a productive and accomplished joiner by the time he reached his early twenties.

In July 1816, Br. Anthony worked with Benjamin Lyon to make a coffin and during that same month made some cupboard doors. Brs. Anthony and Benjamin appear to be co-workers in the joiners' shop during the period covered by Br. Benjamin's journal. They worked together on several projects, although they worked separately on other occasions. In September 1816, Br. Anthony built a chest, and in November he worked with Br. Benjamin to build a case of drawers for the Brethrens' chamber.[1]

Isaac Youngs mentioned in his "Clock Maker's Journal" that in "November 1816, From 25th to 30th, [he] Made two timepieces, No. 3 & No. 4. To have cases."[2] Benjamin Lyon's work journal from this period noted that on November 28, "Anthony goes to work with Isac Youngs, making a case for a timepeas," and that on December 2, "Anthony Bruster finishes the case for the timepeas and sets it up in the spinhous."[3] The second clock was apparently cased by Br. Anthony in early January 1817. Benjamin Lyons recorded in his journal that on January 10, "Anthony finishes his Clock case redy for staining," and that he stained it a week later.[4]

In January 1817, Brs. Anthony and Benjamin worked together to make a case of drawers for the sisters. Br. Benjamin commented in his journal about this case: "Anthony and I tacles in to work at drawers with considerable zeal." During the last week in January 1817, Br. Anthony began work on what Br. Benjamin described as "a sink to wash hands in."[5]

A pine case of drawers from the New Lebanon community has the inscription on the inside of a drawer: "Made by A.B. 1817." Although Faith and Edward Deming Andrews suggest in their book *Shaker Furniture* that the piece was made by Amos Bishop (see ill. 3),[6] it seems more likely that it is a surviving example of Br. Anthony's work from this period.[7]

In November 1818, Br. Anthony moved from the Second to the Church Family and into a room with Isaac Youngs. On that occasion Isaac wrote in his journal, "I shall have to govern myself with some more caution with respect to vanity since Anthony has come here to live, but that may be an advantage to me, if I am wise."[8]

Records of Br. Anthony's woodworking after 1817 refer mostly to his work on buildings rather than furniture. Br. Anthony was suddenly taken with a severe pain in November 1837 and died the following March.[9] At the time of Br. Anthony's death, Isaac Youngs remarked that "his occupation has been that of a joiner & Carpenter till of late he left that & was employed in going out on business for the office deacons &c."[10]

Amos Stewart

(1802–1884) New Lebanon, New York

When Br. Nathan Kendal returned to New Lebanon from a trip to the East in late February 1811, he brought with him a wagon load of fresh fish and three new boys from Shirley, Massachusetts—Charles, Amos, and Philemon Stewart.[1] For nine-year-old Amos it was the beginning of a long sojourn among the Shakers during which he would be elevated to the Church's highest position of spiritual responsibility. He lived in the New Lebanon community until his death at the age of eighty-one in March 1884.

Br. Amos was a leader in the Society for nearly all of his adult life, one of the "first of the Younger class . . . appointed to labour in that calling." The Ministry had appointed Br. Amos to the Elders' Lot in the Center Family one month before his twenty-fourth birthday. Twenty-four years later, on November 14, 1849, he moved to the Church Family, where he held the first position in the Ministry, the highest office in the Shaker Church. In 1858 he was released from the Ministry to take the Eldership in the Second Family.

Meanwhile, Elder Amos's career as a Shaker cabinetmaker spanned at least sixty years. Nathan Kendal, who was one of the early Shaker woodworkers, was appointed to be Amos's guardian at New Lebanon, and it is possible that he introduced Amos to woodworking. The first record of Amos's cabinetmaking, however, shows him at age fifteen working with Benjamin Lyon, who wrote in his journal on July 2, 1817, that "Amos and I begin some panel doars."[2]

Two fine pieces of furniture dating from the early 1830s bear Amos Stewart's signature. In *Shaker Furniture,* Faith and Edward Deming Andrews identify a free-standing cupboard over drawers (Plate 22 in their book) as being signed, "Dec. 1830, made by Amos Stewart." Another piece was signed on the bottom of a drawer, "Made Feb 1831 Amos Stewart" (see ill. 33 and 34). This may be the piece to which a journalist refers in an entry for February 14, 1831: "Amos Stewart has been making a case of draw[er]s for the use of the Boys apartments, we hoist it in to the window this morning, as it is to go in the chamber."[3] On December 30, 1844, Giles Avery noted in his diary that Elder Br. Amos was "employed building a counter to the Garden House for accommodation of the herb business." A little over a year later, Br. Giles recorded that Elder Amos "made a counter with drawers for the Office Sisters," and a month after that, "a case of drawers for the boys' room."[4]

Over the years, Elder Amos's official occupation was listed variously by Isaac Youngs as "mechanic, a great variety" (1840); a "mechanic with a special interest in machinery" (1845); a "tailor-scribe" (1850); and "mechanical jobs of woodwork, etc." (1855).[5] In fact, his knowledge and skill in the mechanical arts led him, in 1864, to patent an "Improvement in Water-Wheels (ill. 35).

Accounts portray Elder Amos as a man who was physically strong, a man with a generous, giving spirit working on behalf of others. A partial list of his accomplishments includes: constructing a new planing machine for the society at Enfield, New Hampshire;[6]

33. Br. Amos's signature on the bottom of one of the drawers belonging to the case of drawers in illustration 34. Both the distinctive way in which Br. Amos wrote his name (using large loops on the letter "A") and the wide beveling of the drawer bottom where it fits into the drawer front and sides may be helpful in identifying pieces thought to have been made by Br. Amos but which lack complete signatures. Note the similarity between the signature on the bottom of this drawer and the initials on the piece shown in illustration 38, which was made more than 40 years later.
Source: Edward and Celeste Koster

34. This case of drawers with cupboards is signed, "Made Feb 1831 Amos Stewart." It was photographed in the home of Edward and Celeste Koster in the 1960s. Its present owner is unknown.
Source: Edward and Celeste Koster

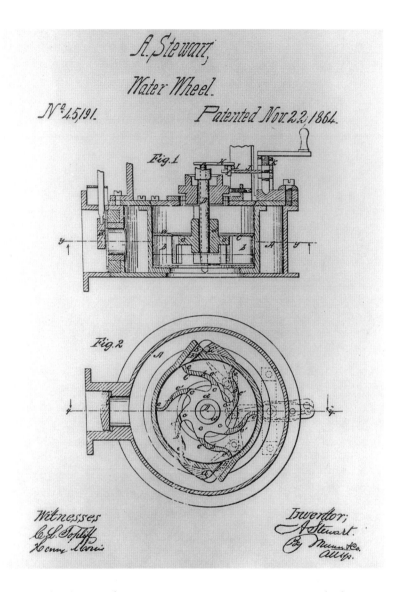

A. Stewart,
Water-Wheel.

Nº 45,191. Patented Nov. 22, 1864.

Fig. 1

Fig. 2

Witnesses
C. L. Topliff
Henry Morris

Inventor;
A Stewart.
By Munn & Co.
Att'ys.

35. This drawing for Br. Amos's "Improvement in Water-Wheels," patented in 1864, illustrates his knowledge and skill in the mechanical arts.
Source: United States Patent Office

building new wagons and making a waterwheel for the stone black-smith's shop at New Lebanon;[7] doing the inside finishing work with George Wickersham on the meeting house in Watervliet; putting on a granary roof; reclapboarding the Ministry's shop; and making the wheel for "a new contrivance of wringing clothes."

Although Amos Stewart's furniture embodies the graceful touches of a master craftsman, he was no stranger to heavy manual labor. Isaac Youngs described a project that required weeks of stren-uous effort: On June 4, 1853, he wrote that Elder Amos began dig-ging, with Daniel Boler, "to prepare for a foundation for an addition to their shop on the west side, 18 by 24 feet. . . . [They] laid the foundation of stone work, a very neat piece of work . . . [and on June 30 they] raised the addition to the Ministry's shop chiefly before break-fast."[8]

Years later, Isaac Youngs paid a special tribute to the Elder's work and spirit:

I could call the attention of the reader to the peculiar case of painting the meeting house this time. It was done by the free will offering of time & service by Elder Amos & Brother Daniel B[oler] They undertook the burden of the job—put up the stag-ings & did the painting, excepting what help they could pick up some of the time. They have shown a great interest for the gen-eral good & a willingness to spend their strength, time & attention, in bearing a burden in a temporal matter as, strictly speaking, does not belong to them; but because help was scarce & much is to be done, they have set an example which I think is worth[y] of the admiration of all.[9]

Elder Amos did not stop to rest. The day after he and Br. Daniel finished painting the meeting house, Elder Amos set out on a trip to assist people in the Canterbury Ministry in New Hampshire, and extended his trip to "Gloucester, Alfred, etc." As an Elder he often traveled to other communities, usually in the eastern Ministries, but

36. This kneehole desk, an unusual one for the Shakers, was made by Amos Stewart eleven years after he lost his left hand in a planing machine. It is proudly signed on the bottom of two drawers, "Made in 1877 by Amos Stewart with one hand age 74." It is made of butternut, cherry, and pine.
  Source: John Keith Russell

37. The bottom of a drawer from the kneehole desk, showing Br. Amos's signature. Note also the treatment of the bevel where the drawer bottom fits into the drawer side and its similarity to the drawer in the 1831 chest of drawers with cupboards shown in illustration 34.
  Source: John Keith Russell

he also made a western tour in 1858 with colleagues from New Lebanon. Elder Amos ministered to others with his "mechanical" gifts as well as with his spiritual ones, and on these trips he always found work to be done.

Elder Amos continued to make furniture, and at least two pieces that he made later in his life are signed and dated. These pieces are exceptional not only because they can be identified as Amos Stewart's work, but also because of the circumstances under which they were made. An inscription on one of these pieces, a butternut kneehole desk (ill. 36), highlights an excruciating trauma for Elder Amos. Written twice, in pencil, on the drawer bottoms are these words: "Made in 1877 by Amos Stewart with one hand age 74" (ill. 37). The story behind this inscription provides dramatic insight into the character of Amos Stewart. In November 1865 he lost his left hand in a planing machine accident. Accounts of the accident and of his recovery appear in a letter and a series of entries in journals and diaries:

> Beloved gospel friends, in sorrow and deep tribulation we now make record of a most melancholy circumstance which has befallen our good and worthy Elder Amos Stewart. On the morning of the 28th of Nov. past, while at work with a Machine plaining boards by poor light & not taking sufficient care, he got his left hand so near the Planiner that the knives caught the fingers of his glove which suddenly brought his hand between the forward roller and Plainer & instantly severed the entire hand from his wrist. . . . Elder Amos bears up under the severe stroke quite as well as could be expected, yet cannot avoid feeling deep regret at the loss of even a left hand. . . . His maimed arm appears to be doing well, but for several days was very painful.[10]

> December 24, 1865: 2nd Order Brethren have been watching with Elder Amos at the 2nd Family the week past. He appears to be getting along verry well. The end of the arm is more than half healed over.[11]

> April 12, 1866: Giles goes to the Second Family to see Elder Amos. He is to start tomorrow to go to Springfield, Mass. and New York, to get an artificial hand.[12]

> April 16, 1866: Elder Amos Stewart returns home from New York, whither he has been after an artificial hand. Succeds in finding a manufacturer who gives him promise of a hand within a few days, of great worth compared with none.[13]

> April 26, 1866: Elder Amos has got a new hand—said to cost $150.00.[14]

After recovering from the planing machine accident, Elder Amos went on to make not only the desk that he signed, but other furniture as well. For instance, an entry in a journal on February 23, 1877, states that Elder Amos made a counter for the Ministry.[15] Two other documented pieces—a cherry counter with pine panels, signed "A S 1873" (ill. 38a and b), and a drop-front desk signed "Made 1873 by Amos Stewart" (ill. 39a, b, and c)—as well as his 1877 desk endure as tangible statements of triumph over adversity. The inscription on the kneehole desk is especially poignant, a written declaration of Elder Amos's personal satisfaction at still being able to serve the community by practicing his craft.

His obituary, written by Giles Avery, appeared in *The Manifesto* of April 1884:

> Elder Amos Stewart, Mar. 7, at Mt. Lebanon, N.Y. Age 81 yrs. 9 mo. and 21 days. He was called to the Gospel of Christ in his early youth, and has ever been one of the most faithful to its principles during his long and very active and laborious life; both temporally and spiritually. A faithful, loving and efficient Elder for nearly sixty years, a part of which time he lived in the Ministry at Mt. Lebanon. He was a bright and living example of the beautiful principles of Christianity and was universally beloved, respected and honored by all who knew him, and rapturously the angels may now sing, Well done, good and faithful servant, enter thou into the joy of thy Lord. G. B. A.

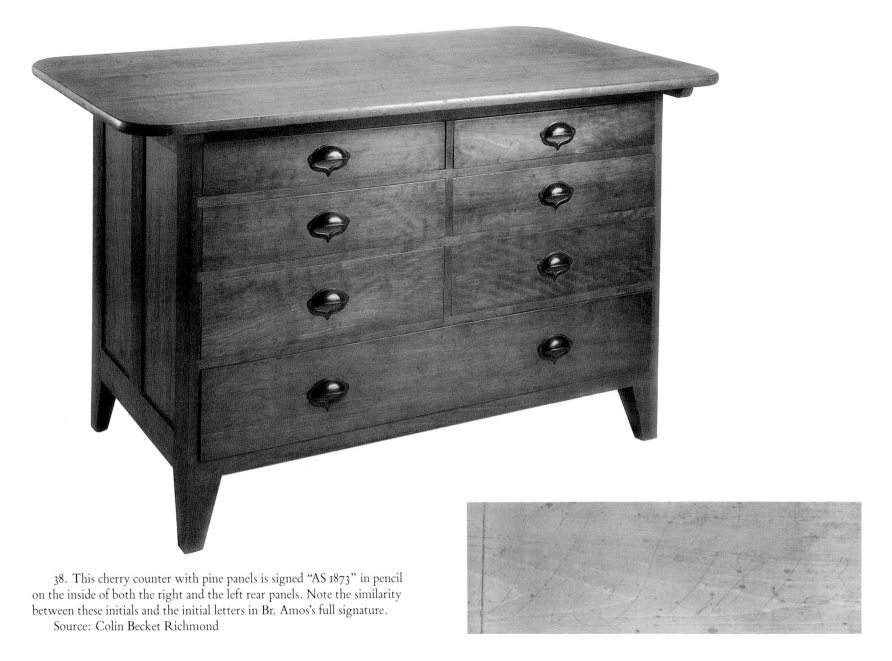

38. This cherry counter with pine panels is signed "AS 1873" in pencil on the inside of both the right and the left rear panels. Note the similarity between these initials and the initial letters in Br. Amos's full signature.
Source: Colin Becket Richmond

a

b

c

39. This drop-front butternut desk is signed "Made 1873 by Amos Stew-art" and includes many characteristic features found on other pieces made by Amos Stewart. Note especially the flush-fitting unlipped drawers and the deep, exposed mortices that hold the front drawer rails.

   Source: John Keith Russell

Robert Johns

(1795–1863) South Union, Kentucky

Robert Johns came to the South Union community as a boy and joined the Shakers along with the other members of his large pioneer family.

Br. Robert is the woodworker most often mentioned in South Union journals. He was foreman of the joiner work on the Church Family dwelling house which was begun in 1822,[1] and through the 1820s and 1830s did other woodworking jobs that included laying a floor in the "yellow carpenter's shop," making the woodwork for the "first carriage made in the society for the ministry," and making shingles, a stairway, and a "large press for medicines." Br. Robert was also a mechanic and made a "flax-dressing machine" in 1826. In the 1840s and 1850s he made chairs for both the Church Family and the North Family.

Elder Benjamin Seth Youngs paid an unusual birthday tribute to him on December 22, 1834, by describing him as "Robert Johns 39 years old today our leading carpenter and wood work man."

The only known piece of South Union furniture with an inscribed date, "August 2nd 1839," may well be the work of Robert Johns. It is a cherry drop-leaf table that has a square top when the leaves are extended (ill. 40a and b).

Robert Johns died of erysipelas on March 15, 1863.

40. This cherry table is attributed to Robert Johns only because of its inscribed date and Br. Robert's activity as a cabinetmaker during that time period. The table escaped the great sale of 1922 because it was being used in the

"preservatory," the building where the Wallace family, caretakers of the Shaker farms, lived at the time. The table was given to Nell McCarley by the Wallaces in appreciation of her voluntary care of their daughter during a bout of typhoid fever. Miss McCarley in turn gave the table to its present owner in 1937 as a birthday present. The table has been altered since it was used by the Shakers. The legs have been lengthened to make it comfortable for dining, and both drop leaves have been added.

Source: Lucy McCarley

Thomas Hammond, Jr.

(1791–1880) Harvard, Massachusetts

Thomas Hammond, Jr., was born on August 8, 1791, in Newton, Massachusetts, a town that is now part of greater Boston. Thomas may have spent his early childhood at the Harvard community, but he also lived in Paris, Maine, for four years, from the time he was eight until he was twelve. He officially joined the Church in 1810 when he was nineteen.

There are few journal entries referring to Br. Thomas's career as a joiner. It was noted, however, that on June 27, 1826, Br. Thomas received help from his brother Joseph in gluing "together the backs & fronts of 15 chairs." And on January 5, 1839, a fellow Shaker recorded that "Elder Brother Thomas Hammond has put four new chairs into the Ministry's kitchen & taken the old ones. He has made all the chairs for many years."[1] Br. Thomas continued to make chairs. A journal entry from April 4, 1841, mentioned that "Elder Brother Thomas Hammond had his eye hurt while turning chair rounds at the mill which laid him up";[2] and on January 28, 1843, another journal noted that Elder Thomas was the foreman of the chair-making operation. That account puts the total number of chairs produced in 1841 and 1842 when he was foreman at 339, and adds, "there was put at the office (for sale) 83 common, 3 rocking chairs with arms, and six small ones—92 in all."[3]

Although many of the journal references to Elder Thomas have to do with his responsibilities as a church leader, including his trips to the New York and New England Shaker communities, mention is also made of other woodworking tasks. On December 15, 1849, Elder Thomas hauled maple logs to the mill for sieve rims; he worked at the mill planing sieve rims with his new machine; and on May 9, 1851, he taught William Patch how to "rim sieves." Also, another Harvard journal notes that on August 25, 1858, "Brother Thomas returned & brot a case of draw[er]s he made at Shirley for his convenience here in the meeting house."[4]

The only piece of furniture possibly attributable to Elder Thomas is a case of drawers made of pine (see ill. 41 and 42), with an inscription on one of the drawers that reads: "Thomas Hammond this belongs to his case of draw[er]s." The piece is not dated, however, and it is possible that it was made by Thomas's father, Thomas Hammond, Sr., who was also a woodworking craftsman at Harvard from 1792 until 1824.

Over the years Elder Thomas kept several journals, and between 1839 and 1850 he further pursued his interest in writing and history by compiling *Sayings of Mother Ann and the First Elders: Taken from Abijah Worcester.* He also wrote, in 1862, *Sketches of Shadrach Ireland Etc.,* essays about the radical New Light preacher who had occupied the Square House at Harvard before the Shakers gathered into a community.

At the age of eighty-nine, after a long life with the Harvard Shakers, Elder Thomas died on December 21, 1880.

42. The case of drawers shown in illustration 41 can easily be removed from its frame, which makes it possible to see how this underslung drawer is mounted in the base. The drawer in the base seems to have been a later addition to this piece.

Source: Hancock Shaker Village, Inc., Pittsfield, Mass.

41. On Shaker furniture, the underslung drawer is common only on pieces made at Harvard, Massachusetts. Bail handles on the sides of this case of drawers in a frame make it an easy piece to move. It may very well be that this piece is the one that Thomas made at Shirley and brought back to Harvard "for his convenience . . . in the meeting house." It would make sense for Thomas to have a chest that he could easily move for he frequently traveled back and forth to Shirley.

Source: Hancock Shaker Village, Inc., Pittsfield, Mass.

Daniel Sering

(1792–1870) Union Village, Ohio

Daniel Sering came to the fledgling Shaker settlement at Union Village, Ohio, in 1805 at the age of thirteen. His father, Samuel Sering, was included in the first gathering there, and several other family members also joined the Ohio Shakers.

Br. Daniel became an elder in the Center Family in 1826, and in 1827, with six other men, went to the community at Whitewater "to put up a large cabin building to make room for an increase of numbers expected from West Union" (the Indiana community at Busro, which closed that year). He lived at Whitewater from 1830 to 1838 "as an aid to Elder Archibald," then returned to Union Village.

During the last thirty years of his life he performed a variety of woodworking and mechanical tasks. He repaired machinery, including a "cooper machine," built a machine for pressing brick, and in 1853 helped construct a steam sawmill at Whitewater. His skill as a mechanic was apparently highly valued, for he was sent to inspect machinery that was to be purchased by the community—a threshing machine in Dayton, for example, and on another occasion, an "engine lathe." He also oversaw the purchase of such construction materials as lumber and building stone.

Elder Daniel worked at the sawmill now and then. In 1842 he was appointed to a committee to draw up plans for "the new centre house." In 1859 he assisted in the construction of a new building at Whitewater, and in 1864 he worked "to put up woodwork of the New Nurse house at second order," where he had "charge of the hands & the sawing & getting of the logs."[1]

The one piece of furniture attributed to him comes from earlier in his life—a butternut case of drawers inscribed with his name and the date November 9, 1827 (ill. 43 and 44)—but he continued his woodworking until he died. In December 1869, the month before his death, Elder Daniel was using pine boards in "making a black board to write music on."[2]

On January 2, 1870, he died "of erysipelas in the hand." At that time a fellow Shaker noted that "Brother Daniel was our principal mechanic for about 50 years. The present meeting house was built by him."[3] Another writer added, "He was a good mechanic in wood and superintended the building of most of the buildings in Union Village, also a number at Whitewater."[4]

43. This case of drawers is dated "November 9th 1827" and is signed "Daniel Sering." It is made of walnut or butternut and poplar.
Source: Warren County Historical Society, Lebanon, Ohio

44. Br. Daniel signed this piece in bold script on the back of one of the drawers.
Source: Warren County Historical Society, Lebanon, Ohio

Richard McNemar

(1770–1839) Union Village, Ohio

Richard McNemar was born in the Tuscarora Valley of Cumberland County, Pennsylvania. He was a bright student in school and became a teacher at the age of fifteen. In his late teens he crossed the Allegheny Mountains to western Pennsylvania, where he lived with his brother Garner and continued to teach school. He spent a year exploring the frontier in Kentucky, working as a weaver and a farmer to support himself, then returned to Pennsylvania and schoolteaching for another year. At the age of twenty-one he again went to Kentucky, this time to study theology. He acquired a reading knowledge of Latin, Greek, and Hebrew. He was married in 1793 and became a Presbyterian preacher in 1797. Richard played a leading role as a revival preacher in the great Kentucky Revival of the early 1800s. In 1802 he moved to Turtle Creek, Ohio, where he later broke away from the Presbyterian church to become a New Light minister.

In 1805 he and his wife, Jenny, who by then had seven children, were converted to Shakerism by three missionaries sent that spring from the New Lebanon community—Benjamin Seth Youngs, Issachar Bates, and John Meacham. Many members of Richard's New Light congregation in turn converted. The land that Richard donated to the Society became the site of Union Village, the first and largest of the western Shaker communities.

Br. Richard became one of the best-known and most influential Shakers of his time. He worked as a missionary to the Shawnee Indians, helped establish the West Union community at Busro, Indiana, and became a writer, composer, printer, bookbinder, and furniture maker. Br. Richard's account of the Kentucky Revival (1807) was the first bound book published by the Shakers,[1] and he worked with Benjamin Seth Youngs in 1823 to revise the third edition of *The Testimony Of Christ's Second Appearing.* He inaugurated *The Western Review,* the first Shaker periodical, at Watervliet, Ohio, in 1834; and he published his own essays and poetry, often under the pseudonym of Eleazer Wright, the Shaker name given to him at New Lebanon in 1811 by Mother Lucy Wright. In her biography, Hazel Spencer Phillips stated that Br. Richard "composed more hymns, anthems and exercise songs for the early Shakers than any other person."[2]

As a mechanic and woodworker, Br. Richard built woodworking lathes and weaving looms; made a grand total of 1,463 chairs; and turned wheels, reels, spools, and "whirls." One surviving piece of furniture attributed to him is a set of drawers cited by Kassay as having been made for Richard's son Benjamin to keep "little tools" in (ill. 45).

A man of formidable talents and a strong charismatic personality, Br. Richard fell prey in 1839 to an invidious effort by Elder Freegift Wells to drive him from Shaker Society, an affair recounted in detail in Phillips's biography. Br. Richard was subsequently vindicated and reinstated by the New Lebanon Ministry and went back to Union Village, but he died within a matter of weeks after his return. He was a notable character on the American frontier, and at the very end of his life he became a tragic figure on the stage of Shaker history.

45. Although according to tradition this piece was made by Richard McNemar, it is interesting to note the similarity in the beading on the drawer fronts of this piece and the case of drawers made by Daniel Sering. It seems to be a detail that one cabinetmaker learned from the other, providing a point of commonality between two pieces of Union Village furniture.

Source: Warren County Historical Society, Lebanon, Ohio

Henry DeWitt

(1805–1855) New Lebanon, New York

John DeWitt, his wife, and their seven children moved from Canada to Watervliet, New York, in March 1813. The two oldest boys returned to Canada, but the rest of the family united with the Shakers and moved to the New Lebanon community the next month.

The DeWitts' son Henry spent his early adolescence making nails in the blacksmith shop, and at the age of seventeen joined his brothers John Jr. and George in the shoemaking trade. Henry wrote in his journal concerning his work as a shoemaker, "I find the shoemaking business does not agree with my health; so I leave it and turn my hands to something else before it is to late."[1] In November 1827 he began working with Br. Levi Chauncey at the business of making spinning wheels and "likewise at making clock-reels, & baskets &c."[2]

Faith and Edward Deming Andrews, in *Shaker Furniture*, quote at length from Br. Henry's journal, which he kept from 1827 until near the time of his death. In this journal Br. Henry describes a good deal of his work at the lathe, turning "closepins,"[3] drawer pulls or "buttons," bobbins, tool handles, banisters, and wheel spokes—besides his work as a reelwright. Although on occasion Br. Henry made some new piece of furniture, most of his work at joinery seems to have involved repairing and modifying existing pieces or working with other joiners to make new pieces. In 1836 he wrote, "I put a pair of rockers to a chair for Molly Bennett," and "lowered the upper story to Frederick S[izer]'s Desk & put legs to it." The next year he wrote, "I put rockers to a chair for Eliza Ann Taylor & took the rockers off a

new rocking chair & lowered it about $1^1/_2$ inches & put them in again."[4] In 1837 he worked with David Rowley to make a number of cabinetmaker's planes (ill. 46), and Br. Henry "did about a fortnights' work" in 1840 assisting Isaac Youngs in making two counters with drawers for the sisters in the tailor shop.[5] In 1854, Br. Henry took on the project of dividing one counter into two for the sisters. He wrote, "I took off [four drawers from] the end of the Counter that's going to the Washhouse for the Drawer basket business; planed the leaf over &c. &c. Expect to smooth it sometime." On March 21, 1854, he continued, "I worked fixing a carcass for the 4 drawers I cut of[f] the Counter . . . for the sisters at the Washhouse."[6]

In the midst of what seemed to be the constant business of furniture repair, Br. Henry occasionally made a piece of new furniture. In March of 1841 he noted that he had "Finished making a counter for the Deaconesses with 12 drawers[;] took between 3 & 4 weeks work."[7] This work continued into the 1850s, with Br. Henry making such things as a "shoe bench for Chauncey [Sears]," "a woodbox with a sink attached to it," and "a small drawer for [his] writing table."[8]

Br. Henry from time to time returned to shoemaking; and in 1841, Isaac Youngs noted that Br. Henry had moved to a different room in the Brethrens' Shop, where he worked at bookbinding (ill. 47 and 48) and making spinning wheels. In June 1845, Br. Henry recorded that he had made "12 spinning wheels and 3 patent heads."[9]

One signed piece of Br. Henry's woodworking at this time is

46. This woodworking plane—from the Church Family workshops at New Lebanon and bearing the impressed initials "HDW"—is undoubtedly one used by Henry DeWitt, although it is a commercially made plane and, therefore, not one of those he made with David Rowley. The plane, a ¹/₂-inch round from which the iron and wedge are missing, was made by "Rowell & Gibson Albany." This imprint appears on planes made by John Gibson and Simeon Rowell between 1825 and 1828.

Source: The Shaker Museum, Old Chatham, N.Y.

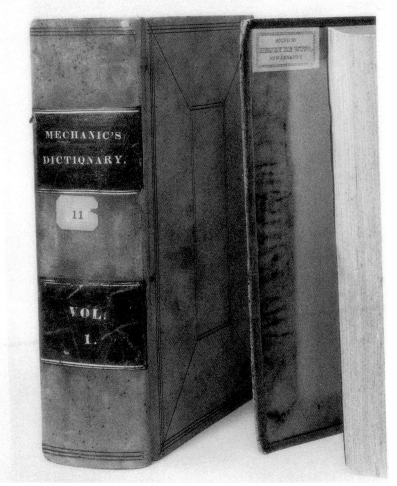

47. The two-volume *Mechanic's Dictionary* was bound by Henry DeWitt for George Wickersham. On December 9, 1853, Br. Henry recorded in his diary the following information: "I get all the covers on . . . my books to day 42 of them 23 Hymn books 2 anthem books for the Hill folx & 7 hymn book 2 large Mechanick's Dictionary on Machinery for Geoʳ Wickersham 11 verse books." The volumes themselves contain Henry's binder's ticket and a rubber stamped inscription stating that the books are from the Church Family Library.

Source: Hancock Shaker Village, Inc., Pittsville, Mass.

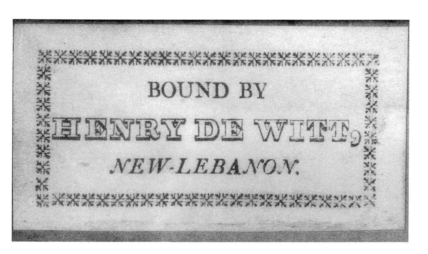

48. Although there were many Shaker bookbinders, this is the only extant example of a signed binding or a binding that contains a binder's ticket. Br. Henry's experience in printing seed and herb labels certainly would have made it easy for him to produce this label for his binding work.

Source: Hancock Shaker Village, Inc., Pittsfield, Mass.

known—a loom signed "H.D.—March—1834" (ill. 49). The date of this piece coincides with the following description in Br. Henry's journal:

> March 1834   The two past weeks, after my days work at making cloth shoes; I have employed myself at making a loom; or began to make one. It is to replace the loom that was bought, it proved nothing at all. In the morning I commenced working on my loom and expect to continue. I have been working at said loom the week past. . . . I finished said loom. It was stain'd yesterday. Eleanor P[otter] & Jane B[lanchard] stain'd it.

Later that month Br. Henry wrote, "I have been about 4 weeks making this spring shuttle loom. I took my new loom over to the spinshop and set it up for weaving. Beamed on about 30 yards of course linen. Betsy Crossman wove some & it went well."[10]

In October 1854, Br. Henry came down "with some disease in his neck & throat, it is hardly understood what it is";[11] and at the beginning of 1855, Isaac Youngs listed Br. Henry's occupation as "printer, now confined." Once taken ill, Br. Henry lived only a little more than one month, dying on February 8, 1855, "after a serious scene of sufferings at 7 minutes past 1 ocl. P.M. aged 49 y. 1 m. 12 d.–"[12]

a

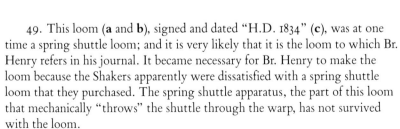

b

c

49. This loom (**a** and **b**), signed and dated "H.D. 1834" (**c**), was at one time a spring shuttle loom; and it is very likely that it is the loom to which Br. Henry refers in his journal. It became necessary for Br. Henry to make the loom because the Shakers apparently were dissatisfied with a spring shuttle loom that they purchased. The spring shuttle apparatus, the part of this loom that mechanically "throws" the shuttle through the warp, has not survived with the loom.

Source: Hancock Shaker Village, Inc., Pittsfield, Mass.

Abner Allen and Grove Wright

(1776–1855)   *(1789–1861)*

Enfield, Connecticut, and Hancock, Massachusetts

A scarcity of surviving written records has until now severely limited the discussion about the history of furniture from the Hancock Bishopric. However, a discovery stemming from the research for this book has stimulated and broadened this discussion considerably. The discovery was that an unusual construction feature of Shaker furniture evolved within the Hancock Bishopric—the sides of the drawers from many pieces are tapered, that is, the wood is thicker at the bottom of the drawer sides than it is at the top edge. This feature has been found on more than thirty pieces of furniture known to have been made either at Enfield, Connecticut, or at Hancock, Massachusetts. Among the Shakers this particular construction is apparently unique to cabinetry in the Hancock Bishopric. Although it is not known why these craftsmen constructed their drawers in this manner, the feature gives the drawers a more delicate appearance without sacrificing strength and leaves us with a distinctive school of cabinetmakers to study.

Although existing documentation does not indicate where and when this style of construction originated, there are a few known pieces of non-Shaker furniture with tapered drawer sides that can be traced to Connecticut cabinetmakers. If the tradition of tapered drawer sides was present in the work of worldly Connecticut cabinetmakers, it would seem likely that the Shakers picked up this practice at Enfield rather than at Hancock. Furniture makers at Hancock either learned the practice from Enfield Shakers who traveled to Hancock to

work or, as is more likely, learned it at Enfield when they were visiting there. The built-in cases of drawers in the 1830 Brick Dwelling at Hancock are the earliest dated examples of Shaker furniture with tapered drawer sides. However, the precision of the skill exhibited in their construction and the existence of undated tapered drawer side pieces appearing to be from an earlier period indicate that the technique was well established by 1830 and may have been practiced a decade or even two decades earlier.

Although Grove Wright and Abner Allen, the two cabinetmakers for whom we have documented pieces with tapered drawer sides, had died by the time of the Civil War, the practice apparently lived on beyond their work. The Ministry at Hancock decided to replace their old shop with a new one in 1873, and on the backside of one of the drawers in these built-in cases is the inscription, "John B Little Sommerville Ct August 13, 1873." Sommerville is the town closest to the Enfield community. Although a John Little is not listed in the Shaker membership records, the fact that these drawers are constructed with tapered sides suggests that either he was a member of the Society at Enfield and the record of his membership has been lost or that he worked with the Enfield brethren and had picked up this style of work from them.

Not all of the furniture makers in the Hancock Bishopric made furniture with tapered drawer sides. Although variations of this construction technique on as-yet-unattributed pieces suggest that other furniture makers were working in this tradition, it is only with the work of Grove Wright and Abner Allen that this feature has been identified on attributable pieces of furniture. As more pieces with tapered drawer sides are discovered, however, other groupings of furniture may emerge, possibly a collection here or there obviously made by the same person. If a piece from one of these groupings can then be positively attributed to a specific individual, the entire grouping in which it is found may be attributable to that furniture maker as well.

This peculiarity of drawer construction in the Hancock Bishopric suggests the possibility of developing a new body of information about Shaker furniture made in all communities through the study of its construction as well as the study of its design.

In a letter dated December 20, 1852, the Enfield Ministry wrote to Elder Grove Blanchard at the Harvard Ministry: "We had forgotten to mention that Abner Allen, had a Paralitic Shock a few weeks ago, which has disanabled him for any business, & the probablility is, he will never be any better. He will be much mised, in the family, and Society, as he was a laborious Brother, a good Mechanic, & the only one who well understood the business of cloth-dressing."[1] Their sorrowful prognosis was, unfortunately, correct. Abner Allen died at the Shaker community in Enfield, Connecticut, on June 21, 1855, at the age of seventy-nine.

Abner was born in 1776 and spent most of his life as a member of Enfield's North Family. Other members of Abner's family also became Shakers, but apart from these facts and the account of the stroke he suffered in 1855, little is known about his life.

However, the furniture that Br. Abner made speaks eloquently about the man as a cabinetmaker. Two signed pieces and several other pieces that may be attributed to him because of the construction techniques used portray Br. Abner as a craftsman who made furniture of exceptionally fine quality and design.

Ironically, Abner Allen's signature has caused confusion about his identity for many years. As illustrated on his two signed pieces, the tail and flourish on the last letter of his signature make it appear to be a *y* rather than an *n,* and until now caused him to be known as "Abner Alley." Those who recorded his name on Shaker documents, however, spelled his surname "Allen." Since there is no one known in Shaker records by the name of "Alley," one explanation for the confusion could be that Abner simply was making an *n* with a fancy swirl at the end of his name. Another possibility is that Abner's surname was Alleyn or Allyn, which he shortened to Alley, while those who officially recorded his name wrote it the way they had always heard it, Allen.

The first known piece bearing his signature is a cupboard and drawers, dated 1830.[2] The second signed piece is a small case of drawers marked, on various drawers, "Enfield, Conn. May 16, 1849. Abner Alley. A.E. age 66" (ill. 50).

The drawer sides of these two pieces are tapered in a fashion similar to those made by Grove Wright, and in addition, have another feature in common with drawers built by other joiners from the Hancock Bishopric—the inside of the drawer front is chamfered along both the top and the bottom edge. But two features distinguish Abner Allen's work from the work of other joiners, particularly from Grove Wright's. In Br. Abner's work, the sides of the drawers are flat on top, unlike Elder Grove's, which are rounded; and the outside back edge of the drawer is heavily chamfered, evidently with a plane after the drawer was assembled (ill. 51).

If one takes a closer look at other Hancock Bishopric cabinetwork with these construction details in mind, it becomes possible to attribute eight additional pieces to Abner Allen: five washstands, a small chest of drawers, a cupboard and drawers, and a long work table (ill. 52, 53, 54, 55, 56, and 57).

Such features of style as the size and shape of the splashboards on his washstands and the beveled molding on his drawer fronts that he

50. This small pine case of drawers (**a**) is signed on the backs of the drawers "Enfield, Conn. May 16, 1849. Abner Alley. A.E. age 66." The dovetailing of two pieces of wood with the grain running two different directions, as was done with the front rail dovetailed into the sides of this case (**b**), is most unusual.

Source: J. J. Gerald McCue

51. The details of the corner joints of these two drawers from pieces made by Abner Allen (see also ill. 50b) show some of the characteristics of his work that allow similar pieces to be attributed to him. The top of the drawer back has a distinctive chamfer on its back side. This chamfer, which is also seen on the inside of the front of the drawer, is not carried into the corners where the sides meet, and thus apparently was done after the drawers were assembled. The tapering of the drawer sides, which can be seen in the dovetails, is found on many pieces signed by or attributed to Br. Abner.

Source: J. J. Gerald McCue

b

52. This washstand over a cupboard with a drawer is dated on its back in chalk "Sept 18, 1850." The bottom is pine and butternut, and the flared top is curly maple. The piece is assumed to be the work of Br. Abner based on how the drawer is constructed.

Source: Bedelia Croly Falls

53. A second washstand over a cupboard with a drawer is a close match to the piece in illustration 52. Although it is undated and unsigned, it probably was also made by Br. Abner around 1850.

Source: Hancock Shaker Village, Inc., Pittsfield, Mass.

54. This washstand over a table (**a**) is made of curly maple. The flaring dovetailed top (**b**) and the drawer construction are similar to features on other pieces thought to have been made by Br. Abner. The heavy chamfer used as a decorative molding on the drawer front also appears on several other pieces illustrating Br. Abner's work.

Source: Helen Upton

55. The flaring dovetailed top on this washstand over a case of drawers is constructed in the same manner and with the same kind of wood as the top on the washstand over a table in illustration 54. The case of drawers is made of butternut, and the drawer construction is similar to that found on other pieces thought to have been Br. Abner's work.
Source: Bedelia Croly Falls

56. This washstand—made predominately of curly maple and with a flaring dovetailed top—seems to be closely related to the other pieces attributed to Br. Abner.
Source: Donald Sprowls

57. The drawer construction and the dominant curly maple top of this worktable with drawers seems to indicate that it is also the work of Abner Allen. The construction of the drawers under the overhanging ends is different from those within the table's base, and they may have been added at a later date by another craftsman. The two pieces of curly maple used for the top of the table both taper slightly in width, but in opposite directions. Thus the top still has parallel outer edges. The taper may have resulted from the cabinetmaker's desire to use the tapering boards coming from a sawn maple tree trunk without sacrificing the bit of wood that would be lost in ripping the boards to produce parallel edges.

Source: Hancock Shaker Village, Inc., Pittsfield, Mass.

favored also provide clues that help to identify Abner Allen's furniture. Viewed in conjunction with the construction features of the drawers he made, these details can be seen as characteristics developed from repetition as the furniture maker worked at his craft over a period of time. Detailed comparisons show them to be an invaluable composite "signature" for Abner Allen in much the same way as Grove Wright's

finishing techniques and drawer lettering and numbering system distinguish his furniture.

In 1792, John and Cynthia Wright "embraced the gospel of Christ's second appearing."[3] "It fell to my happy lot," wrote their son Grove, "to be bro't up & educated in the gospel school among believers from early childhood." Grove and his parents may have continued living in their family home even though they had accepted Mother Ann's testimony. Grove recalled, "When I was 9 years of age, it was felt to be the gift for me to leave my father's house & move to Tyringham, 18 miles distant." Little mention is made of Grove in surviving records until his name appears on the 1816 Tyringham Covenant. Two years later Daniel

Goodrich was released from the Ministry, and Br. Grove moved from Tyringham to Hancock to take his place as assistant to Elder Nathaniel Deming in the Ministry.[4] Elder Grove remained a part of the Ministry for more than forty years, becoming the First Elder of the Hancock Bishopric in 1845, when Elder Nathaniel died. He continued to serve in this position until 1860, when he resigned because of ill health.

Living and working at various times in all three communities of the Bishopric, Elder Grove was known in each place as a woodworking craftsman. He was involved for part of the time in the production of articles for sale, including pails and swifts, and he can be identified as a preeminent builder of furniture at Hancock.

On January 1, 1846, Thomas Damon, a joiner from the Enfield Shaker community, was appointed to be Elder Grove's assistant in the Ministry. A tall case of drawers made later indicates that Br. Thomas also worked with Elder Grove in the joiners' shop (ill. 58). The case, made of butternut and pine, is now at Hancock Shaker Village, and contains this handwritten inscription on a label glued inside: "This Case of Drawers were made by Elder Grove and Brother Thomas and placed here thursday, January 13th, 1853. It was the day our Ministry expected to return to the City of Peace [Hancock], but were detained

58. There are similarities between the work of Grove Wright and that of Abner Allen. Both use tapering drawer sides and have the habit of chamfering the inside edge of the drawer fronts. This tall case of drawers was made prior to January 13, 1853, by Elder Grove Wright and Br. Thomas Damon, as indicated by a paper label attached to the inside of the case. The facing parts of the case, the drawer fronts, the rails between drawers, and the facing glued to the fronts of the sides are of butternut, whereas the rest of the piece is made of pine. The drawer pulls are of walnut. The drawer construction used in this piece is similar to that found on pieces thought to have been made by Br. Abner, but with some distinctive differences. The top edges of the drawer sides and back are rounded, and the back edge is not chamfered.
Source: Hancock Shaker Village, Inc., Pittsfield, Mass.

on anccount of the snow storm which occured on that day"[5] (ill. 59).

An earlier piece—a tailor's rule inscribed "Clarissa Ely's. Made by Eld[er] Grove Wright. A.H." (ill. 60)—is the only other known piece on which Elder Grove's name appears. The tall case of drawers, however, contains clues in the workmanship that in effect place Grove Wright's cabinetmaking signature on several other pieces of furniture, which will be discussed later in this chapter.

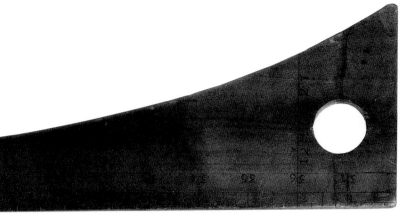

a

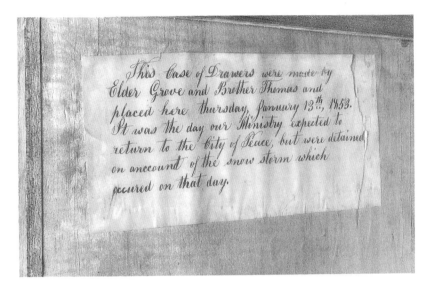

59. A paper label glued inside the tall case of drawers shown in illustration 58 identifies its makers and date of construction.
Source: Hancock Shaker Village, Inc., Pittsfield, Mass.

b

60. This tailor's rule (**a**) is dated "12M 1827" and has a paper label (**b**) identifying it as the work of Grove Wright. The label reads, "Clarissa Ely's. Made by Eld[er] Grove Wright. A.H."
Source: Helen Upton

Like most of the other Shaker craftsmen, Elder Grove was adamant in his desire to keep working, even in the face of the declining health he experienced during the last years of his life. His health had become a topic of concern in Elder Grove's journals as early as April 1850, when he spent some time taking the "Western treatment" at Northampton, Massachusetts. In August 1853 another Hancock journal mentioned that Grove "started for the seaside in quest of health . . . [and] they finally located at Watch Hill in Westerly, R.I. a prime place for bathing—good accommodations."6

He had a bout of illness after this trip; but as he was recuperating in January 1854, he found the strength to begin making pine pails. In a letter dated February 10, 1854, he wrote to Elder Grove Blanchard of Harvard that he had made 116 pails, which had been ready to paint by January. He insisted in the letter that he had done it all by himself, "besides other considerable work, so you will see that I have not been confined to *bed* all the time."7

Later that year Elder Grove made thirty-eight oak pails, steps for the office stairs, and "a sort of cupboard to put swift stuff in to stand in the East room." Thomas Damon was in charge of manufacturing yarn swifts (used to hold a skein of yarn while it was being wound into a ball), and Grove assisted him, noting in his journal that in 1854 they made a total of 910 swifts.8

Elder Grove had, however, spent four weeks at New Lebanon that September being "nursed up a bit," and in October of 1855 he felt unwell enough to propose that he be released from his official duties in the Ministry because of ill health. The Church response, as recorded in a Hancock journal, was simple enough: "Request not granted."9 So Grove continued in the Ministry. During the next five years he submitted other requests asking for permission to resign, but these also were denied.

In January 1860, Elder Grove finished making a "little loom for weaving palm leaf braid," and for several months of that year helped Thomas Damon at the business of making swifts, even as he con-

tinued to suffer from failing health. In July he traveled to Saratoga Springs, New York, where he spent two weeks "under treatment at the Water Cure." He returned to Hancock feeling much better, but his renewed strength soon faded.

A Hancock journal recorded that on October 3, 1860, "The New Lebanon Ministry came to Hancock to consider the subject of Elder Grove's release from the Ministry, his declining health having prompted him on a number of occasions to prefer his request to that end. The day was spent without arriving at any satisfactory results as to successorship &c. The reasonableness of the petition is not questioned."10 Finally, on October 7, his old friend and colleague Thomas Damon was appointed to take over the responsibilities of First Elder in the Ministry. An observer commented that "Elder Grove Wright was released from his care and burden in the ministry order having stood in it 41 years. Said to be an almost perfect man."11 Elder Grove's own comments at that time related to his work. "Have wound off with swift business for the present," he wrote in his journal on October 10, "and probably for life."12

He wanted to spend the winter at Enfield, and on October 29 moved to that community, where he continued working as a joiner in spite of his poor physical condition. Journals from November and December show how persistent he was:

November 9:   Getting out and preparing stuff for a large cupboard in the North farmer[?] room. . . .
November 15:   I work on the cupboard, put the outside together, dovetailed the sides & bottom & top. . . .
November 17:   I work at fitting the back & the sisters stain the inside of the cupboard. . . .
November 22:   I finish the doors, (4) and fitted them in ready to hang. . . .
November 23:   Finished off the cupboard and put it up. Elder sister stained it. . . .

November 28:   I worked at finishing a sort of real [that is, reel] for Olive Stebins. . . .

December 3:   I work at making a sort of chair stairs to get up to high drawers. . . .

December 6:   I made a little flight of portable stairs or steps. . . .

December 8:   I put a lot of spring ketches on to cupboard doors. . . .

December 11:   Work at repairing an old bed stead and a drawer cupboard. . . .

December 14:   I am at work making a sort of clothes culender. . . .

December 15:   I worked at the clothers culenders & moving some of the cooper tools from the ministries shop. . . .

December 27:   I began to get out timber for some portable folding stairs for the sisters. . . .

December 29:   I worked at fixing two chair stairs or steps.[13]

Elder Grove's condition worsened, and four months later (on April 25, 1861) he died at Enfield, at the age of seventy-two.

On May 2, 1861, the Hancock Ministry (that is, Thomas Damon) sent the Ministry at New Lebanon a letter that contained praise of Elder Grove Wright:

No one felt any embarassment in holding up his godly example, his pure life, his interested and devoted labor in the cause of truth and holiness, for no one feared exaggeration where it seemed impossible to do justice to the reality. Those qualities which call down blessings upon the meek, the merciful, the pure in heart, the peacemakers, were his in a preeminent degree, and he had exemplified them in a long life of unwearied and unflinching devotion to the best cause that was ever bequeathed to mortals . . . and we have laid his remains by the side of one who is endearingly remembered by all the household of faith as the "Altogether Lovely Father James."[14]

By carefully examining the tall case of drawers with the 1853 inscription shown in ill. 58 and comparing it to built-in butternut and pine cabinets in the Brick Dwelling at Hancock (ill. 61 and 62) one can see that Grove Wright made both the cabinets and the cases of drawers. Grove Wright's cabinetmaking signature is embodied in the way the drawers of these pieces were made, and although Thomas Damon

61. The fourteen built-in case of drawers and cupboard units on the first two floors of the 1830 Brick Dwelling House at Hancock Shaker Village, one of which is shown here closed and open, are apparently the work of Grove Wright. The drawers in these pieces seem to have been made by the same hands as the drawers in the tall case of drawers signed by Elder Grove and Br. Thomas (ill. 58). The date 1831, found on one of the drawers of the built-ins, indicates that the drawers were made the year after the building was started. Thomas Damon, who was between the ages of eleven and twelve in 1831, certainly was not the master craftsman who made these drawers. Thus it is likely that Grove Wright made the drawers for the 1853 tall case of drawers while Br. Thomas probably worked on the carcase.

Source: Hancock Shaker Village, Inc., Pittsfield, Mass.

62. A closeup of the joinery of a drawer made by Elder Grove shows both the taper of the drawer sides (reflected in the bottom-to-top decrease in the width of the dovetail pins) and how he rounded the top edges of drawers' sides and back.

Source: Hancock Shaker Village, Inc., Pittsfield, Mass.

worked on the case of drawers with him, the drawer construction points to Elder Grove as the primary architect and builder of that piece as well as the maker of some fourteen built-in cabinets in the Brick Dwelling. First, the drawer construction is similar to drawers in other cabinetwork from the Hancock Bishopric in that the sides are tapered. Second, the drawer fronts are chamfered on the inside top and bottom edges, which is a characteristic of furniture made by both Abner Allen and Grove Wright. Two other salient features of the drawer construction, however, distinguish the drawers from the work of Abner Allen and other Hancock joiners—the top edges of Grove Wright's drawer sides and backs are rounded, and the top edge of the drawer backs are not chamfered (ill. 63). The idiosyncratic features of the drawers of the 1853 case are present in the drawers of the built-in cabinets, indicating that the same joiner built them. This person is shown, by a process of elimination, to be Grove Wright rather than Thomas Damon. Thomas Damon was only eleven years old in 1830 when the Brick Dwelling was built, and even though he may have been an apprentice in cabinetmaking at an early age, he would not have been a master

63. This comparison of a drawer thought to have been made by Br. Abner (top) to one made by Elder Grove (bottom) shows the difference in the way they each finished the top edge of a drawer's sides and back. It is interesting that in examples of Elder Grove's work the drawers are assembled "backwards." Cabinetmakers usually construct drawers so that the part of the dovetail joint that is shaped like a dove's tail is visible on both ends of a drawer's sides. This arrangement makes the drawer resist the tendency to pull apart when it is opened and closed. Elder Grove made the drawer in this illustration so that the front of the drawer is dovetailed in the traditional manner but with the back of the drawer dovetailed in the opposite way. Thus this back joint is best at keeping the drawer sides from spreading, a job usually left to the rails on which the drawer slides or to the sides of the case itself.
Source: Hancock Shaker Village, Inc., Pittsfield, Mass.

joiner by the time the built-in cabinets were made for the interior of the dwelling. In addition, Br. Thomas was not living at Hancock—he was living in the Enfield, Connecticut, community at the time—and although other joiners from Enfield may have traveled to Hancock to work on the dwelling in 1830 and 1831, it is doubtful whether they would have taken an apprentice along with them. Even if Thomas Damon had come to Hancock to work on the Brick Dwelling at that time, he would not have had the responsibility for building such cabinets. Grove Wright, on the other hand, had been living at Hancock for many years and was old enough to have established himself as a master craftsman.

Finally, the handwritten letters and numbers on the 1853 case of drawers are in a style and script that seem, if one compares writing samples, to have been made by Grove Wright, not Thomas Damon. The numbering of drawer parts and their positions in the case is identical in format and style to the numbering found on one of the Brick Dwelling built-ins that is dated 1831.

Grove Wright's cabinetmaking signature appears on other significant pieces of furniture (ill. 64 and 65). This look at Elder Grove's furniture and the study of unique stylistic traits in Abner Allen's work have shed new light on Shaker furniture. This new way of attributing specific pieces to individual craftsmen is a method that undoubtedly will be refined and applied in the future to other Shaker furniture makers from different communities in different parts of the country.

64. This small two-drawer case is, judging from the construction of the drawers, an example of Elder Grove's work. The piece is made of butternut. Further evidence of his workmanship is found in the way he chose to number the pieces of the drawers (that is, how he kept all of the different joints from getting mixed up when they were put together). His script and the placement of the penciled numbers in the corners of the drawers is consistent throughout the various pieces thought to be his.
Source: Hancock Shaker Village, Inc., Pittsfield, Mass.

65. The drawer construction of a tailoring counter of extraordinary design and beauty may very well be Elder Grove's work.
   Source: Anne R. Whipple

Orren N. Haskins

(1815–1892) New Lebanon, New York

Toward the end of his life Orren Haskins wrote a credo for work that contained echoes of the Shaker "Holy Laws of Zion" and "Millennial Laws" prohibiting the manufacture of ornate or superfluous articles. With an evangelical fervor, Br. Orren exhorted his fellow Believers, especially children, to strive for high quality in their work rather than to be infatuated, as the world was, with ephemeral styles. Writing on January 18, 1887, at Mount Lebanon, he presented the crux of his thesis:

> Why patronize the out side world or gugaws in our manufactures, when they will say we have enough of them abroad? We want a good plain substantial Shaker article, yea, one that bears credit to our profession & tells who and what we are, true and honest before the world, without hypocrisy or any false covering. The wourld at large can Scarcely keep pace with it self in its stiles and fassions which last but a short time, when something still more worthless or absurd takes its place. Let good enough alone, and take good common sense for our guide in all our persuits, and we are safe within and without.[1]

His words reflected beliefs about his life and work that Br. Orren had espoused for more than sixty years—and the furniture he made over the decades embodies those same principles. Many signed pieces of his work throughout his career illustrate the variety of his cabinetwork and at the same time can be seen as essential links in a narrative about his life.

Orren Haskins was born December 3, 1815, in the town of Savoy, in western Massachusetts. His parents became interested in the Shakers, and Orren was listed among the "Young Believers" in Savoy in 1819. At age five, his parents moved to New Lebanon, and on July 7, 1823, eight-year-old Orren was taken into the Church Family.

Little is known about his early training in woodworking,[2] but evidently Br. Orren had completed an apprenticeship by 1833, the date of his first signed piece of furniture. Although the current whereabouts of this first piece is unknown, it is identified by Faith and Edward Deming Andrews as a pine case of drawers with a cupboard top, stained red. Inscribed on the bottom of the drawer just below the cupboard are the words, "March 27, 1833. Made by Orren H."[3]

A lap or table desk made by Br. Orren the next year is in the collection of the Shaker Museum in Old Chatham, New York. This desk is from the New Lebanon Church Family, and on the bottom are the initials "O.H.," written with distinctive curlicued flourishes, and the date "June 6, 1834" (ill. 66).

Philemon Stewart recorded in his journal on March 13, 1835, that Orren was making a workbench for him. In the beginning of January 1837, Orren apparently completed work on a three-door cupboard or top to a now-missing desk, which is in the collection of the Shaker Museum in Old Chatham, New York. The cupboard is dated and signed on its back in red crayon, "January 26, 1837 O.H." An 1838 lap desk from New Lebanon is the next documented piece. Although its location is currently unknown, its inscription, in pencil on the drawer bottom—"February 6th 1838 by Maker Orren N. Haskins. R.B."—was recorded by Faith and Edward Deming Andrews, who suggested that this desk was "probably a presentation piece to the owner (Rachel Bacon?) whose initials conclude the inscription."[4]

A piece made later in 1838—a desk of pine, butternut, and cherry (ill. 67)—bears two penciled inscriptions. Large cursive letters going with the grain of the wood across nearly the whole bottom of the desk state: "Orren Haskins Maker Dec 18th 1838 John Allen." The second inscription, in a similar cursive style but with much smaller letters written cross-grain in a corner, states that Orren Haskins made the

66. This pine table desk was acquired from the Church Family Shakers at Mount Lebanon, New York. There it had been used in later years by Sr. Emma Neale. On the underside of the drawer in faint pencil is the inscription "O.H. June 6, 1834," in a curlicue style characteristic of Br. Orren's writing.
Source: The Shaker Museum, Old Chatham, N.Y.

desk in 1838 for John Allen, who used it at the seed shop for "upwards of two years" and then put it on legs and moved it into the house in 1841 (ill. 68).

Br. Orren used his joinery skills for more than just furniture. A tape loom made by him in 1839 and stamped "OH" (ill. 69) and a beater for a similar loom (ill. 70) dated 1836 and stamped in the same manner were used for weaving such narrow material as chair webbing, belting, and rug binding. Adding more detail to a portrait of Br. Orren at work are three planes that belonged to him in this period, now in the collection of the Shaker Museum at Old Chatham (ill. 71, 72, and 73). All three are stamped with his initials, and two have dates stamped on them as well, one 1833 and the other 1838.

Br. Orren performed a great deal of general carpentry over the years. He framed and repaired roofs—tin roofs, shingle roofs, and cloth roofs—and he repaired floors. He built "a new house for accommodation, called a Back house privy or Jake's house,"[5] did the framing for barns and other buildings, and also made coffins on occasion.

As was true for the other Shaker cabinetmakers, Br. Orren held a variety of jobs throughout his life. He turned his hand to mechanical work— for instance, remodeling the community's threshing machine and building a mortising machine for use in making doors—and for a time in the 1830s he turned broom handles for the Shakers' use or for sale. Here a journal entry from 1837 showed a mild competitive spirit among the Shakers, for it described Br. Orren "beating all brags" by turning a record 1,000 handles in one day.[6]

On April 19, 1848, at age thirty-two, Br. Orren moved from the Center Family to the Church Family to work as a carpenter and joiner. His occupation was listed as "a joiner, carpenter &c." in the 1840 and 1845 five-year censuses kept by Isaac Youngs. In 1848, Youngs wrote that Orren was moved "to officiate as Woodworkman. This seems to be highly necessary as we have had no one to support that occupation since the absconding of Braman W[icks]."[7]

68. A closeup of inscription on the bottom of the drawer of the desk in illustration 67.

Source: Richard Janosko

67. The history of this desk is best told by the inscriptions left on it: "Orren Haskins Maker Dec 18th 1838 John Allen Made by Orren Haskins December 18th 1831 for John Allen & used at the seed shop upwards of two years. It was then put upon legs by John Allen & taken into the house on the first monday in January. 1841 1841." The desk is made of pine, butternut, and cherry.

Source: Richard Janosko

69. This loom was made for weaving narrow fabric such as that used as chair webbing and rug binding. The date "1839" and Orren's initials are impressed into its breast beam. The initials "OH" are stamped into the wood with a single tool whereas the date is stamped with the dies for individual numbers that were used for marking rulers and other measuring tools. The "OH" stamp was used by Br. Orren to mark several woodworking planes and the 1836 and 1839 looms. It apparently was common for Shaker craftsmen to mark their tools and occasionally those things they made with such stamps. The initials were impressed into the wood by hammering an iron or steel stamp into the wood. The stamps were made either to press in the background (leaving the letters protruding to the level of the original surface of the wood) or to press the letters below the original surface. The "Revised Millennial Laws of 1845" (reprinted in Edward Deming Andrews, *The People Called Shakers*) allow for the marking of tools but dictate that "the initials of a person's name, are sufficient to put upon any tool . . . for purposes of distinction," and that "it is strictly forbidden unnecessarily to embellish any mark."

Source: Milton Sherman

70. This loom beater once belonged to a loom similar in size and function to the one in illustration 69. It is dated "1836" and is marked in the middle of the top cross-bar with the same "OH" stamp as the 1839 loom.
Source: Hancock Shaker Village, Inc., Pittsfield, Mass.

71. The woodworking plane on the left is for rounding. The plane was made in Albany, New York, by "Bensen & Crannell," planemakers. Nicholas Bensen and Matthew Crannell, Jr., manufactured planes under this name between 1844 and 1862. The plane on the right is a moving fillister (or filletster), used for cutting rebates along the edge of a board. This plane bears the manufacturer's stamp, "J. & J. Gibson." It should be noted that this stamp was only used on planes manufactured by Joseph and John Gibson in Albany, New York, in the years 1837 and 1838 and that this plane was dated "1838" by its user.
Source: The Shaker Museum, Old Chatham, N.Y.

After he took Braman's place, Br. Orren was mentioned on different occasions as working on specific jobs of carpentry with other furniture makers—Benjamin Lyon, David Rowley, Elisha Blakeman, and George Wickersham. All of these men were living in a communal family (Orren Haskins and Elisha Blakeman were roommates for a time), and they shared work just as members of any large family might have done.

An example of Br. Orren's own work from this period is a fifteen-foot-long workbench (ill. 74), which he signed and dated on the bottoms of three drawers. The inscriptions include two different dates—the date it was made, February 1853, and the date it was moved into the Church Family's brick Brethrens' Shop, February 9, 1871.

In December of 1855, Br. Orren took charge of the shop formerly occupied by the Family's "master" cabinetmaker, David Rowley, who had died the month before.[8] This line of succession indicates that Br. Orren's skills as a joiner were held in high esteem, and it is another reminder that many of the best joiners in New Lebanon were contemporaries.

After six years in charge of the joiners' shop, Br. Orren moved into the Brick Shop on May 29, 1861, "to work at mechanical jobs, for common accommodations, fixing wheels &c. &c. &c. &c."[9] Orren's

72. This trying plane was acquired from the Church Family workshops at Mount Lebanon and bears Br. Orren's stamped initials and the date "1833." It is also marked with the initials "HR" and the date "1851." The reason for the later initials and date is not known. The only brother in the First or Second Order of the Church Family with these initials in 1851 was Hiram Rude. Although Br. Hiram was a blacksmith, he was also known for his mechanical skills and very well may have been the second person whose initials appear on the plane.
Source: The Shaker Museum, Old Chatham, N.Y.

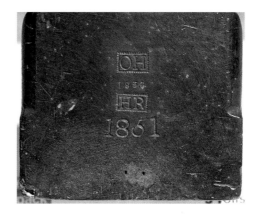

73. The initials and dates stamped on the front end of this trying plane (see ill. 72) suggest that two different craftsmen had possession of this plane at different times.
Source: The Shaker Museum, Old Chatham , N.Y.

presence in the Brick Shop endured beyond his work there, and even beyond his life span. In the 1930s the new residents of the Church Family, the staff and students of Darrow School, still referred to the room where Br. Orren worked as "*Orrin* Haskins Workshop" (ill. 75).

In November 1862, Isaac Youngs noted that Orren, "takes charge of [the] Ministry's horses . . . [but] retains his mechanical business, variety of woodwork, taking care of the paint &c. for the present."[10] Because of his work with the Ministry's horses during the 1860s and 1870s, Br. Orren was often out of the community chauffeuring visitors from other communities around to the various families or to the springs and other sights around New Lebanon. He took the Ministry to Hancock and Watervliet, and often met them at train stations when

a

74. The arrangement of drawers and vises on this workbench (**a**) is somewhat out of the ordinary. In addition to the ten drawers on the front of the bench, four shallow drawers are found on the back of the bench just under the bench top. These shallow drawers slide in over the top front drawers. In addition, three larger drawers just off the floor on the back slide in under the bottom front drawers, while yet another drawer on the back fits under the overhanging top at the end of the bench where the tail vise is located. The bench was made to stand in the middle of a room so that it could be used from both sides. The back side is finished, and a third vise is attached to the back just opposite the tail vise. This workbench was made by Orren and was signed by him (**b**).

Source: Mount Lebanon Shaker Village, Inc., New Lebanon, N.Y.

b

they returned from trips on "the cars." And it was Br. Orren who took Elisha Blakeman to the depot when Elisha left the community to go into the world in 1871.

Meanwhile, Br. Orren was still making furniture. A table (ill. 76), now at Hancock Shaker Village, has an inscription designating it as a piece made by him. This worktable is made of cherry and butternut, with white china knobs, and is inscribed on a drawer in pencil: "Cornelia French May 17, 1874 No. 3 O.H." (ill. 77).

The last known reference in Shaker journals to Br. Orren's work as a joiner was on February 10, 1875, when he made two privy boxes, "one for the Office & one for the Elders."[11] Undoubtedly this work was made necessary by the disastrous fire set by an arsonist on February 6, 1875, which destroyed eight buildings at the New Lebanon Church Family, including the Great House, the family's main dwelling.

Two pieces of furniture attest to the continuation of Br. Orren's furniture making beyond the evidence recorded in Shaker writings. A pine dairy counter, dated 1876 and signed by Br. Orren, was recorded in a watercolor rendering by an *Index of American Design* artist in the mid-1930s (ill. 78). And in 1881 he made a cherry worktable (ill. 79), which is similar in design to the one he made for Cornelia French in 1874. This table bears an elaborate and intriguing inscription written in pencil on the bottom of one of the small drawers from the upper gallery (ill. 80):

75. The room shown in this photograph is in the Brethrens' Brick Shop of the New Lebanon Church Family, which at present is known to the staff and students of the Darrow School as "Orrin Haskins Workshop." Br. Orren's connection with this room is apparently through the recollections of the Shakers living at Mount Lebanon when the Darrow School started, some of whom had known Br. Orren for over thirty-five years.

Source: Historic American Building Survey, National Park Service

76. This worktable is signed in pencil on the underside of one of the six drawers in the upper gallery: "Cornelia French May 17, 1874. No 4 [i.e., drawer number 4] OH." The table itself may or may not have been Br. Orren's work. It seems clear that the two parts were made at different times if not by different hands.

Source: Hancock Shaker Village, Inc., Pittsfield, Mass.

Sarah H. Winton
Our Shaker Sister
Worth her weight in gold:
Please accept this little token
Of my approving love;
Altho' tis small it measures more
The half has not been told;
God bless you ever ever more,
To rest in our clean fold
While on this mortal shore.
       O.N.H., June 11ᵗʰ 1881
       Mount Lebanon Columbia Co N.Y.

Br. Orren made the table and his declaration of affection for Sarah Winton when he was sixty-five and she was fifty-four years old. Sarah left the community eight years later, in 1889, three years before Br. Orren's death.

Br. Orren had several bouts of illness in 1892, and he died on September 15 of that year at the age of seventy-six, after a long and richly documented career as a Shaker cabinetmaker. He had been a productive cabinetmaker for more than half a century and a Shaker for sixty-nine years, living and working according to the principles that he believed would keep him healthy in body and soul, "safe within & without," as he had averred in 1887.

77. Cornelia French (1840–1917), a sister whose name appears along with Orren's initials on this 1874 worktable shown in illustration 76, was apparently the recipient of the piece.
Source: Hancock Shaker Village, Inc., Pittsfield, Mass.

78. This watercolor of a pine dairy counter was executed by an *Index of American Design* artist in the mid-1930s. The counter was from the New Lebanon Church Family. The information accompanying the *Index of American Design*'s artwork stated that the piece was signed on a drawer by Orren Haskins and was dated 1876. The counter was owned by Faith and Edward Deming Andrews at the time that the watercolor was done.
Source: MASS-FU-16 DAIRY TABLE; watercolor rendering of a piece made by Orren Haskins; Index of American Design; National Gallery of Art, Washington

79. This worktable was probably once a table to which a gallery has been added. The underside of the tabletop has mortices for the hinges that once supported a drop leaf. There are also screw holes that apparently once held the guides for the pullout that supported the drop leaf. The table once had three small pegs on the side of the apron that have since been cut flush with the side of the apron. The bottom drawer is a later addition. The joinery on the table portion of this piece, as with the Br. Orren's 1874 worktable, seems to have been the work of different hands. The underside of the upper middle drawer in the gallery is signed by Br. Orren and is dated "June 11, 1881." The legs and pulls of this worktable are cherry; the aprons, top, and drawer fronts are butternut. The fancy-grained wood around the top of the gallery is probably a quilted birch or maple.

Source: Hancock Shaker Village, Inc., Pittsfield, Mass.

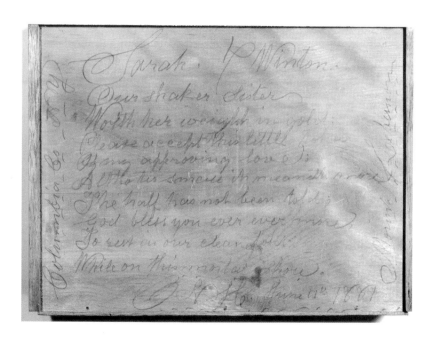

80. The inscription on the underside of the upper middle drawer of the 1881 worktable shown in illustration 79.
Source: Hancock Shaker Village, Inc., Pittsfield, Mass.

Elisha D'Alembert Blakeman

(1819–1900) New Lebanon, New York

Poetry, music, mechanical devices, and furniture all had a basic element in common for Elisha Blakeman: He saw them as worlds inviting the application of his inventive gifts. Elisha was a Renaissance man who combined lyrical and mechanical talents to make ingenious contributions to each of these spheres.

Elisha's father, Elisha D'Alembert Blakeman, Sr., was a medical doctor from Clyde, New York, a small town located south of Lake Ontario, twelve miles from the Shaker community at Sodus. On occasion the Shakers called upon Elisha Sr. for medical assistance, and on visits in 1828 and 1830 he introduced his wife Chloe and his son, Elisha Jr., to the community. Chloe Blakeman died from an illness in October 1830, and two months later her husband and Elisha Jr. went to live in Sodus with the Shakers.

Over the next several years, Elisha Sr. and his son remained with the Sodus Shakers, but neighbors and former patients continued to come to Elisha Sr. for medical treatment. This not only took up his time but also made it difficult for him to attain the kind of separation from the world which the Shakers saw as necessary for his spiritual development. The Church's solution was for Elisha Sr. to move to another Shaker community farther away from his hometown. Writing in his journal, Elisha Jr. later explained how this had happened. Elder Richard Bushnell from New Lebanon, hearing of the circumstances and realizing that "it must be hard for him to make much if any pro-

gress in things spiritual while in that situation; accordingly went to the Ministry & got permission to have my Father come to Lebanon, to live in order that he might get clear of such calls. . . . It was allso thot best for me to come with him as I was young & considerably attach'd to him."[1]

In 1834 father and son traveled together to New Lebanon, where Elisha Sr. took up his residence at the North Family. His son was brought into the Church Family, and shortly after his arrival fifteen-year-old Elisha went "into the brick shop to work at joinering with David Rowley," the master cabinetmaker.[2]

Meanwhile, back in western New York, the Sodus Canal Company was proposing to dig a canal connecting Lake Ontario with the Erie Canal, a project that eventually forced the Shakers to sell their property on Sodus Bay for a right-of-way. When the Shakers subsequently purchased land 170 miles to the southwest at Groveland, New York, where they expected to relocate, Elisha Sr. requested that the Ministry at New Lebanon allow him to return to the community where he was first "gathered." He suggested that the move would provide sufficient distance between the community and his former patients for him to lead a proper Shaker life.

The Ministry agreed, and before he left New Lebanon, Elisha Sr. had an interview with his son at the Church Family's office. In their meeting, Elisha Jr. later recalled, his father "remarked that he knew it would be impossible for me as I was yet young to get a beter home than that wich I now enjoyed here in the Chh. He considered that the gospel which we had embrac'd was the true and only true one on Earth & furthermore . . . he desired that I would keep my faith & live & grow in the way of God to the end of my days."[3] Elisha Jr. by then had gained a variety of experience as a woodworking apprentice, and when his father settled up with the Trustees at New Lebanon and was given some money, he used it to buy a trunk and some medical books for himself, and some tools, which he presented to Elisha as a gift at his departure, encouraging his son to hone his skills as a joiner.[4]

On January 17, 1837, Elisha Sr. returned to Sodus, and on March 15 moved with the rest of the community to Groveland. He arrived at Sodus not only with a trunk and some medical books, but also with notions about the "science" of phrenology. Although the Shakers would eventually embrace phrenology, at this early date they did not, and a conflict arose between Elisha Sr. and the Church leaders.

"The truth of the case is," wrote the Elders at Groveland in describing the situation to Stephen Munson at New Lebanon, "[Elisha Blakeman, Sr.] was ashamed to confess what he had been about. He brought a book with him when he came from the East that he pretends to tell the disposition of people by feeling of the head. And of corse he must practice alittle seing he was a Doctor, of corse a Doctor must have the liberty to examin young females heads, or they would not no how to Doctor them when they was sick. He has practiced some on some of the young females & told them to be sure not to let the Elders no it, for believers was very Swift against such thing[s], but he thought it to be a butiful studdy." The result was that Elisha Sr. quietly withdrew from the Society on October 9, 1838. "But we are thankful to be able to say that he has gone alone," the Elders wrote, "& we hope no one will be foolish enough to follow him."[5]

Elisha Jr., however, remained a Shaker and continued to gain woodworking experience. In New Lebanon he had worked with David Rowley in the joiners' shop, had helped build the belfry for the re-cently enlarged Great House, and had worked at laying floors and making ladders.

In April 1835 he took up his "residence with Luther C[opley] in the joiners shop"; and when Luther "moved from the Joiners' Shop up to the machine shop to take charge there," Br. Elisha went with him to work as "mechanic." Following nearly two years of work with Luther, Br. Elisha returned to the joiners' shop, this time to work with Stephen Munson, a house carpenter and maker of herb and seed boxes.

The first indication that Br. Elisha had begun to make furniture came on January 7, 1840, on an occasion that he proclaimed with a poem:

Friend Daniel C. came unto me,
With maple sticks for me to fix
As then he bid a low bedstead
At which I went with good intent.[6]

Br. Elisha noted in his journal four days later that he had finished and set up "a low bedstead," a trundle bed in room 13 of the Great House.

This was the time of year when many of the men not engaged in farm work went to the community's Washington Mountain woodlot to cut firewood and timber for lumber, and Br. Elisha was scheduled to be in this group. However, Derobigne Bennet, another joiner, wanted Br. Elisha's help with a project. "As the weather was bad," Br. Elisha wrote, "& Derobigne B[ennet]. felt desireous of my assistance to work at a counter & case of drawers under it & cupboard, he agreed to go to Washington with me next week if I would help him at his counter this week. And in union with the Deacons & Elders I staid home to assist him."[7]

Subsequently, Br. Elisha wrote that he "took up & rough[ed] off some stuff for a counter, with a case of drawers & a cupboard under it."[8] Work on the counter progressed well, for on February 1, Henry DeWitt recorded that "Derobigne & Elisha, has been to work for the convenience of the herb department, having been to work about the business for 9 days past. Put up a number of shelves and made a counter 8 feet long with seven drawers in it & 2 cupboards; finished all but top board & doors."[9]

After helping in the woodlot, Br. Derobigne and Br. Elisha returned from Washington Mountain around the middle of February and finished up the counter, with Br. Elisha making two panel doors on February 17. Then Br. Elisha took some time to settle into his shop. He made a "trying plane stock, single iron," fixed up a large cupboard for tools, and dressed over and leveled off his workbench before the end of February.

Br. Elisha's journal for this period ends in December 1840, but he continued at cabinetmaking until March 19, 1844, when he "left the Carpentry business & went to tanning."[10]

A rather dramatic change in his life came with a new work assignment. On September 2, 1844, Br. Elisha wrote, "Elder Daniel C[rosman]. came to me & bade me follow him to their room in the great house.—I obeyed with quick steps which soon bro't me on the floor of the aforesaid.—My heart beat for fear every second for the waters were troubled & crosses were to be seen afloat on every hand & side. . . . I was presently informed that it was the gift to have me take some burden & care of the Boys!!!!!!!—this in many respects loaded down my boat to its last degree of capability of sailing on the ocean of time."[11]

In the weeks that followed, Br. Elisha was kept busy assisting John Allen, the brother with whom he shared responsibility for the boys, but he was relieved of that responsibility in November. On November 20 he wrote gleefully in his journal:

> I'm now released from the boys
> And from a deal of din and noise
> And John is left to rule the roost
> Without a second mate to boost
> My Elders gave me a good name
> So I do leave devoid of shame

> Ha ha he he how glad I be
> I've no more boys to trouble me.[12]

In September 1846, however, Br. Elisha had to take up that cross once more. John Allen, along with Derobigne Bennet and two other New Lebanon Shakers, left the Society in an episode of mass apostasy, and Br. Elisha was again saddled with the care of the boys, a job which he held for the next seven years. In that time he never wanted for things to occupy his time. His activities included cutting wood; harvesting corn and potatoes; cutting and stooking acres of rye;[13] gathering chestnuts and walnuts; harvesting and selling prodigious quantities of apples, blackberries, and elderberries; painting and shingling buildings; and making bobsleds, a new broom machine, and thousands of brooms and brushes. Not surprisingly, he also went to stay for a few days in Saratoga Springs, New York, for his health.

There was also the need and opportunity for him to apply his skills in cabinetmaking. In December 1850, when most Shakers were sleeping two to a bed, Br. Elisha made his most curious (though nonextant) contribution to the Shaker furniture tradition. As Isaac Youngs described it: "Elisha Blakeman has been getting up a new contrivance for a bed; it being a long bedstead, long enough for 8 boys side by side, it takes up much less room than 4 bedsteads. He has put it up today & thinks it is fine!"[14] Br. Elisha described this invention as a "large newfashioned double bedstead."[15]

Br. Elisha's furniture making during these years was not restricted to beds, for in December 1850 he also mentioned "making a work stand for Harriet G[oodwin]," the caretaker of the girls. In March 1852 he made "a clothes box or chest to keep the boys winter wearing appearal in," and in December of that year he made two book cupboards for the Sisters.[16]

Late in April 1853, Br. Elisha was finally allowed to resign his commission with the Boy's Order, and at that time he went "into the

Joinering business with O[rren] H[askins]," an association which lasted for nearly two years. On January 18, 1855, Br. Elisha "left working with Orren and went into the Shop occupied of late by Henry DeWitt to do printing [of herb labels] that Henry has done,"[17] but he did not stop making furniture, for in November of that year he made "a large cupboard to set in the water cellar Brick shop for storing paper in."[18]

In June of 1860, Br. Elisha traveled to western New York, where he visited his father, who was living near the town of Clyde and was seriously ill; and he also visited the Groveland Shakers. In November of that year, Br. Elisha returned to the Groveland community and spent the winter teaching school, returning to New Lebanon on March 29, 1861. Isaac Youngs noted in his journal on the occasion of Br. Elisha's return that "he has succeeded well in teaching their school the winter past; (a great help to them)."[19] As he formally changed from one vocation to another, Br. Elisha continued making furniture. A revolving stool (ill. 81) made in New Lebanon the following year may be a signed example of his work. Currently in the collection of the Duxbury Art Complex, this piece bears the inscription "E.D.B. 1862."

Descriptions of joinery work done by Br. Elisha after 1862 refer mostly to altering bedsteads, a job made possible and desirable by demographic changes within the New Lebanon community. When the population of the Church Family was still near its peak, there was a need for space-saving trundle beds; and in 1850, Br. Elisha's bed for eight boys had been a timely invention. But by the mid-1860s a decline in the number of members in the family gave the Shakers more room, and they began to abandon the space-efficient double beds, trundle beds, and beds for eight in favor of single beds. This new trend continued so that when Isaac Youngs noted that "Samuel White introduced a new bedstead into room No. 9" in July 1868, he was able to add that "nearly all now have single beds."[20] Ironically, Elisha Blakeman may have been one of the exceptions, for not until December 1868

81. This revolving stool is signed on the bottom "E.D.B. 1862" and was probably marked as such to identify its user. It is possible that Br. Elisha did make the stool for it is known that he was engaged in doing odd jobs of woodworking during 1862. The stool has a pine seat, a bird's-eye maple pedestal, a brass ferrule to keep the narrow top of the pedestal from splitting, and a cast iron flange to hold the revolving steel shaft to the wooden seat.

Source: The Art Complex, Inc., at Duxbury, Duxbury, Mass.

do records show that he "turned a set of bed-stead legs for himself—cherry."[21]

Br. Elisha had announced the beginning of his joiner's career in 1840 with a poem about a trundle bed, and so it seems curiously fitting that the last references to his Shaker cabinetmaking also show him working on beds. In December 1869, a journal notes that Br. Elisha narrowed and shortened a bed for a boy by the name of Franklin Thomas, and went on to add that "This is the first beginning to introduce single beds for the boys."[22] The progress he made was noted three months later in a record showing that "Elisha . . . narrowed up nine bedsteads for the boys so they all have single beds but two little boys."

The fact that Br. Elisha was making beds for the boys at this time is also linked to other changes in his life. Sometime during the 1860s, Br. Elisha had again taken up the care of the boys; and the work he performed with them, gardening and basketmaking, is described in detail in various records. To make baskets, Br. Elisha first hauled "some white oak sticks with an old oxen from the Island—great swamp . . . to work up into basket rims, bales & handles." He then made blocks for forming quart baskets and planed basket splints for the boys to use as they worked. The boys had different tasks. Some turned the stand-ups over the rim splints, and others plaited the bottoms and filled (that is, wove) them while Br. Elisha prepared splints and made "rims, ears & handles."[23]

The boys were involved in basketmaking in November and December of 1867. Early that winter Elisha made three board sleds for them to play with; and later in the winter, at the beginning of March 1868, Br. Elisha finished off and "put iron shews onto a nice little frame, play, hand sled—to be called 'Reindeer'"—thereby adding a fillip of playfulness to his work with the boys.[24]

In fact, Br. Elisha had had a change of heart toward the boys since he had written the poem celebrating his great good fortune on being relieved of their care back in 1844; he now had great affection for them. On his birthday in March 1869, he wrote another poem, which reads, in part:

> Fifty years old this day.
> Thus half a cent'ry has vanished away
> And here I am, with the dear little boys
> Enduring with patience their prattle and noise;
> Fourteen in number; and quite good they are;
> This truth with pleasure, I now do declare,
> And may they all live in peace love and joy
> And in Mothers gospel their time well employ.
> I love them sincerely, and for them I live;
> To help them to God my time freely I give.[25]

While he was a Shaker, Br. Elisha also applied his hands and creative imagination to the realm of mechanical devices. In the early 1850s, in addition to inventing his eight-boy bed, he "drew a plan for an improvement on the wind mill—Appending a spiral spring as a self regulator."[26] In 1855, while he was working as a printer, he demonstrated his engineering skills by building "a self regulating ventilator for lodging rooms &c—to be set under or over the sash of the windows &c— Operated by the wind." Then, in 1857, when the Church Family had lost the water power used for churning butter, Br. Elisha was again "trying his inventive faculties" by building "a kind of Gymnastic Swing, to which the churn is attached. One, two or more, then get into the Swing, have the delicious pleasure of a Swing, while the Churn is bringing forth Butter."[27]

Isaac Youngs chronicled a stage of Br. Elisha's next invention. In November 1858, he wrote in his journal that Br. Elisha had returned home from New York, where he had taken "a model of a fly-trap he has late made, with a view to show it to Munn, the editor of the 'Scientific American,' to see if a patent may not be obtained for it. He saw Munn; & wrote a man at Washington, who does business in that line, a reply is expected shortly. . . . This fly-trap is an excellent article & well worth a patent."[28] Br. Isaac's judgment proved correct, for in 1859, Br. Elisha patented an "Improved Fly-Trap" (ill. 82).

Br. Elisha's contribution to the world of music came next. Responding to the Shakers' recent acceptance of instrumental music in the early 1870s, Br. Elisha built "a new instrument by which to learn music: a monochord, can play tunes on it, a piano in miniature, or a one string fiddle."[29] The monochord soon became an "improved monochord," which evolved into an "extended eight-string monochord," which in turn became a "dualichord." When Br. Elisha applied for a patent in March 1871, the patent broker, Munn & Co., editors of the *Scientific American,* dubbed his instrument the "Piano-violin" (ill. 83 and 84); and it was with this name that Elisha secured letters patent on May 9, 1871. He noted that on May 6 a musical concert was held at New Lebanon "on my new instruments, 'Piano-Violins.' The two built of chestnut wood in tune with each other, and my old big cherry, built two years since which carried double base—for the first trial of the three in harmony, the music was very fine." By the next month, Br. Elisha was receiving inquiries from people who wanted to be sales agents and advertisers for his Piano-Violin, and in the months that followed he was busy building some instruments himself and arranging for the manufacture of others by a company in Pittsfield, Massachusetts. It was an exciting time as Br. Elisha sold his invention and gave demonstrations of it to public school teachers and administrators, who were convinced that the instrument should be used as an aid in the teaching of music.

Br. Elisha also saw his invention as a means of ministering through music to people in the world and as a way of attracting converts to the Shaker faith. This idea, however, was apparently not regarded favorably by the Ministry, and the lack of encouragement from that body seemed to have played a part in Br. Elisha's deciding to leave the faith. In March 1872, Br. Elisha ended his active life in the Shaker community and went into the world.

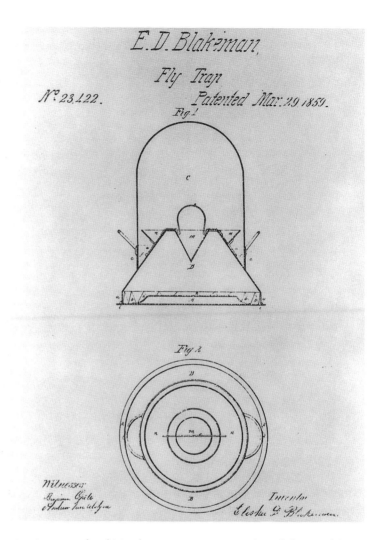

82. A patent, dated March 29, 1859, was granted to Elisha D. Blakeman for a fly trap. The patent was witnessed by the Church Family's Trustee, Benjamin Gates. Flies are attracted into the narrow funnel by molasses or some other sweetener. They then are diverted by light from another chamber, in which they find additional food, this time, however, of a poisonous nature.
Source: U.S. Patent Office

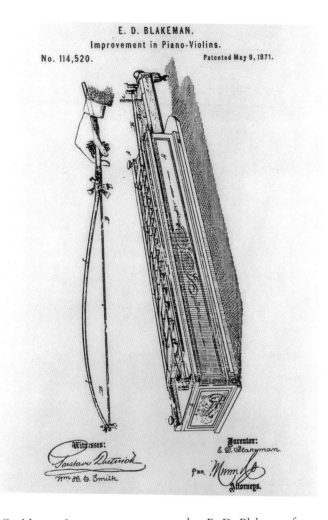

E. D. BLAKEMAN.
Improvement in Piano-Violins.
No. 114,520.   Patented May 9, 1871.

Witnesses: Inventor:

83. On May 9, 1871, a patent was granted to E. D. Blakeman for a musical instrument called a piano-violin. Br. Elisha believed that this instrument would be most helpful in instructing people in music and apparently hoped that it could be used in evangelizing efforts to increase the Shakers' membership. Munn & Co., the New York–based publishers of *Scientific American*, assisted Elisha in obtaining this patent.
Source: U.S. Patent Office

A letter from Philemon Stewart addressed to "Beloved Ministry, March 1872" provides some background for Br. Elisha's decision:

> Had they said to Br. Elisha Blakeman. You seem to feel a great interest for the increase of the Gospel, and you also feel that their might be considerable made in your Instrument of Music, we have labored upon it, and feel to bless you, in taking 40 or 50 dollars with you, and go out and do what you can in gathering souls to the Gospel, and with your Instrument; stay just as long as you feel you can do good and enlighten souls in the work of Salvation. Had this been done 4 or 5 weeks ago in my oppinion he would have long before this time been home, and much more satisfied and contented in his feelings. But as things are now held we shall certainly loose him entirely, and many others unnecessarily so in my oppinion.[30]

Polly Reed of the New Lebanon community chronicled Elisha's departure. On March 16, 1872, she wrote:

> How solemn the story we mention this day.
> Our poor Elisha B. has concluded to stray.
> He was taken by Orren to Shaker Depo . . .
> For he to the world was determined to go.
> The way is too narrow, the path is too straight.
> The crosses too many, the burdens too great.
> For ease & indulgence he's laid a new plan,
> So here is the end of poor Elisha Blakeman.[31]

However, far from being the end of Elisha, his departure was the beginning of a new life for him. He eventually married, and he wrote a book entitled *Two Hundred Poetical Riddles. For the Instruction and Amusement of Children and Youth,* which was published by Derobigne M. Bennet, Elisha's old cabinetmaking associate at New Lebanon.[32] From collaborating on cabinetmaking and working in the Washington Mountain woodlot in the 1840s, the two friends had gone on to work together as writer and publisher.

The riddles included an intriguing variety of Elisha's observations from the natural and civilized worlds around him, and some, as in the following examples, related to his work as a cabinetmaker:

No. 17

I have a back, legs and arms you see,
Though feet were never given me,
Yet aged people think me nice;
Who'll guess my name by trying twice?
    [rocking chair]

No. 27

Four legs I have, only one foot;
Two wings, one head without an eye;

Full well my character I've put,
Guess what I am—come now and try.
    [bed]

No. 157

Curls and ringlets very good,
And ribbons nice we make of wood,
Whose dingy substances oft grows bright,
As we by toil bring it to light.[33]
    [cabinetmaker's plane]

Working in words now rather than wood, and part of the world now rather than separate from it, Elisha continued to use his creative gifts to "invent" things for the "Instruction and Amusement" of others.

Elisha died at the home of his sister in Chillicothe, Ohio, twenty-eight years after leaving the Shakers. By then an octogenarian and a widower, he died of appendicitis on April 11, 1900.

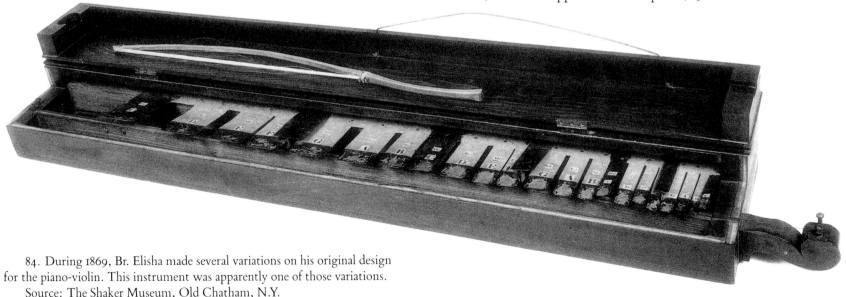

84. During 1869, Br. Elisha made several variations on his original design for the piano-violin. This instrument was apparently one of those variations.
Source: The Shaker Museum, Old Chatham, N.Y.

Samuel Humphrey Turner

(1775–1842) New Lebanon, New York, and Pleasant Hill, Kentucky

Of all the known Shaker cabinetmakers, Samuel Turner was one of the earliest converts to the Shaker faith. He was born in Hancock, Massachusetts, and went to live in the community at New Lebanon, New York, in 1788, when he was thirteen years old.

As a young man Samuel proved himself a leader, and in 1806 he was part of a group selected to go West to help organize the fledgling Shaker communities in Ohio and Kentucky. In 1808 he was appointed Elder; and that year he set out from Union Village, Ohio, for Pleasant Hill, Kentucky,[1] with several other leaders to take charge of the families in that community. For twenty-eight years Elder Samuel stayed in Kentucky. One of the few personal glimpses of his life during those years comes from a letter he wrote from Pleasant Hill to Calvin Green at New Lebanon on April 26, 1827. "I also thank you kindly for the nice comb you sent me," Elder Samuel wrote. "I have a few hars left on my head yet, but they are getting quite gray. But I think you would still know me if you was to see me."[2]

Elder Samuel returned to New Lebanon in 1836, and shortly after his arrival it was determined that he should reside at the Church Family. Once settled there he began working in the joiners' shop. During the same year it was noted that he had made "a new kind of stove pattern," and "a parcel of round leafed stands, for furnishing the great house."[3] A "round leafed" stand bearing the inscription, "ELDS. RUTH. SR. ASENETH. 1837.," was sold by Skinner's Auctions in Bolton in March of 1989. Eldress Aseneth Clark and Sr. Ruth Landon

were the Ministry Sisters at New Lebanon in 1837. The style of the inscription, stamped into the wood with individual metal letter stamps, each word followed by a period, clearly associates this stand with Br. Samuel, and this stand is probably one of the "parcel" on which he was working at the end of 1836.

A ruler at the Shaker Museum in Old Chatham bears the stamped signature, "S. TURNER. TO. SETH. Y. WELLS. 1839." (ill. 85). Elder Samuel may have been responsible for a number of rulers, yardsticks, and squares made during the last five years of his life. A yardstick-maker's jig in the collection of Laurent Torno, Jr., is stamped "SAMUEL TURNER 1837" with the same metal lettering and numbering stamps that were used to mark the ruler in illustration 85 and the stand in illustrations 86 and 87. Paired with this jig is a yardstick-maker's plane. Together these two tools allowed the craftsman to prepare a piece of wood to a precise and even thickness. This piece was then marked with a knife or scriber and was punched with letters and numbers to produce a measuring stick.

All of the extant items signed by Elder Samuel seem to have been presentation pieces. Two hat forms—one with the imprint, "CALVIN REED 1837," and the other stamped, "TO. ELDER. BENJAMIN. 1830" on one end and "SAMUEL TURNER" on the other—both appear to have been made by Elder Samuel as gifts.[4] The largest "gift" and the only piece of furniture that can at present be documented as the work of Elder Samuel's hands, is the previously mentioned stand shown in

illustrations 86 and 87, which is stamped in his distinctive manner, "SAMUEL. TURNER. TO. RUTH JOHNSON 1837." It seems impossible to learn which of two Ruth Johnsons was the recipient of this stand. Both of them appear to have had associations with Elder Samuel that would have encouraged such a gift.

Elder Samuel continued to work as a cabinetmaker after his return to New Lebanon, as is clear from a January 1838 journal entry, which records that "Samuel Turner made a new case of drawers for the elder Sisters' room."[5] Although no woodworking pieces except a hat block can be attributed to Elder Samuel while he was in the West, the quality of the workmanship on the signed piece he made at New Lebanon the year after he returned suggests that he may have left a rich legacy of fine cabinetwork to the Shakers in Kentucky and Ohio, where he spent most of his life.

85. One side of this ruler is calibrated in inches and is numbered 7 through 23. The other side, which is stamped "S. TURNER. TO. SETH. Y. WELLS. 1839.," is numbered 10 through 150 and is calibrated in units that are each equal to three millimeters.
Source: The Shaker Museum, Old Chatham, N.Y.

87. This detail of the inscription on the stand in illustration 86 clearly shows the similarity in the way that Br. Samuel marked the products of his hands.
Source: Robert Hamilton

86. The form of this stand and the date at which it was made suggest the influence of the western Shaker "style" with which Samuel had lived for most of his Shaker life. The stand, stamped "SAMUEL. TURNER. TO. RUTH JOHNSON 1837," is made of cherry and butternut.
Source: Robert Hamilton

Giles Bushnell Avery

(1815–1890) New Lebanon, New York

After Freegift Wells died in 1871, the records in Giles Avery's diaries[1] indicate that he frequently worked in Freegift's shop while he was at Watervliet on his Ministerial visits. He was building complex pieces of furniture for the use of the community as well as for sale to the world. Although Br. Giles (see ill. 88) was not known as a major cabinetmaker, he had been doing woodworking for many years, and by the time he was in his late fifties and early sixties, he had become an important figure in the Shaker Ministry at New Lebanon. He was an important and interesting enough man to have other Shakers urge him to write an account of his life, which he did in 1880.[2]

Giles's father and mother, with their two youngest children, Eliza and Giles, moved from Saybrook, Connecticut, to join the Shakers at New Lebanon in 1819—after they had left two older children with the Shakers at Enfield, Connecticut. In 1821, at the age of six, Giles was placed in the Center Family, where he lived for the next thirty-eight years. Benjamin Lyon, an early New Lebanon cabinetmaker, was appointed as his guardian, and it is likely that Giles first learned cabinetmaking from him.

In his autobiography, Br. Giles fondly related his earliest childhood recollections of living near the seashore and went on to describe himself as an extremely sensitive young man growing up in New Lebanon. He was filled with awe by beautiful landscapes and sunsets; he wept in sadness at "sights of want and misery—even an old forsaken homestead going to ruin and decay"; and he wept for joy when he saw health, life, industry, and prosperity—"outward signs that bespoke an inward sense of beauty."

When he was fifteen, he began teaching school; and in his early twenties, he took charge of the family farm for three years. Br. Giles wrote that "there was little leisure for reading or study," because he was so busy with physical labor. But during this period he became intrigued by music, and he recalled that when he drove the team of horses on the farm, he "frequently wrote a song on the plough-beam while the team was resting."

"In the fall of 1837," Br. Giles wrote,

a marvelous outpouring of the Spirit commenced among the juvenile portion of the Society of Believers at Watervliet, N.Y. There were visions, trances, revelations and communications from the spirit world. These persons would lie entranced for several days, during which time they were traveling and sightseeing in the land of souls. They would move their limbs as if flying, and would relate with all the interest and imagery of an aeronaut voyager, the beautiful scenes through which they passed. . . . In that state they would converse with spirits as freely as with mortals. . . . In the course of seven years many mediums were developed to speak, to sing and to act for the spirits, while thousands of inspired songs, and other communications, verbal and written, were poured out upon the inhabitants of Zion from the realms of spirit life.

88. Giles Bushnell Avery (1815–1890).
Source: The Shaker Museum, Old Chatham, N.Y.

For eight years, Br. Giles was "subject to inspirational influences," and he was a singing and speaking medium for several of those years. "During one year of this period," he wrote, "I was apparently lifted above the earth. I wearied not with the most fatiguing hand labor for sixteen hours in succession, and performed more than twice the amount I could have done in my normal state. . . . Earthly attractions and worldly affections vanished, and my attachment to the things of time had scarcely the strength of a gossamer thread, for these were halcyon days."

During this time, when he was twenty-five, Br. Giles was appointed to live with Elder Amos Stewart as his junior in the Elder's Lot. He remained an Elder in the Center Family for twenty years, nine of which were under the direction of Elder Amos. Elder Giles continued learning woodworking, among other things, from his mentor. Elder Giles listed his manual employment as: "the repairing of buildings, digging cellars for foundations, stone masonry, sawing stone for a new dwelling, plumbing, carpentering and plastering. I had some experience at cabinet work and wagon making, and even made wooden dippers . . . trimmed and grafted many hundreds of old apple trees; and prepared cisterns for holding liquid manure for fertilizing."

In 1859, Elder Giles became an associate with Elder Daniel Boler in the Order of Ministry, and he remained in the Ministry for the next thirty-one years. During these years he traveled to other communities from Maine and New Hampshire to Ohio and Kentucky, doing the work of the Ministry. In his later years he spent much of his time at Watervliet, as was his duty as a member of the Ministry. As previously mentioned, during the time he spent there, he made furniture in the shop left vacant when Freegift Wells died.

For years Elder Giles had made great quantities of beehives and seed boxes at New Lebanon, but except for dippers he made in 1845 and a writing desk in 1864, no specific woodworking projects or pieces of furniture are mentioned in his diaries. However, at Watervliet in

1873 he made a sewing machine counter probably similar to the one shown in illustration 6; put backs on benches for the singing school in October 1874; made a secretary for the Eldresses' room between November 1874 and May 1875; and built counter drawers in 1875. In 1877, he made a cupboard and drawers; and in 1879 he finished another cupboard case. He spent much time in 1879 moving furniture from one house to another at Watervliet. Later that year he made a shoe box for the Ministry and book boxes for the school.

In 1880, working "at Freegift's little saw bench at the mill," Elder Giles sawed lumber for work tables for the sisters, which he then proceeded to build, along with a dining room table. In February and March 1880 at Watervliet, Giles had made three little bureaus for sale to the world; and that November he made a desk and a "secretary for Eldress Polly," which was also referred to as a "Ladies Parlor Beaureau."[3]

From the last week of May 1880 to the first week in July, Elder Giles kept a cash account of supplies he purchased and the time he spent making a set of work bureaus or desks for sale, in which he figured the cost of his time at twenty cents an hour (see ill. 89). This account, which can be compared side-by-side to journal references about the actual cabinetwork he did, is one of the few records of its kind.[4] This accounting of his time and materials gives some insight into the actual hours of labor necessary for the construction of furniture. Since the intention was to sell these "little bureaus," the careful accounting may have been necessary in order to determine a fair price for the pieces.

Elder Giles died in Watervliet on December 27, 1890; and his funeral, which was held on December 30, was attended by many Believers who journeyed from Hancock and New Lebanon despite the fact that the weather "was intensely cold and somewhat stormy, the roads badly drifted and the traveling exceedingly unpleasant."[5] A postscript published with Elder Giles's autobiography includes an

a

account of his funeral and many letters and elegiac poems written by Shakers from nearly every community, who had been his friends. The letters and poems are glowing tributes that portray Elder Giles as a noble leader and teacher, an unselfish worker and friend. He was venerated by those who knew him as "one chosen of God for special work," and had been looked upon in his own lifetime as "an Angel of the Lord."[6]

89. These pages from Giles Avery's "Diary for 1880" (OClWHi, Shaker Collection, V B 120) are representative of the records he kept of the time and money spent building three small "worktables" or "ladies' beaureaus for sale." Such accounting was apparently necessary in order to establish a sale price for these pieces. (**a**) Br. Giles's entry for July 2, 1880, clearly states that these pieces of furniture are being made for sale. (**b**) Note especially that the lumber for the worktables is cherry (May 24), that the worktables will be on casters (May 27),

and that Br. Giles will use "trimmings" (possibly moldings) to finish the piece (May 27). (**c**) Note the number of hours Br. Giles worked on these worktables each day and that he valued his time at twenty cents per hour. (**d**) It is easier to picture these worktables if one knows that they have commercially made "knobs & casters" and "mouldings" and that they apparently were highly finished with varnish.

Source: The Western Reserve Historical Society, Cleveland, Ohio

George M. Wickersham

(1806–1888) New Lebanon, New York

Although he was a cabinetmaker, George Wickersham's work as an architect also produced furniture for the New Lebanon Church Family in a curious way. "A new case of drawers & cupboard," wrote Isaac Youngs on February 28, 1859, "was bro't into the house for No. 10—they were made by Shumway—at the North house. He was paid for it, by the North family in consideration of George Wickersham's service in drawing a draught for a new barn, (which they are calculating to build the ensuing season,) & his assistance in planning the work &c."[1] (see ill. 90). Br. George was well thought of as an architect and mechanic, and when the Great House, the dwelling for the New Lebanon Church Family, burned in the fire of 1875, he designed the plans for a new house.

George was raised in Philadelphia, Pennsylvania, and at the age of fourteen moved with his family to Valley Forge to live in a community inspired by the English socialist Robert Owen. There George worked for about a year in a machine shop, then returned to Philadelphia, where he spent another year overseeing his father's wire-working business. His father returned from Valley Forge and took over the business when George was sixteen. At that time, George expressed a desire to become either a carpenter or a machinist. His father, who had a long-standing interest in socialist communities, offered him the opportunity to investigate the Shaker community at New Lebanon as an alternative. George soon traveled to New Lebanon, where he lived for the rest of his life. He developed his skills at both of his desired trades,

as it turned out, and became a furniture maker as well. Interestingly, George's brother, John Wickersham, who remained in Philadelphia, became an architect and an inventor.[2] He also was a maker of furniture, although his pieces, in stark contrast to George's, were made of iron and were of Victorian design. George was also an inventor and in 1863 developed a new kind of stove called an "ironing arch" used for heating flat irons while shielding the room from the additional heat produced by ironing in the summer.

A tool chest thought to have been used by Br. George and containing tools marked with his initials are in the collection of the Shaker Museum in Old Chatham, New York (ill. 92 and 93). A signed and dated lap desk that he made has also survived, although its location is now unknown. It bears the inscription, "Made by George Wickersham 1841 North Family Phebe Ann Jones."[3]

Inspired by the record of Giles Avery's life as a Shaker, Br. George wrote an essay entitled "How I Came To Be A Shaker," which was published as a small pamphlet by the Shakers at East Canterbury, New Hampshire, in 1891.[4] Br. George died on Christmas Day of that year, and a Shaker sister wrote a footnote to his passing: "We have sweet surprise with our little girls all dressed in white bearing a bough in their hands appearing in the dining room to sing a Christmas song. Immediately after we hear Br. George has finished. Pretty coincidence."[5]

90. The North Family's Great Stone Dairy Barn was started in 1859 following the architectural plans drawn by George Wickersham. The North Family compensated for Br. George's time by having a case of drawers and cupboard built for the Church Family by a cabinetmaker named Shumway, a non-Shaker from the town of New Lebanon.

Source: Hancock Shaker Village, Inc., Pittsfield, Mass.

91. This portrait of George M. Wickersham was taken in his room in the Church Family's new brick Dwelling House, which was built in 1875 to replace the Great House that had been destroyed by arson. Br. George was the architect for the new dwelling, which is now the administration building for the Darrow School and bears his name. The architectural floor plans for this building are in the collection of the Western Reserve Historical Society, Cleveland, Ohio (ms. XIV-8).

Source: The Shaker Museum, Old Chatham, N.Y.

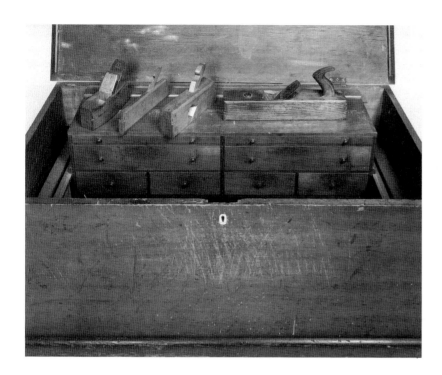

92. This tool chest with its interior drawers, trays, special fixtures, and racks is thought to have been made and used by George. When it was purchased by the Shaker Museum, it contained woodworking planes and tools bearing his initials.

Source: The Shaker Museum, Old Chatham, N.Y.

93. A number of common woodworking planes that have the initials "G.M.W." impressed into their front ends are in the collection of the Shaker Museum in Old Chatham, New York. Most of the planes were made by Richard and Leonard Carter of Troy, New York, and are marked with the imprint, "R. & L. Carter Troy," which was used only between 1842 and 1846. The set includes ordinary rabbet (or rebate) planes, a half-set of hollows and rounds, a jack plane, a trying plane, a jointer, and several special-purpose planes.

Source: The Shaker Museum, Old Chatham, N.Y.

Alfred Merrick Collier

(1823–1884) Harvard, Massachusetts

Thomas Tucker Collier, a potter by trade, was married in Bristol, England, in 1812 and traveled alone to America in 1818. His wife, Harriet, and their three children followed him several years later, landing in this country in 1822. Their son Alfred was born the next year on January 20, in Cambridge, Massachusetts. They had ten children in all (two of whom died in infancy). Thomas Collier later deserted his family and moved to Virginia, leaving his wife with the burden of raising the children alone.

Even though the two oldest boys went to work in an attempt to help make ends meet, the care of such a large household was more than Harriet could manage. She arranged for two of her daughters to be taken in and raised by a family in East Cambridge; and in March 1831, Alfred who was then eight years old, was taken to live with the Shakers at Harvard.[1] Alfred stayed in the Boy's Order until March 1838 when he and Elijah Myrick, who was just a year younger, moved together to the Church Family.[2]

Records from Alfred's youth touch upon his suffering from bad colds, pulled teeth, and a sprained ankle; and there are signs that in his late teens Alfred had more serious difficulties in adjusting to life with the Shakers. His father, who was living in Richmond, Virginia, came to visit him at Harvard in July 1840, and one of the things he did in the course of a two-day visit was to lecture his son "in consequence of his shortcomings." Whatever their nature, Alfred's problems were significant enough so that the following month Elder Grove Blanchard wrote of Alfred that they in the Ministry also had "much labor with him in consequence of his shortcomings."[3]

The remonstrative efforts of his father and the Elders apparently strengthened Alfred's resolve to overcome his failings, but although he became an energetic worker as a member of the Church Family and remained at Harvard for twenty-four more years, his life there was seemingly never without some discontent. As a young man, Br. Alfred often worked with Thomas Holden. When the two were put in charge of the farm for a period of time beginning in March 1842, Elder Grove noted that although "they take up their crosses cheerfully . . . both [are] in trouble now & again, probably because [they are] young men."[4] In later years, however, Br. Alfred's discontent turned to disillusionment. He saw many of his close friends leave the Society during a period when very few new members were joining, and eventually he too left the community following a confrontation with the Ministry.

The first indications that Br. Alfred was involved in woodworking come from 1842 and 1843 journal records that show him working at the sawmill with Thomas Holden and Elijah Myrick on different occasions. These records include an account of an accident at the saw in which Br. Alfred "cut his great toe badly" when he was twenty.[5] Br. Alfred also worked as a mechanic, and in February 1843 he made and installed a frame for the saw at the mill. Thomas Holden and Br. Alfred hauled logs to the sawmill; and they shingled the sheep barn together in the summer of 1843. Through the 1840s, Br. Alfred worked at other tasks that included hauling rocks, planting trees, building roads, and making cider.

As time went on, Br. Alfred was mentioned more and more often in the journals as performing carpentry tasks on his own. In December 1847 he did extensive mechanical work to put the sawmill in working condition, and from that time on he was involved almost exclusively with woodworking, occasionally helping out with other kinds of work and also performing the duties of a Church Deacon.

In the first months of 1848, Br. Alfred jointed and matched the boards for the roof of the dry-house and then made doors and sashes for the building. In the same year, he collaborated with Thomas Holden on at least one occasion to make a coffin. And he was very active at the mill. A journal reference on March 13, 1848, recorded that Br. Alfred "runs the sawmill with but little intermission day or night"; and an entry on October 12, 1849, noted that he and another Shaker brother worked "at the mill until after midnight."[6]

A journal kept by Br. Alfred in 1857 and 1858 mentions many pieces of furniture that he made during those years. These entries confirm that after the late 1840s he made a transition from carpentry to cabinetmaking.

A desk made of pine, maple, and chestnut is the one known piece of furniture that can be attributed to Br. Alfred (ill. 95). It has the name "Alfred Collier" on the underside of the lid, inscribed with chalk. It may be this desk to which Br. Alfred refers when he records in his journal on January 31, 1861, "I work in the Shop & work on a Desk for Elder Grove [Blanchard]." The project was put aside for several months and was finished in June. On July 4, Br. Alfred wrote in his journal, "I went over to the S[outh] Family & got my Desk I made for Elder Grove [Blanchard]";[7] while an entry from the same day in

94. Alfred Collier (1823–1884).
Source: Dorothy B. Collier

another journal stated that "Elder Gr[ove Blanchard] received a new desk from Alfred Collier."[8]

One of the most intriguing aspects of the furniture that Br. Alfred made in 1857 and 1858 is that a number of the pieces were made for people who were not Shakers. He made a cupboard and a "Trunk Desk" for his natural brother Charles, who lived in Charlestown (on the outskirts of Boston); and he made a sink and a cupboard for "Samuel Bacon in Mill Street," presumably in the village of Harvard. And in his journal entry for the afternoon of November 27, 1857, Br. Alfred noted, "I work in the Shop & blind dovetail a writing desk for my niece in Charlestown."[9] (Blind dovetails, a form of joinery in which none of the dovetail joint is visible once the piece is assembled, is rare in Shaker furniture.)

On several occasions Br. Alfred also mentioned that he was working on boxes, "little boxes for some friends far away," friends who obviously were not in the Harvard community.

During these two years Br. Alfred also made cupboards for the Harvard Ministry as well as several other cupboards for different people and locations within the community, but the focus in his journal during this period was clearly on things outside the Shaker village. This journal shows Br. Alfred to be a man in a personal quandary. He often found himself torn between a commitment to being a Shaker and a desire to pursue a richer, more fulfilling life among friends in the outside world. A farewell to 1856, written on December 31 of that year, begins this segment of his journal; and in this statement Br. Alfred introduced two major topics that were to become increasingly

95. The form of this tall desk, its green color, and the original bail handle, all unusual in Shaker furniture, are more understandable coming from the hands of Br. Alfred, whose attraction to the world outside his Shaker home might have caused him to challenge traditional Shaker styles. The underside of the lid is signed with white chalk in script, "Alfred Collier."
Source: J. J. Gerald McCue

important in his life—changes in his views of religious matters, and the loss of friends. "My mind has been subjected to some changes in my views of religious matters," he wrote, "but not as yet to effect a change in my manner of life. I have at times felt very sorrowful but the loss of friends has effected me deeply & has at times wrung out the bitter tears of agony . . . but finally 1856 farewell."

Br. Alfred may have been writing here about friends from whom he was alienated by differences of opinion on religious issues, but he was soon to experience the loss of friends who would leave the Harvard community. He chronicled the first and most poignant of these departures on March 12, 1857, when he wrote, "With pain and grief I record the exit from this place of Charles Henry Collier [his nephew; see ill. 96]. He became dissatisfactioned with his home and peacibly with drew from this Society this morning. [He] left on the Noon Train for Charleston, the place from where I took him. He came to live with me on the 3rd day of Sept 1849. He was then 10 years of age [and] he will be 18 years of age on the 18th of July next. O! I love him! I love him! I love him!"

On March 14, Br. Alfred resumed his mournful soliloquy: "This day I do nothing but walk round. I have suffered so much in my mind of late on Henry's account that I could not find rest to the Sole of my foot anywhere. It seems that my heart became liquid & I have poured it out like water. It seems that there is no Sorrow like my grief."

Br. Alfred's anxiety persisted, and he lost twenty-five pounds in two and a half months. At this time he was making furniture for members of his family who were not Shakers, and he began to grow closer to them and to other people outside the Harvard community. On June 23, 1857, he went to Concord, where he had a very enjoyable visit with Henry and met other "kindred spirits and old friends." Stimulated by these contacts and subsequently feeling downcast upon his return to Harvard, Br. Alfred wrote three days later, "I feel very much discontented in my social position in these days. I have nought against people or place, but I want to step out into freedom!!!"

96. Br. Alfred and his nephew Charles Henry Collier (1839–1858). This picture, copied from a daguerreotype taken in the early 1850s (well before Charles Henry left the Shakers), is certainly one of the earliest photographic images of Shakers.
Source: Dorothy B. Collier

His depression deepened to the point where he was prompted to write on June 28, "I hope for better days or for death ere long." But Alfred had glimpses of better days as he gravitated toward other members of his family who were in the world. The next month he went to Boston to see his mother and sisters and his nephew Charles Henry, and he found it difficult to leave them to return to Harvard. Alfred wrote on July 23, the second day of his visit, "We had all of the Collier name of our family together & went over to Boston & had an ambrotype of all of them taken in a group and the same hung up in Charles[s] house" (see ill. 97). On July 25, Alfred added, "We went to the Atheneum & spent the forenoon among pictures and statuary. We were highly delighted. I received noble ideas of the human intellect & came out with better feelings than when I entered. PM—I prepared for coming back [and] then came the tug of war. I had spent 4 days of exquisite delight with kindred spirits where I loved & was loved. These few days are the happiest of the year so far and [it] was very hard to part for we loved each other well."

That October, D. Lafayette White, a friend of Br. Alfred's whom he called "my almost constant companion for 26 years," left the Harvard community to live in Lowell, Massachusetts. Lafayette's departure was another severe blow to Br. Alfred's spirit and served to deepen his melancholy. "He left many weeping friends," Br. Alfred wrote, "[and] his loss is irreparable."

Within a few days, Alfred went to Charlestown to see Charles Henry again, only to learn that his nephew was planning to go to New Orleans. The prospect of not seeing Charles Henry for perhaps several years was a sad one for Alfred; but as always, visiting with Charles Henry delighted him, and this helped him to accept the idea of Charles Henry's venture with some equanimity.

In November, Charles Henry sailed for New Orleans on a ship carrying ice to that southern port. Two months later, on his birthday, Alfred made these remarks in his journal, reflecting his general dissat-

97. "We had all of the Collier name of our family together & went over to Boston & had an ambrotype of all of them taken in a group and the same hung up in Charles['s] house." This July 23, 1857, entry from Br. Alfred's journal leaves little doubt about when this photograph was taken. Br. Alfred is in the center. Charles Henry (at the far right), pictured without his Shaker clothing, had left the community four months earlier.

Source: Dorothy B. Collier

isfaction: "This is the 35th anniversary of my birth. At 20 min p 8 o'clock AM I have arrived to the meridian of life allotted to mankind in this age of the world. If I am Suffered to live out the rest of my days as I have lived the past, I shall be a strange being in very deed."

Br. Alfred continued on as a Shaker, but although he made furniture for the community and specifically for the Ministry, he allowed a hint of antagonism toward the Harvard leaders to creep into his journal. On occasion he referred to the Ministry as "the Party in power," writing in a tone that intimated some resentment if not disrespect.

He also continued to be attracted to the outside world. In April 1858, upon reading a sermon by Reverend Theodore Parker of Boston, Br. Alfred remarked in his journal that "there is considerable excitement on the Subject of Religion among the Outside but is as dumb as a Churchyard among us." For his part, Br. Alfred nurtured his own interest in worldly people and their ideas. That May, he had "some very agreeable conversation with Ralph Waldo Emerson's wife and daughter," who had come to visit the Shakers at Harvard; and in June, he visited the "Cambridge Colleges & went into the museum there & the library & read some very valuable books & had some very agreeable conversation with the Librarian & students. [I] also went into [the] Botanical Garden—all of which I enjoyed very much because I felt my self intellectually & morally improved."

He continued to pursue this path of inquiry, seeking out people who were alive with ideas and energy. Two days after his trip to Cambridge, Br. Alfred visited Theodore Parker in Boston and spent an hour and a half conversing with him. He was very much impressed with Parker's erudition and wisdom and expressed the thought that, by comparison, his own intellectual growth had been stifled by the Shakers. The tone of his comments is not so much an accusatory one as one of dissatisfaction with what he had done thus far with his life.

On August 27, 1858, Alfred "received the sad news that my boy Charles Henry Collier is no more. He died of the Yellow Fever in New Orleans." Alfred was once again swept into grieving for Charles Henry, perhaps the person he had loved most dearly of all his family and friends.

Br. Alfred's sadness was prolonged. His description of a Thanksgiving dinner in 1858 has about it a heavyhearted air, a sense of impending, inevitable doom. On November 25 he wrote, "PM we have a dinner got ready for us. I bought a Turkey & things to make us Savory meat that we may eat and bless each other before we Separate. Elijah Myrick, Alfred Collier, Elisha Myrick, Lyddia Grover, Angelina Whitier, Elizabeth Persons, & Caroline Meahan. We all sat down at one table in the Bakers room & passed one hour in happiness at the table & did Justice to the vittuals. This is the first time in all our lives that we all eat together at one table and it may be the last. We gave thanks that there were so many of us left. But perhaps we may never meet again."

Eating in mixed company with the sisters, something that bordered on the heretical or sinful, certainly did not improve Br. Alfred's standing with the Ministry, but then he did not appear to be especially solicitous of their favor. Less than a week after Thanksgiving, he went to Charlestown to spend more time with old friends and noted wistfully that he returned to Harvard "with a heavy heart from warm friends to Cold ones here." As time went on, the balance of Br. Alfred's affections seemed weighted more and more heavily in favor of people he knew outside the Society.

Br. Alfred's farewell to 1858, written on December 31, contains observations on the decline of the Shaker Society that are imbued with his personal melancholy:

This day closes the year, with a darker hue, than last year, our number still grows less & as the day fades into evening so does our light & prosperity wane[.] [I]t is abundantly evident that we are on the decline[.] [W]e number less than ever before[.] [W]e have but 65 in the Church all Counted (. . . 21 males, 6 boys, 3 men over seventy). So the Society is on the Decline in Numbers & power[.] [T]here is not near the ability in the Society as there was 10 years ago, there is now but one in the Church on the Brethren's side that has come in on their own faith for 30 years & that is William Davidson of Aberdeen Scotland . . . there is none on the Sisters side that came in on their own faith within 30 years in the Church.

So now 1858 Farewell & while I set writing these few lines my Soul is pained with the aweful stillness of this Shop. Not one breath of mortals Song is heard nor yet the sound of mortal footstep is heard. All, all have gone to seek their fortune over the Worlds vast domain. Nearly all those who set out on the Journey loving & Cheerful have one by one drop[p]ed from my side till I alone am left to tell the sad story. Elijah & Elisha are all the ones left in the Church (Warren Sparrow was about to go to the South Family) & we are not often together because our business causes us to be sepperate. Once our house rang with echo of cheerful Mirth at times to the disturbance of elderly people who used to signify their dislike in unmistakeable terms. But Alas! They have gone to the "Hills of the Dead."

The decline continued. Little more than a month later, on February 3, 1859, Elisha Myrick left the Harvard Shakers to go to work in Boston. Br. Elisha had lived at Harvard for more than thirty-one years, and he and Br. Alfred talked "long & profoundly" the night before he left. The next day Br. Alfred found himself with one less old friend at the Harvard Shaker Village, and he again was moved to comment in his journal on the diminishing number of believers.[10]

Br. Alfred, however, at least had not lost his physical health and strength. He described himself as follows on January 20, 1860, his thirty-seventh birthday: "though age and hard work has had some effect on me, Physically I am still as blithe as ever. My hair is not grey, my sight is not in the least impaired but my beard is a little grey on my chin. My weight is 175 lbs., my health is very good and I was never so

strong in my life. I can shoulder 200 lbs. & walk off with it with comparative ease."

He continued to make furniture and built a cupboard and a chest during that January and February. On February 13, he wrote that "I . . . began a little trunk for myself," and the next day he "veneered the two ends of it." In 1861 he helped Elijah Myrick make herb boxes, he finished the desk for Elder Grove, and he also finished a flour chest that he had "been makeing at odd jobs."[11]

But as Br. Alfred continued to work, more Shakers were leaving the community. In 1862, Warren Sparrow and Thomas Holden left. Both were long-time friends of Br. Alfred's, as well as fellow cabinetmakers. Br. Alfred had grown up in the Shaker village with Br. Thomas, and the two had worked together for several years when they were young men.

Br. Alfred could see prospects of life in the sect becoming progressively more gloomy, and it seems that the cumulative effect of these departures and disappointments might have been enough to persuade him to leave the Shakers. There was, however, one last straw—a final conflict with "the Party in power," the Ministry headed by Elder Grove Blanchard. In June 1864, Ida Rich, a Shaker sister, was taken away from the Harvard community by her father for reasons having to do with her friendship with Br. Alfred. However, the two evidently continued to keep in touch while Ida was with her family in Boston. Two months later, Br. Alfred was forced to give up to the Ministry letters that Ida had sent to him, and on September 12, 1864, he was dismissed from the community by the Ministry. He left the same day "for the world on the noon train," and Elder Grove stated for the record that a settlement had been reached with Alfred "in perfect good & kind feelings, and parties well satisfied."[12]

Elder William Wetherbee and Sr. Nancy Fairbanks went from Harvard to Boston the next day to see Mr. Rich, who confronted Ida and "caused her to yield up letters sent her from A. Collier." Afterward, "perfect good & kind feelings" notwithstanding, Elder Grove wrote in his journal that when Ida gave up the letters, "Sister Nancy Fairbanks then and there informed her that she could not be received here among Believers again. And so one more very disagreeable and awful case is closed," he concluded, "and especially so of A. Collier, an infamous Heretic of quite an age." This censorious remark intimated that Elder Grove had had a long-standing suspicion of or disaffection for Alfred and his maverick tendencies—feelings that possibly went back as far as 1840 and the occasion of his taking Alfred to task for his "shortcomings."

The other administrative details were perfunctory. On September 22 a part of Alfred's clothing was sent to him, at his written request, at an address in Brooklyn, New York, where his sister Maria was living, and his temporal connection with the Harvard community was no more.[13]

For many years Alfred had been drawn to the world of people and ideas beyond the pale of the Shaker Society, and now he found himself a part of that world. From Brooklyn, Alfred moved to the Titusville and Oil City area of Pennsylvania, where he established a connection with the oil business. A great nephew, Arthur Luke Collier, wrote in a family memoir that while Alfred was there, "it is said that . . . he worked with a man called 'Coal Oil Johnnie,' and that his prospects of gaining great wealth never materialized because of the unscrupulous methods of some of his competitors. . . . In all probability others got the better of him and he, in his simple Shaker faith, was 'taken in' by them."[14]

Alfred had better fortune in other respects. He married Margaretta D. Thomas in Oil City on May 18, 1871, and a daughter, Carrie May, was born to them on August 6, 1872, followed by a son, Charles Edwin Collier, on May 24, 1874.

Alfred died on August 29, 1884, and his wife died the next year.

Alfred's mother, Harriet Collier, had moved to Cincinnati by 1846 to live with her daughter, and while there she became a member of the New Jerusalem Church. Whether Alfred followed his mother into this faith is not clear. He was, however, buried in the Old Swedenborgian Cemetery in the Philadelphia suburb of Upper Darby.[15]

Elijah Myrick

(1824–1890) Harvard, Massachusetts

Elijah Myrick was born on February 18, 1824, and was taken to Harvard in 1830. As a teenager he worked at the sawmill with his brother Daniel. A journal entry for January 9, 1843 notes that Br. Elijah was sawing boards at the mill, and an entry for February 24, 1843, mentioned that he was "making a sink for the wash-house."[1] Later that year Elijah and his brother Elisha worked together with Thomas Holden to build the fence around the clearing used for worship on Harvard's Holy Hill.

At this time Br. Elijah was also working as a mechanic. On February 17, 1843, he finished a shingle machine; and in September 1843, he was making a pump for the hog house. In January 1844, he "made a machine to move Abigail Blanchard with. She is helpless and has to be lifted off and on to her bed often."[2] That January Br. Elijah also finished making parts for one of the looms, and on January 13 it was noted that "Elijah Myrick makes a lot of broom handles."[3]

In 1845, Br. Elijah was the foreman for the job of framing one of the farm sheds. It was "his first Building as chief," an observer wrote, and "it came together very well."[4]

Br. Elijah became a Trustee, and through the 1840s and 1850s he spent much of his time traveling in New England. He often went to Boston, sometimes with produce and articles for sale and sometimes to purchase livestock, molasses, bricks, stoves, or fresh herring. Many of his trips were "seed journies" to sell garden seeds, along special routes that took him to Brattleboro, Peterboro, Nashua, New Bedford, Salem, Boston, Lowell, and Cape Cod.

98. This portrait of Elijah Myrick was probably taken before the Civil War, when he was still in his thirties.
Source: Hancock Shaker Village, Inc., Pittsfield, Mass.

99. While this once-built-in pine cupboard isn't particularly unusual, the inscription on its back, left by its maker, adds considerable interest to the piece. The inscription reads: "Made by Elijah Myrick March 1869 While reflecting on the improving element in our government telling as it does with irresistible effect on the whole world. Differing from the past by the alliance of integrity with intelligence in the highest council of the Nation. Massachusetts may well feel a laudible pride in the providential selection to their consideration of her past empire of thy gratified designs possessing the power and ability which integrity and intelligence only can give."

Source: Fruitlands Museums, Harvard, Mass.

During the 1860s he continued to travel, but his pace slowed somewhat, enough, at any rate, to allow him to make furniture back at Harvard. The one documented piece of furniture made by Br. Elijah is a large cupboard that was built to fit into a recess in the kitchen or in one of the dining rooms (ill. 99). A penciled inscription on the back begins, "Made by Elijah Myrick March 1869" and goes on to make a grandiloquent political statement praising the government of Massachusetts, a curious and unique expression on a piece of Shaker furniture.

Br. Elijah was also an inventor of sorts. In 1869 he engineered an improvement in chimney caps, involving cast-iron caps, "made in sections, corresponding to the size of bricks by which any chimney can be capped as readily and as easily as a course of brick can be laid. The sections . . . all firmly locked together, making a solid cast iron cap"[5] (see ill. 100). Br. Elijah's chimney caps were patented and apparently were marketed for a time. In 1873, Elder John Whitely of Harvard made a trip to New Lebanon and took with him, to show the members of that community, "a new style of lamp shade" that Br. Elijah had invented.[6] And the August 1881 issue of *The Manifesto* describes "an ingenious device to protect the curtains [in carriages] when rolled up," also invented by Elijah Myrick.

In 1874 and 1875 Br. Elijah made trips to other Shaker communities in New York and New England, and in 1876 he traveled to Philadelphia for the Centennial and to visit the Believers in that city.

Br. Elijah became an Elder in the Harvard Church Family in 1883. He died on February 9, 1890, nine days before his sixty-sixth birthday. Two surviving photographs of Br. Elijah give a visual perspective to his life over a period of time. One is a portrait of Elijah as a young man (ill. 98), whereas the other shows him as a Church Elder much later in his life (ill. 101).

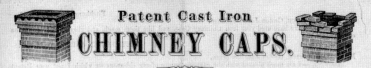

Patent Cast Iron
CHIMNEY CAPS.

Cheap, Durable and Ornamental.

THESE Caps are made in sections, corresponding to the size of bricks by which any chimney can be capped as readily and as easily as a course of brick can be laid. The sections are all firmly locked together, making a

SOLID CAST IRON CAP,

consequently no brick can ever be displaced by the action of the elements. Common observation and experience is the best argument to prove their necessity and utility in preserving Chimney Heads, for where the top course is secured their need be no fear of the rest. It is well known that the top bricks, (and frequently in a very short time,) become loose and work off, and many times drop down the flue, and lodge in such a way as to stop the draft, and can only be removed at much trouble and expense. And when they fall outside on slated roofs they break the slate, and do other damage many times far exceeding the cost of *capping the chimney*.

Added to the unsightly appearance of a dilapidated Chimney, the displaced brick cause the draft to be irregular, often blowing down the chimney, and sending the smoke into the room. Such chimneys are generally left a long time before being repaired, it being a disagreeable, difficult and expensive job to do.

It is desirable to have the top of a chimney enlarged. But it has always been attended with the objection that the overhanging bricks become loose and work off, and often the whole head parts in the centre. This Cap overcomes that objection.

They can be put on in connection with any arrangement used to assist the draft, and add very much to their stability, and *especially* is this the case in cities, where funnels are applied to each separate flue in a chimney (having many flues) to extend the draft upward. They can also be applied to the base of chimneys, and chimneys already built. They are as convenient to keep in a store as other kinds of hardware, and a set can readily be selected to fit any size chimney.

This invention was brought to public notice only a few months last season, and received the unqualified approval of our intelligent mechanics, masons and builders, and all who have used them, and no one can fail to appreciate how great a want they supply; and their ready adaptation, utility and cheapness, together with the neat and tidy appearance, so desirable to house and village, bespeak their merits better than a multitude of testimonials, a few only of which are subjoined.

TESTIMONIALS.

Groton Junction, Mass., June 14th, 1869.

Mr. E. Myrick,

Dear Sir,—I have used your Patent Chimney Caps, and am so well pleased with your improvement, I shall recommend them as being the one thing needful on every chimney. Their cheapness and usefulness can but commend them to general favor. In my opinion they should be reckoned on the side of economy.

Respectfully yours,

FRANCIS SWAN, Mason.

Boston, June 18th, 1869.

Mr. Elijah Myrick, Groton Junction, Mass.

Dear Sir,—Your Patent Chimney Caps have our unqualified approbation, and should be applied to every chimney to complete, protect, and ornament it. Please place one in our warehouse in Boston for exhibition. Such a valuable improvement shall have our best efforts to promote the general introduction and sale of the same.

Faithfully,

AMES PLOW CO., H. C. TURNER, SUP'T.

Groton Junction, Mass., June 15th, 1869.

Mr. E. Myrick,

Dear Sir,—I see no reason why your Patent Chimney Caps should not be introduced wherever they are known. They effectually secure the chimney head, are so easily obtained, so completely adapted to all sizes of chimneys, and so cheap as to be within the means of all. Their general adoption would be a great saving, and give a neat appearance to houses and villages. I shall without reserve recommend them.

Respectfully yours,

JOEL E. FLETCHER, Builder.

Fitchburg, June 17th, 1869.

Mr. Elijah Myrick, Groton Junction, Mass.,

Dear Sir,—We have used your Iron Chimney Caps, and like them much, and they should be put on every chimney. Yours,

WETHERBEE & DERBY, Masons.

Mr. Elijah Myrick, Groton Junction Mass.,

Dear Sir,—I am much pleased with the neat appearance of my chimneys on which I put your Patent Chimney Caps. They present a striking and favorable contrast to those around them. While I have the satisfaction of knowing that mine are lastingly secure.

L. J. SPAULDING, Road-master, Fitchburg R. R.

Chicago, Ill., Aug. 14th, 1869.

Friend Myrick,

I think your invention a good thing. I see the necessity from the condition of my own chimney tops of something of the kind. Yours very truly,

E. S. CHESBROUGH, City Engineer.

Concord, Mass., March 1st, 1870.

Mr. Myrick,

Dear Sir,—We are very much pleased with your Chimney Caps, and highly recommend them to the public as the best thing made for preserving the tops of chimneys. Yours truly,

CYRUS FLETCHER & CO., Masons.

Leominster, Feb. 11th, 1870.

Mr. E. Myrick, Groton Junction, Mass.,

Dear Sir,—We have long seen the need of a real protection to chimney tops which would come within the means of all. We think your Patent Chimney Cap supplies the deficiency admirably.

Very respectfully,

SMITH & SPRING, Masons.

Bolton, Mass., Feb. 15th, 1870.

Mr. Myrick,

Dear Sir,—You may use my name as agent for your Chimney Caps. I think very highly of them, and shall recommend them as much as possible, Respectfully yours,

AMOS BRYANT, Mason.

Beverly, Mass., Feb. 12th, 1870.

Mr. E. Myrick,

Dear Sir,—I have put on ten of your Patent Chimney Caps, on both new and old chimneys, they all give first-rate satisfaction, Respectfully yours,

CHAS. F. DODGE, Mason.

West Hartford, Vt.

Mr. E. Myrick,

Your Patent Chimney Caps are liked very much, and in the Spring I shall order a number of them. Very truly,

AUSTIN HOWARD, Mason.

For information or Caps address

E. MYRICK, Patentee, Groton Junction, Mass.

OR HIS AGENTS.

A. D. Otterson, general agents, Nashua, N. H. Ames Plow Company, Boston. Wetherbee & Derby, Fitchburg. E. H. Hayward, Groton Junction. White & Conant, Worcester. Weston & Stevens, Nashua, N. H. Smith & Spring, Leominster. T. D. Bailey, Lowell. George Bowdich, Salem. C. F. Dodge, Beverly. Amos Bryant, Bolton. Ripley & Shattuck, Burlington, Vt. I. S. Kinsman, Keene, N. H. Edmonds & Co., Charlestown, Mass.,

PRICES OF CHIMNEY CAPS.

16 x 16 — $2.00	16 x 20 — $2.25	16 x 24 — $2.50	16 x 28 — $2.75	16 x 32 — $3.00	16 x 36 — $3.25	16 x 40 — $3.50
20 x 20 — 2.50	20 x 24 — 2.75	20 x 28 — 3.00	20 x 32 — 3.25	20 x 36 — 3.50	20 x 40 — 3.75	20 x 44 — 4.00
24 x 44 — 4.25	28 x 28 — 3.50	24 x 24 — 3.00	24 x 28 — 3.25	24 x 32 — 3.50	24 x 36 — 3.75	24 x 40 — 4.00
28 x 32 — 3.75	28 x 36 — 4.00	28 x 40 — 4.25	And in the same proportion for other sizes.			

☞ I would refer customers to Burditt & Williams, No. 20 Dock Square, Boston, who would gladly continue the agency were it not for the want of space in this already overcrowded store.

---

100. This advertising handbill for Elder Elijah's patented cast-iron chimney caps fails to mention his connection with the Shakers, giving his address only as Groton Junction, Massachusetts.

Source: Hancock Shaker Village, Inc., Pittsfield, Mass.

101. This photograph shows Elder Elijah later in his life.
Source: Hancock Shaker Village, Inc., Pittsfield, Mass.

Elijah Myrick   131

Thomas Damon

(1819–1880) Hancock, Massachusetts

During his fifty-five years of Shaker life, Thomas Damon had the opportunity to work at various woodworking trades in all three of the Hancock Bishopric communities. His work at Hancock and Tyringham, Massachusetts, as well as at Enfield, Connecticut, illustrates the importance of looking at Shaker furniture in terms of its regional origin and characteristics rather than trying to tie it to a specific village.

Thomas was born in Johnston, Rhode Island, on the day after Christmas 1819, to Arthur and Olive Damon, who were introduced to Shakerism several years later. "In February 1825, the believers came from Enfield," Olive later wrote, "and opened the testimony of Christ's second appearing to us. . . . The believers visited us often, and taught us how to come in at the door of mercy and be saved. And a number set out to bear their crosses according to the testimony which they had received. They rejoiced, and felt exceedingly happy, and spake with new tongues, and praised God in the dance."[1]

In April 1827, the Damon family moved to the Enfield community in Connecticut, and Thomas Damon began his life as a Shaker. He lived at different times with the Center and West families at Enfield, and became an Elder at the Center House. His formal association with Grove Wright began in January 1846, when he moved to Hancock and was appointed as Elder Grove's assistant in the Ministry.

Thomas Hammond, a Shaker cabinetmaker from the Harvard community, visited Hancock in September 1846. As part of the record of his visit, he made one of the few known references to Thomas Damon actually working with wood at that time, mentioning that he had observed "Br. Thomas turning &c."[2] Nevertheless, Thomas Damon had been making furniture. In December 1846 he wrote a letter to George Wilcox, a cabinetmaker from Enfield, in which he described a desk he had made, which had an unusual false drawer face:

> Not having anything of importance to write about, I will proceed to comply with your request respecting the desk although I fear you will hardly obtain 5 cts. worth of information. Length 23 in. Width 21½ in. as wide as the bench would admit. Depth, back side 4½ in. front side 2¾" including lid & bottom. The desk is made precisely as any common desk, and slides in & out exactly like one of the drawers. When it is shoved in, it slides sufficiently far to admit of a *false drawer face* (about ½ in. in thickness) which is hung with brass butts so as to turn down to admit the desk's sliding out & in freely: this and all the rest that I have said relative to it, would no doubt have occurred to your mind, but as you requested the particulars I have been thus explicit. You will please suit yourself as to size and formation, "For where there is no law there is no transgression."[3]

The whereabouts of Elder Thomas's desk is not known at this time, and it is uncertain whether George Wilcox proceeded to make a similar piece. In any event, the letter provides an illustration of Shaker craftsmen sharing information about their furniture making.

Elder Thomas spent a good deal of time with Grove Wright working on church business, but a tall, signed case of drawers indicates that they also worked together in the joiners' shop. This handsome piece of furniture (described in detail in the portrait of Grove Wright) contains a handwritten note glued to the inside of the case identifying the two men as the craftsmen who built it sometime prior to January 13, 1853.

In the 1840s and probably into the 1870s, Elder Thomas was in charge of the manufacture of table swifts at Hancock. The swifts, umbrellalike folding devices used for winding yarn, were made and sold in three sizes (see ill. 102 and 103). Shakers visiting Elder Thomas in his shop recorded that he had "constructed machinery for cutting out and dressing up the various parts of the kind of swifts that are screwed to a table for use. . . . He is the inventor of these swifts and manufactures them by the wholesale at 50 cts per pair, and was at this time filling an order for 20,000 pair at that rate. Several of the Sisters were aiding in this Job, at such parts as they could perform, which were not a few."[4] Although Elder Thomas was not the inventor of the folding table swift, he certainly developed a distinctively recognizable design for those swifts made by the Shakers at Hancock. It is also doubtful that Elder Thomas was filling orders for 20,000 swifts. Production statistics from 1854 to 1860 indicate that he made on the average 920 swifts each year.[5] It is more likely that Elder Thomas was making 20,000 slats for swifts, which at 24 slats per swift meant that he could assemble over 830 swifts that year. Like many Shakers, Elder Thomas was inclined toward mechanization, and the arduous task of making 20,000 swift slats apparently motivated him to make mechanical improvements. He noted in his journal entry for October 10, 1854, that he "Started a new machine for planing & edging Swift slats, it worked charmingly and bid fair to be the 'Ne plus ultra' in that line" (see ill. 104 and 105).[6] This machine, now in the collection at the Shaker Museum at Old Chatham, illustrates Elder Thomas's mechanical ingenuity and woodworking skills, a combination of talents that

102. Thomas Damon had charge of the swift business at Hancock for many years. Swifts such as these were made to be mounted on tables rather than to be free standing on bases. They were used in a variety of tasks associated with textiles but most commonly held a skein of yarn while it was wound into a ball for knitting or onto a shuttle or quill for weaving. The form and design of the adjustable table-mounted pin cushions seem to have been associated with Elder Thomas's swift manufacturing.

Sources: Timothy D. Rieman (swift), and Hancock Shaker Village, Inc., Pittsfield, Mass. (pin cushion)

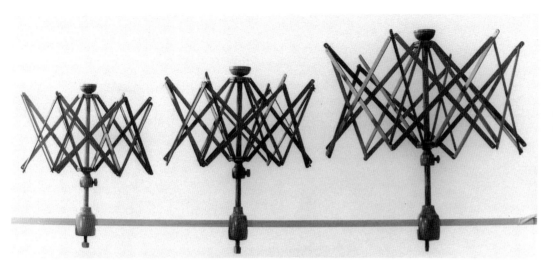

103. Yarn swifts were manufactured in three sizes, each with either a cup or a ball on top of the shaft. The cups were used to hold a ball of yarn mid wind.
Sources: Timothy D. Rieman (small); Jerry V. Grant (medium); Hancock Shaker Village, Inc., Pittsfield, Mass. (large)

104. The "Ne plus ultra," a four-sided planer/shaper, was devised and built by Elder Thomas to speed up the tedious job of making the slats used to assemble the freely turning "basket" that holds the skein of yarn on a swift. Each swift has twenty-four slats. The machine smoothed both flat sides and put a slight round on the edges—all in one pass through the machine.
Source: The Shaker Museum, Old Chatham, N.Y.

was fairly common among the best of the Shaker furniture makers.

At a Ministry meeting on October 7, 1860, Elder Thomas was appointed to take the place of Grove Wright as first Ministry Elder of the Hancock Bishopric. A journal entry made on that occasion notes that "Elder Grove being feeble & unable to speak has wrote a piece which was read by Br. Rusel expressing his feelings of quiet submission also a piece of recommendation for Elder Thomas from the Lebanon Ministry & the union of our leaders respecting the matter."[7]

It is not certain whether Elder Thomas continued to make furniture, but there are enough existing journal references to indicate that he spent the remainder of his life as an active Shaker leader. Records show Elder Thomas traveling to Shaker communities in New York, Massachusetts, and Connecticut during the 1870s, as well as making business trips to Boston, Hartford, and Albany. In 1877 he attended a "singing school" at New Lebanon with George Wilcox, to whom he had supplied the desk plans; and he traveled to Enfield, Connecticut, in May 1880, just two months before his death on July 28, 1880.

105. This closeup of the cutting mechanism on the device in illustration 104 shows both the vertical planing heads (for smoothing the sides of the slats) and the horizontal molding heads (for rounding their edges).
Source: The Shaker Museum, Old Chatham, N.Y.

Emmory Brooks

(1807–1891) Sodus Bay and Groveland, New York

With his father, mother, three brothers, and one sister, Emmory Brooks joined the Shakers at Sodus in May 1827; and although the rest of his family left in April of the following year, Emmory remained. He served the community in several positions of leadership. By the time the Sodus community moved to Groveland, New York, in 1837 and 1838, he had become a Trustee. During this time he was appointed to be associate Minister with Elder Jeremiah Tallcot, a position he held until May 12, 1851, when he was appointed to succeed Elder John Lockwood as first in the Ministry. When the Ministerial Order was dissolved in 1859, he was assigned to be Elder of the Gathering Order; and in 1861, Emmory became First Deacon of the West Family.

Elder Emmory made many pieces of furniture for the Groveland community between 1860 and 1890. His furniture is easily identifiable by its distinctive style and by his extensive use of black walnut, a wood not unknown but uncommon in Shaker furniture. Many of the pieces made by Elder Emmory can be traced back to 1895 when the Groveland community closed and much of the furniture was moved to Watervliet. In the 1930s several of these pieces were obtained from the Shakers by the New York State Museum and remain in that collection today.

Although Elder Emmory's signature has not been found on any of the pieces associated with him, documentation of his cabinetmaking comes from information supplied by Shakers who knew him—Srs. Jennie Wells, Polly Lee, and Ella Winship. In 1943, Jennie Wells wrote a letter to Charles C. Adams, the director of the New York State Museum, in which she noted that Emmory Brooks "made all the [Groveland] Sisters a black walnut bedstead." She included a letter written by Emmory Brooks to Eldress Polly Lee, dated January 1869, in which he cautions, "I am coming home after a while to finish your bedstead so do not let others medle with it or try to have it finished before I return"[1] (see ill. 110).

In 1892, Genevieve DeGraw, writing in the "Home Notes" in the *Manifesto,* sadly informed Shaker brothers and sisters everywhere that Elder Emmory had died. "He received the welcome which to him was 'glad tidings of great joy,'" she wrote, "for he had 'fought the good fight, finished his course and kept the faith.'"[2]

106. In the summer of 1930, photographer William F. Winter visited the South Family at Watervliet, where he took this photograph of a Shaker sister's retiring room. It is thought to have been Eldress Anna Case's room. Both the bed and the cupboard over a case of drawers are attributed to Emmory Brooks. The chair is typical of those made by Freegift Wells in the middle of the nineteenth century.

Source: New York State Museum, Albany, N.Y.

107. This little walnut stand is attributed to Br. Emmory because its construction is similar to other pieces that appear to be made by him, especially the pulls on the four smaller drawers and the unusually thick drawer fronts.
Source: The Shaker Museum, Old Chatham, N.Y.

108. Sr. Jennie Wells recalled that this walnut cupboard over a case of drawers was made by Br. Emmory. It is a fine example of his work and shows that he exercised considerable restraint in his attempt to update the traditional Shaker form of a cupboard over a case of drawers to the modern Victorian style, which was becoming more acceptable to the Shakers by the late 1860s. It is possible that the cupboard was made at a later date and attached to the top of what had been a case of drawers.
Source: New York State Museum, Albany, N.Y.

109. This walnut case of drawers was given to the New York State Museum by the Watervliet Shakers. It was attributed to Br. Emmory by Sr. Jennie Wells. In addition to the panel and frame construction and the use of walnut, two other details on this piece are associated with Br. Emmory's work. First, the drawer pulls are assembled from three separate pieces—a two-inch "stepped" cap, a collar between the cap and the drawer front, and the tenon (which is glued into the cap, passes through the collar, and is fastened into the drawer front). Second, the drawer fronts on this piece are exceptionally thick, nearly $1^1/_2$ inches. The reasons for these two peculiarities found in Br. Emmory's work are not known.

Source: New York State Museum, Albany, N.Y.

110. This walnut bedstead was purchased in the early 1930s from the Watervliet Shakers by Gertrude Reno Sherburne. Mrs. Sherburne had been raised by the Shakers at Watervliet and was able to purchase the bed that she recalled as having belonged to Eldress Polly Lee. The bed was sold to the Colonie Historical Society in 1978. If this is the same bed that Emmory referred to in his letter to Eldress Polly, in which he wrote, "I am coming home after a while to finish your bedstead so do not let others medle with it or try to have it finished before I return," this piece would date to the time of the letter, January 1869.

Source: Colonie Historical Society, Colonie, N.Y.

112. This walnut bedstead, one of at least a pair made by Emmory in this rather fanciful style, is very close in design to the bed photographed by William F. Winter in 1930 and may in fact be the same bed.
Source: The New York State Museum, Albany, N.Y.

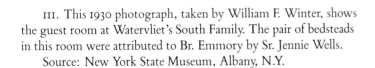

111. This 1930 photograph, taken by William F. Winter, shows the guest room at Watervliet's South Family. The pair of bedsteads in this room were attributed to Br. Emmory by Sr. Jennie Wells.
Source: New York State Museum, Albany, N.Y.

Eli Kidder

(1783–1867) Canterbury, New Hampshire

Eli Kidder's parents joined the Shaker community at Enfield, New Hampshire, in 1792, the year in which that community was formed. Eli, who was nine years old, and his brother Thomas were sent at that time to the Shaker village at Canterbury, some forty miles southeast of Enfield. The Canterbury community was also in its first year of existence.

James Daniels, another cabinetmaker at Canterbury (1767–1851), also joined the community in 1792, and it is likely that Eli learned the joiner's craft from Br. James, who was sixteen years older. The two men lived in the same village for many years, and their initials on several homemade planes suggest that a working relationship existed between them. These woodworking planes, perhaps made by them as well as used by them, have the initials "EK" and "ID" stamped in the wood (see ill. 113),[1] and are now at Hancock Shaker Village and the Shaker Museum in Old Chatham, respectively.

Br. Eli became an active leader in the church. In 1821 he was appointed second in the Elder's Lot in the Second Family, and from 1826 to 1848 he served as First Elder. He lived in the Church Family from 1848 until 1861 and then returned to the Second Family, where he remained in the position of First Elder for the rest of his life.

Apart from milestones that are noted in journals, the personal details of Elder Eli's life are rather sketchy. Early in his life, Eli was at one point thought to be near death from consumption, but he "miraculously recovered";[2] and although he was not a robustly healthy man, he lived to be eighty-three years old. He was described as a man who was "universally beloved,"[3] and he was genuinely mourned when he succumbed to lung fever in 1867.

Two documented pieces of furniture made by Elder Eli provide significant links to other pieces attributed to him, all of them sewing desks. On a drawer of the first desk, made of maple, bird's-eye maple, and pine (ill. 114), the following words are inscribed in ink: "Work stand made by Bro Eli Kidder aged 77 years. Jan 1861 Moved into by MEH Jan 18, 1861" (ill. 115). The second desk, made of pine, cherry, maple, and bird's-eye maple (ill. 116), bears this inscription in ink on a drawer: "Made by Br Eli Kidder ad. 77 yrs. For Almira Hill ad 40 yrs. January 1861. Chh Canterbury N.H. U.S.A." (ill. 117).

A detailed comparative analysis of these and two other sewing desks (ill. 118 and 119)—one in the collection at Hancock Shaker Village and one from a private collection—shows a close stylistic relationship that may be used to make an attribution to Elder Eli as the cabinetmaker who made all four of them.

113. These three woodworking planes at Hancock Shaker Village are part of a large set of planes that once belonged to Eli Kidder and, before him, to James Daniels, both of Canterbury, New Hampshire. The front of this ovolo sash plane at the right is marked with Br. Eli's initials (EK) and those of James Daniels (ID). A few planes marked in the same way are in the collection at the Shaker Museum in Old Chatham. Thus many of the planes used by these two craftsmen are still extant.

Source: Hancock Shaker Village, Inc., Pittsfield, Mass.

114. This piece bears the inscription, "Work stand made by Bro Eli Kidder aged 77 years. Jan 1861 Moved into by MEH Jan. 18, 1861." The initials MEH probably indicate that the workstand was made for the use of Marcia E. Hastings, who lived in the Church Family at Canterbury.

Source: The Shaker Museum, Old Chatham, N.Y.

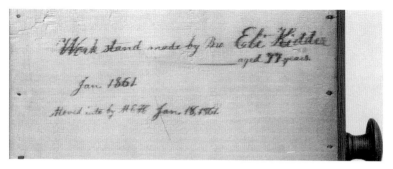

115. Br. Eli's inscription is on the bottom of one of the small drawers in the gallery of the worktable shown in illustration 114.
Source: Shaker Museum, Old Chatham, N.Y.

116. A second worktable, apparently made at the same time as the one in illustration 114, is inscribed, "Made by Br Eli Kidder ad. 77 yrs. For Almira Hill ad 40 yrs. January 1861. Chh [Church Family] Canterbury N.H. U.S.A." The similarity of this sewing desk to the one in illustration 114 and the fact that they were both produced in the same month may indicate that Br. Eli made them as a pair. The existence of other, similar sewing desks suggests that he may have made several more of these worktables.
Source: Philadelphia Museum of Art; given by Mr. and Mrs. Julius Zieget

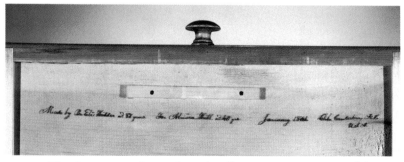

117. The signature on the workstand in illustration 116 is on one of the larger drawers in the lower portion of the case.
Source: Philadelphia Museum of Art; given by Mr. and Mrs. Julius Zieget

118. This worktable—one of two others seemingly related by their construction and design to the signed worktables made by Br. Eli—was once in the collection of Mrs. John Spring, who acquired it from the Shakers at Canterbury in the 1920s. The key for the upper right drawer has a tag labeled "L.2. DESK." stitched to the key. The "L" refers to a building at Canterbury and the "2" to a room in that building. This marking is consistant with the Shakers' method of labeling other materials that originated at Canterbury. The worktable has a bird's-eye maple work surface.

Source: Hancock Shaker Village, Inc., Pittsfield, Mass.

119. The other worktable related to Br. Eli's signed ones also shares a conspicuous similarity to the unsigned one in illustration 118. On both signed worktables the panels on the front of the desk are vertical whereas on the two unsigned examples they are horizontal. If the two unsigned pieces were made at the same time, as was apparently true in the case of the signed pieces, it would help to explain this difference in design between the signed and unsigned pieces. This worktable has a curly maple top. It has almost precisely the same dimensions as the piece in illustration 118.

Source: J. J. Gerald McCue

Henry Clay Blinn

(1824–1905) Canterbury, New Hampshire

The story of Henry Blinn's early years is that of a young boy with a love of books and learning who persisted in his desire to further his education during economic hard times.

Henry was the last of seven children born to Sarah Blinn and James M. Blinn in Providence, Rhode Island. Henry's father, the captain of a merchant ship that sailed between Providence and the West Indies, died of a fever in Kingston, Jamaica, the year after Henry was born, leaving his widow, Sarah, to raise their children.

Henry attended a primary school in Providence and then the city public school, but he was permitted "to enjoy the privilege only a few years, as it was found that so large a family of children was fast reducing the small income that had been left in the charge of [his] mother."[1] His parents were not members of any church, but Henry attended the Unitarian Sunday school at the church where his sister Sarah was a member. "Being privileged to take books from the [Sunday school] library," Henry recalled, "I became very much interested."

Books figured prominently in his life from early childhood, when he was given story books as presents; and he could recall buying his own first book for a penny at a bookstore run by an old man. "For the running of errands," he remembered, "I gathered a few pennies from time to time and purchased many more of these little books, and when I had saved enough to be the owner of a 'Mother Goose's Melodies' and a 'Peter Prim's Pride,' I thought myself quite wealthy."

At the age of twelve, however, economic necessity forced him to leave school and to take a job. He first worked in a clothing store in Providence. Here, as he later described, his tasks were:

> to open the store in the morning, build the fires, sweep the room, and then through the day and evening carry garments to the makers or to customers in every part of the city.

> This first experience in the business relations of the world did not please me, especially as I was obliged to go long distances at a late hour of the night and when the streets were poorly lighted. Stories of kidnappers were not uncommon. They were represented as being a class of men who stole children and sold them for slaves.

> There was an object in having the children hear these fables, as it evidently kept them more at their own homes. The effect, however, upon the minds of the children, did more harm than good, as these kidnappers or "bug-a-boos," who were said to steal children, did not exist. Such incentives to fright no doubt, increased the timidity of the listeners and made the dark, stormy nights doubly frightful.

When he was thirteen Henry became a jeweler's apprentice in the northern part of Providence. He was the youngest apprentice, and therefore his work consisted largely of chores—which he did from 7 A.M. to 6 P.M. At the request of Edward Knowles, the jeweler, he and the other apprentices attended the Knowles family's Baptist church. Henry was "kindly offered the privilege of attending an evening school during the winter," but because he lacked warm winter clothing and had to walk a mile through an obscure section of the city that frightened him, he gave it up after one night. "By this," he later wrote, "I lost the opportunity to add to a limited stock of education, very much to my regret."

Henry could read and write quite well, and he pursued his education by reading on his own. Nonetheless, he was anxious to find a place where he could earn his living and get a formal education at the same time. After eighteen months, he left the jeweler's and returned to live with his mother while he searched for a new job and a new home. Guided by "a holy light," as he later put it, Henry persuaded his mother to go with him to see a Shaker who was visiting Providence. They met Nathan Willard, a Shaker brother from Canterbury, who told Henry "of the kindness of the people, of their religious services, of their schools, and of their fields, orchards and gardens; so that [Henry] became fully determined to accompany him to his home in New Hampshire."

"It was the journey of a young Pilgrim," Henry wrote of his leaving Providence with Nathan Willard in September 1838.

At Boston we took the cars for Lowell, the terminus of the railroad at that date, going north. From Lowell, we rode to Concord, N.H., in a stage, and then hired a private conveyance to Shaker Village. Our trip from Concord was over the pine plains, through Loudon Village and over Beck's Hill. On reaching this last elevated spot, the whole of the Church Family was presented to view, and the presentation was a beautiful picture on the mind. At that date, the white and light yellow houses with bright red roofs, heightened the beauty of the village very much and "to my youthful mind," after a long and tedious journey, it seemed to be the prettiest place I had ever seen.

Everything at the Shakers was new and strange, and yet they received me with the kindest of care. My first impressions of the place and of the people were very pleasant, although I was among a new class of people, whose language, dress and manners were so unlike those of the city; yet their kindness found access to my heart, and at once I began to feel quite contented. That the people said yea and nay, instead of yes and no, had no bearing on my mind, and the plainness of their dress was rather agreeable than otherwise.

It was the auspicious beginning of a new life for Henry. He would spend the next sixty-seven years in the Shaker Society, and he was to become a printer, teacher, historian, author, beekeeper, stonecutter, tailor, dentist, cabinetmaker, and one of the most beloved and distinguished of the New Hampshire Shakers.

Henry was placed in the First, or Church Family, and James Johnson, an associate Elder who had charge of the mill and the wood-turning machinery at Canterbury, became his guardian. The first order of business was to counsel Henry regarding spiritual matters, and then he was put to work. In his first months at the community, Henry helped saw staves for pails (at the time, the Church Family made about a thousand pails a year for sale), he worked on the farm with other boys, and he served as an assistant in the blacksmith's shop.

That December, to his great delight, Henry began attending school again (there was a twelve-week winter term for the boys and a twelve-week summer term for the girls) and quickly began to make up for lost time away from the classroom. He was kept busy before and after school mending tinware and heading broom nails for Br. Thomas Hoit (who, as Henry later wrote, "was a universal chore man, and enjoyed the euphonious name of tinker"); but after three winters of formal school sessions, Henry became the boys' schoolmaster at Canterbury.

During the summer Br. Henry worked at the wool-carding machines for three months. Then, after helping the brethren with the

120. This photograph of Elder Henry tending his bees was part of what eventually became a series of fifty-eight stereopticon views of the Shaker Village at Canterbury. The pictures were made and sold by W. G. C. Kimball, photographer, of Concord, New Hampshire.
Source: Hancock Shaker Village, Inc., Pittsfield, Mass.

fall harvesting, he returned to school in the winter. At the close of the school term in 1842, Br. Henry was appointed to be schoolmaster, a position he held for eight years.

One of the few regrets he recorded during his first years as a Shaker was the occasion when he had to give up his books for inspection by the Elders, who were forming a library in the village. "This touched quite keenly my love for self," he wrote,

> and my little stock of books, brought from the city, which had been so choice, moved very slowly toward the place of deposit. Some of them were sent to the office, as not suitable for the family. They were stories about the Indians, battles on sea and land, or the history of some nation. Such books, we were told, encouraged a warlike disposition in the reader. Only a few of my books were saved, and among these were copies of "The Penny Magazine." These books, so full of illustrations and interesting stories, may be found in a good state of preservation in the library at the present date, 1899. This was to be my first prominent lesson in a united interest, and it was, no doubt, a very useful one. A small Bible was soon after presented to me as a better book for study, and I trust I made good use of the exchange. . . . At first, the reading of the Bible was a mere question of obedience, but ultimately it became a real pleasure and profit.

In the spring of 1843, Br. Henry was sent to the printing office at Canterbury to learn to set type and work the press; and his first job was to print the historic *Holy, Sacred and Divine Roll and Book.* "The acceptance of the work which would involve a book of some four hundred pages was a heroic venture on the part of the family," Br. Henry wrote, "as no one fully understood the business." But he helped to make it succeed.

In 1844, Br. Henry directed the printing and binding of one thousand copies of the "Juvenile Guide, or Manual of Good Manners," a manuscript from New Lebanon, New York; and during the same year he oversaw the printing of a four-hundred-page book entitled "Millennial Hymns." In 1848, Br. Henry drew a map of the Canterbury community,[2] part of his work as a historian that exists today as an invaluable guide to the village as it was then.

In January 1849 the *Divine Book of Holy Wisdom,* an inspired manuscript written at Watervliet, New York, was received for printing at Canterbury. This became a book of nearly seven hundred pages, and it took Br. Henry most of that year to direct the publication of an edition of twenty-five hundred copies. He wrote that he "was removed from the charge of the children and the school, as [his] whole attention was to be given to printing." He completed the project in December 1849.

Br. Henry subsequently resumed the care of the children and remained with them until 1852. Thomas Hammond, Elder and cabinetmaker from Harvard, visited Canterbury in 1851 and commented in his journal in June that he had gone "to the printing establishment managed by Henry Blynn, who also teaches the boys' school & takes care of the boys' spiritual matters. The Sacred Roll, & Divine Book of Holy Wisdom were printed here. They print hymns, anthems &c., with the notes attached to them. Henry set the types for the printing of the Sacred Roll & Holy Mother's Book; according to his statement. He is about 27 years old."[3]

In March 1852, Br. Henry was appointed to the Order of Elders; and though he was sorrowful at leaving the children, whom he dearly loved, in retrospect he saw this as a change that greatly broadened his horizons in life. After only a few months as an Elder, Henry was appointed as an Elder in the Ministry, and in this position he formed many new friendships in both the Canterbury and Enfield, New Hampshire, communities. He was for part of this time engaged as a tailor. Then, "as the demand for artificial teeth was on the increase," he became a dentist, "a form of work that was far more congenial, which gave [him] sufficient employment."[4] In November 1859 he

121. This portrait of Henry Clay Blinn was taken in the studio of
W. G. C. Kimball, of Concord, New Hampshire.
Source: Hancock Shaker Village, Inc., Pittsfield, Mass.

moved from the Ministry to become First Elder in the Canterbury Church Family.

Elder Henry continued his involvement with the printing operations at Canterbury, and he also made many trips to other communities besides Enfield as a member of the Ministry and as a Church Family Elder. In 1873 he took an extended trip to the New York, Ohio, and Kentucky communities, and became the first New Hampshire Shaker to visit the villages in Kentucky. Polly Reed of New Lebanon wrote of Elder Henry's visit there, "He is low spirited & out on a tour south & west for his health."[5] She added that Elder Henry was depressed because of a remark that had been made recently at the Canterbury community—"to this import that Elder Henry's influence was a detriment to the prosperity of that Society. This cut him to the heart & made a lasting wound."

Evidently the trip buoyed his spirits, for Elder Henry returned to Canterbury and led an active life for thirty-two more years. During that period, along with his other accomplishments, he became the author of *Advent of the Christ in Man and Woman,* a work published at Canterbury in 1896.

In addition to his other contributions, Elder Henry also left in the form of journal observations a historian's vividly detailed view of Shaker life in New Hampshire as well as glimpses of the other places and people he knew from his extensive travels as a Shaker leader. He also found the time and energy to become a furniture maker. We have this addendum to his autobiographical notes in the published *In Memorium,* covering the period after 1899:

Elder Henry lets fall the thread of history at this point. His amanuensis lifts it to connect the golden cord, which runs through the remaining six years of his stay with us.

Gradually, gracefully, he seemed to outgrow the responsibilities of earth. While to the last maintaining nominally the office of Minister and Trustee, he willingly resigned active duties to younger companions in both orders, depending upon them more and more.

That he might have all the care needful in his decline, apartments at the Infirmary were kept at his disposal; though he was never better pleased than when able to spend the day at his carpenter's bench, engaged in light cabinet work, a favorite occupation.[6]

Another account, written after his death, speaks of the work he accomplished late in his life: "Through declining years, Elder Henry gave us many specimens of his handiwork, neatly and lovingly wrought, and when the feeble hands laid aside the tools, and he sought the rest promised to all that labor, we heard his voice in words of blessing and assurance, which beautifully completed the closing record of his life, placing thereon the seal of love, peace, gentleness and goodness." [7]

One signed piece of furniture provides a documented illustration of Elder Henry's work as a cabinetmaker—a sewing desk, illustration 122, with inscription on the drawer.

a

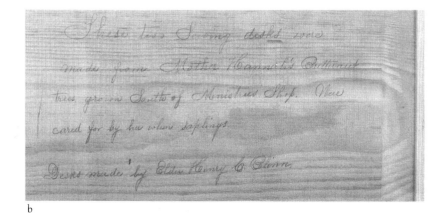

b

122. This sewing desk (**a**) has the following inscription written on the bottom of a small drawer in the upper gallery (**b**): "These two Sewing desks were made from Mother Hannah's Butternut trees, grown South of Ministries Shop. Were cared for by her when saplings. Desks made by Elder Henry C. Blinn."

Source: The Shaker Museum, Old Chatham, N.Y.

Henry Clay Blinn 151

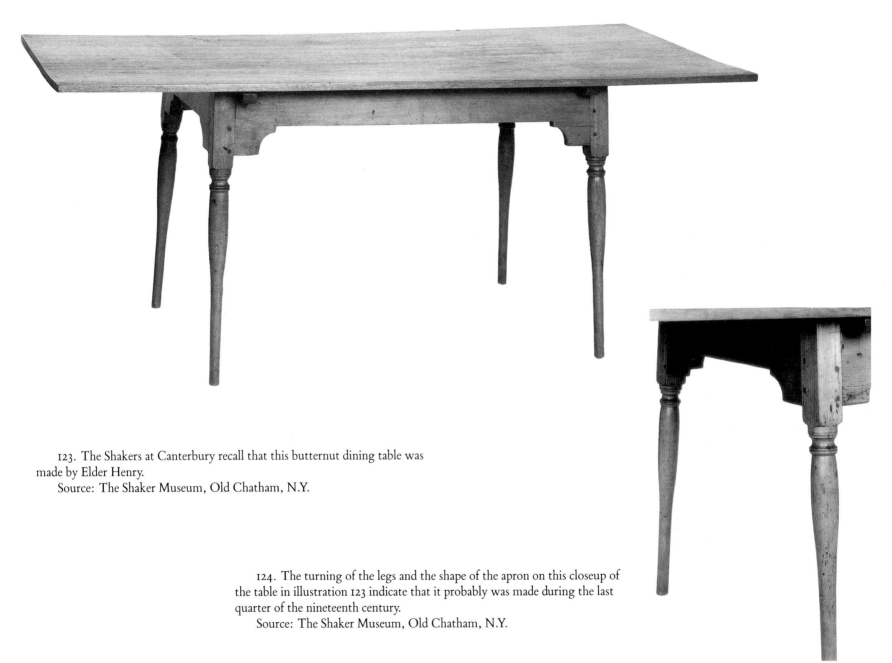

123. The Shakers at Canterbury recall that this butternut dining table was made by Elder Henry.
Source: The Shaker Museum, Old Chatham, N.Y.

124. The turning of the legs and the shape of the apron on this closeup of the table in illustration 123 indicate that it probably was made during the last quarter of the nineteenth century.
Source: The Shaker Museum, Old Chatham, N.Y.

Several other pieces of furniture can be attributed to Henry Blinn on the basis of museum records, oral history among the Canterbury Shakers, and inscriptions that relate to *The Manifesto*. These include a dining table at the Shaker Museum in Old Chatham, New York (ill. 123 and 124); two large cabinets in the Canterbury community, one of which is shown in illustration 125; and a secretary from a private collection.

A posthumous tribute was created with the publication in 1905 of *In Memorium: Elder Henry C. Blinn,* a volume that includes Elder Henry's "Autobiographical Notes" and more than ninety pages of eulogy in the form of letters, essays, and poems from his many friends. Some of the friends whose writings are included were, of course, Shakers, but many were citizens of the world from nearly every walk of life, including clergymen, physicians, and political leaders. The deep feelings and extremely high praise in their reminiscences about Henry compose the portrait of a man who left an indelible impression of charity and kindness on the people he knew in the course of his life as a Shaker. If there is such a thing as a Pantheon of Shakers, Henry Blinn is certainly commemorated in it by these people.

125. This chestnut cupboard with drawers is attributed to Elder Henry by Eldress Bertha Lindsay.
Source: Shaker Village, Inc., Canterbury, N.H.

Henry Green

(1844–1931) Alfred, Maine

Henry Green joined the Shakers at Alfred, Maine, when he was fifteen years old. He became a woodworking apprentice to Elder Joshua Bussell, and during the 1870s and 1880s made many pieces of furniture that have since been attributed to him by Shaker brothers and sisters who knew him at the Alfred community.

Br. Henry made all of his furniture during the years of the Shakers' numerical decline, and although much of it has the plain lines and distinctive proportions of earlier traditional Shaker furniture (ill. 127), other pieces such as writing desks that he made for the sisters in the 1880s (ill. 128) clearly show the inroads of Victorian influences. Interestingly, he made both the traditional pieces and the pieces with the modern, worldly features during the same period of his life. Although Henry made furniture in later years—for instance, a secretary with a bookshelf in 1905 (ill. 129)—and oval boxes in the years after that, he made few pieces of furniture after 1890.

Br. Henry was a schoolteacher, and he also served as a business agent for the Shakers for more than fifty years. He made innumerable trips to the New Hampshire mountains and to seashore communities in Maine and New Hampshire, where he sold at resort hotels such Shaker "fancy goods" as sewing baskets, sweaters, and other small household items. On these trips he used a folding table of his own design to display his wares, a surviving example of which is known to have been made by Br. Henry around 1880 (see ill. 130).

As Mary and Charles Carpenter relate in an article about Henry, he gained the respect and friendship of the people with whom he came in contact, and in later years he became known affectionately as "the Old Man of the Mountain."[1] Br. Henry became an elder in the Alfred Church Family in 1896, and fulfilled administrative duties in that capacity until the community closed in the spring of 1931. Elder Henry then moved to Sabbathday Lake, where he died that September at the age of eighty-seven.

127. This tailor's counter, made by Elder Henry around 1875, is similar in design to Shaker tailoring counters of the pre–Civil War period, although the use of oak as a primary wood would have been unusual earlier than the 1870s.
Source: Collection of The United Society of Shakers, Sabbathday Lake, Maine

126. Elder Henry Green.
Source: Collection of The United Society of Shakers, Sabbathday Lake, Maine

128. This sister's writing desk, thought to have been made in the mid-1880s, is one of more than a dozen desks of this style known to have been made by Elder Henry.

Source: Collection of The United Society of Shakers, Sabbathday Lake, Maine

129. Elder Henry made this secretary and attached bookshelf for Otis Wallingford, a non-Shaker laborer at the Alfred community. It is thought to have been made within a few years of the turn of the century. The piece is made of oak, walnut, maple, and pine.

Source: Collection of The United Society of Shakers, Sabbathday Lake, Maine

130. Elder Henry built this folding table to display the fancy goods that he sold on his many trips into the White Mountains of New Hampshire and to the Maine coastal resort towns. The table, which remains in the Sabbathday Lake community, is still useful for selling their products.

Source: Collection of The United Society of Shakers, Sabbathday Lake, Maine

Thomas Fisher

(1823–1902) Enfield, Connecticut

Noted for his deviation from earlier Shaker styles, Thomas Fisher carried the Enfield cabinetmaking tradition into the twentieth century. Br. Thomas, a Church Family carpenter and chair maker, was mentioned by Faith and Edward Deming Andrews in *Shaker Furniture* as "a Scotch convert at Enfield, Connecticut, whose prolific output is marked by decadent designs of Victorianism."[1] Br. Thomas used distinctively different woods in making his furniture, sometimes joining light and dark woods in striking contrast on the same surface plane, and he crafted some pieces in solid oak in a late Victorian style replete with carvings. A large quantity of oak furniture made by Br. Thomas was removed to Canterbury, New Hampshire, after the sale of the Enfield, Connecticut, property; and several pieces of this work bear his signature.

A small chest in a private collection bears the following inscription, written in ink on the side of a drawer: "Brother Thomas Fisher, cabinetmaker in the Enfield, New Hampshire [i.e., Connecticut] society, made this spice chest T. Fisher 1887." On the side of an adjacent drawer are the words, "Enfield Shakers 1887." In April 1977, a small lift-top box signed, "Sister A. Brooks, T. Fisher, '99," was sold at auction. Abigail Brooks, for whom the box apparently was made, lived in the North Family at Enfield until her death on April 13, 1901. Many other pieces that have been attributed to Br. Thomas based on their late-1800s Enfield provenance and style are in museum collections.

a

b

131. These cases of drawers are credited to Br. Thomas. Both are made of oak with walnut tops.

Sources: (a) Harriet S. Dickinson; (b) anonymous

132. This oak octagonal dining table was made by Br. Thomas.
Source: Shaker Village, Inc., Canterbury, N.H.

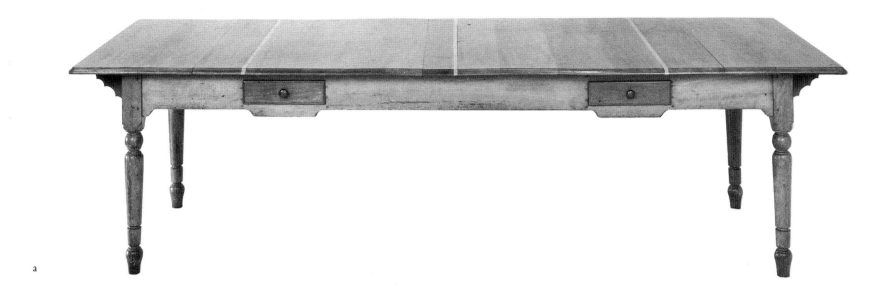

a

133. This table (**a**) is thought to have been made by Br. Thomas. The style of drawer construction (**b**) certainly is related to other pieces made at Enfield, Connecticut, and at Hancock, Massachusetts. It seems more than likely that Thomas reused drawers from some now-forgotten bank of small, tapered-sided drawers for the group of similar tables that he made. (**c**) A closeup showing decorative detail.

Source: Hancock Shaker Village, Inc., Pittsfield, Mass.

b

c

Thomas Fisher 161

Delmer Charles Wilson

(1873–1961) Sabbathday Lake, Maine

Delmer Wilson was placed in the Sabbathday Lake community by his mother in 1881, when he was eight years old. By his late teens he had become a skilled woodworker as well as an orchardist and a dairy herdsman. He was also to become a beekeeper, barber, and dentist; and he later developed artistic skills as a painter and photographer. In 1910, Delmer built a garage for the Shakers' first automobile, a 1910 Seldon.

As a woodworker, Br. Delmer was best known as a maker of oval boxes. He made many thousands of boxes in his lifetime, and a 1923 photograph (ill. 137) pictures him with a stack of 1,083 boxes that he had made during one winter's work. He was given the honorific title "Dean of the Carrier Makers" in a memorial tribute published in *The Shaker Quarterly* in 1961.[1]

In the same spirit as the many Shaker craftsmen who were his predecessors, Br. Delmer strove for excellence in all that he did, and *The Shaker Quarterly* declared that the work of his hands was a living memorial in the form of the boxes, furniture, carpentry work, paintings, photographs, and carefully cultivated orchards he left behind. Br. Delmer's expertise in different trades was sorely missed after his death in 1961, and posthumous tributes were paid to him when the remaining Shakers at Sabbathday Lake found it necessary to hire specialists from a variety of different fields to do the work that Elder Br. Delmer had taken care of by himself.

One piece of furniture, a pine and maple desk, is attributed to Delmer by Br. Theodore E. Johnson in *Hands to Work And Hearts to God*.[2]

134. Delmer C. Wilson.
Source: Collection of The United Society of Shakers, Sabbathday Lake, Maine

135. The Shaker community and all who join them at meals dine on tables that were made by Br. Delmer.
Source: © Ann Chwatsky from *Four Seasons of Shaker Life,* 1986

136. A pine and maple desk, made by Br. Delmer in 1896.
Source: Collection of The United Society of Shakers, Sabbathday Lake, Maine

137. In one of the most famous photographs ever taken of a Shaker craftsman, Br. Delmer is pictured in his shop, finishing his tally of the oval carriers he had made that winter—an astonishing total of 1,083.

Source: Collection of The United Society of Shakers, Sabbathday Lake, Maine

Epilogue: Light Out of Shadow

By incorporating relatively brief vignettes of the lives of certain brothers, the geographic scope of this book has been expanded to include all seven of the Shaker Bishoprics. We thus are afforded a broad view of Shaker society, a picture painted on a canvas that spreads from New Lebanon East to New England and West to Ohio and Kentucky. Taken together, the lives of these craftsmen also extend the chronological sweep of our view from the early flowering of the society into the years of its gradual decline. The composite group portrait that emerges is in some ways more intriguing and rewarding than any one definitive "life" could be.

The story of the Shakers in America is in essence a drama extending from colonial times to our own day. Although their history is known from beginning to denouement, this book provides the first full and in-depth portrayal of the furniture makers as players in this drama. At times we see an individual character only in a brief scene, sometimes with that person in silhouette or shadow. Nonetheless, as one reads on, new relationships begin to emerge—of the craftsmen to one another and to their work—and the puzzle pieces of the entire Society begin to fit together into a coherent whole. The full import of natural family ties and personal friendships, of a political or spiritual struggle here or a love story there, is often left to one's imagination.

But that is perhaps as it should be, as it always is to a degree in a real-life drama.

At times the appetite is whetted for more details, which aren't available. It may indeed be fitting that some of these individuals remain in partial shadow, their biographies incomplete. One effect is that the resulting group portrait emphasizes the larger community of Shaker brothers and sisters, which was always more important than any individual. It also reminds us that for these craftsmen true personal completion involved an *inner* spiritual harmony, which at best can be reflected only partially by the work of their hands and by the outward circumstances of their lives.

The Shakers believed in an eternal spirit energized by the communion between God and mankind. Elements of this communion are visible in the work left to us by the unique craftsmen of the sect; the spirit is still nourished in the daily life and worship of the Shakers who live today in Canterbury, New Hampshire, and Sabbathday Lake, Maine. Regardless of whether or not there is ever another great gathering of souls to the Shaker faith and community, there will always be a kindling of their spark whenever one senses the spirit embodied in the consecrated labor of Shaker hands.

Notes

Abbreviations

DLC: Library of Congress, Washington, D.C.

DeWint: Henry Francis DuPont Winterthur Museum, Winterthur, Del.

KyBgW: Western Kentucky University, Bowling Green, Ky.

KySP: Shakertown at Pleasant Hill, Harrodsburg, Ky.

MHarF: Fruitlands Museum, Harvard, Mass.

MPH: Hancock Shaker Village, Inc., Pittsfield, Mass.

N: New York State Library, Albany, N.Y.

NNASPR: American Society for Psychical Research, New York, N.Y.

NOC: Emma B. King Library, Shaker Museum, Old Chatham, N.Y.

OClWHi: Western Reserve Historical Society, Cleveland, Ohio.

Introduction

1. Anna White and Leila Sarah Taylor, *Shakerism, Its Meaning and Message; Embracing an Historical Account, Statement of Belief and Spiritual Experience of the Church from its Rise to the Present Day* (Columbus: Press of Fred. J. Heer, 1904), p. 73.
2. Ibid., p. 76.
3. Peter Whitney, *The History of the County of Worcester in the Commonwealth of Massachusetts* (Worcester: Isaiah Thomas, 1793), p. 163.
4. Inventory of property the "Widow Abigale [Abigail] Hawkins brought with her," OClWHi, Shaker Collection, IV A 30.
5. Samuel Banta, "Inventory," Church Family, Pleasant Hill, Ky., KySP.
6. "Daily Record of Events of the Church Family, Union Village, Ohio," OClWHi, Shaker Collection, V B 230.
7. *National Intelligencer* (Washington, D.C.) 20 (December 25, 1819), p. 1.
8. "An Inventory of the property of Nathan [and Betsy] Hasking [Haskins] taken the twelfth of January in the year of our Lord one thousand eight hundred and twenty two," OClWHi, Shaker Collection, II A 8.
9. Issac Youngs, "A Domestic Journal of Daily Occurrences," Church Family, New Lebanon, N.Y., N, Shaker Collection, Accession Number 13500.
10. "Some Account of the Shaking Quakers," *The American Museum and Universal Magazine* 10 (August 1791) 100–101.
11. [Benjamin Seth Youngs], *Testimonies of Christ's Second Appearing, Exemplified by the Principles and Practice of the True Church of Christ* (Albany: Published by the United Society, Called Shakers [Van Benthuysen, Printer], 1856), p. 630.
12. Edward Deming Andrews and Faith Andrews, *Shaker Furniture: The Craftsmanship of an American Communal Sect* (New Haven: Yale University Press, 1937), pp. 42–43.
13. Ibid., p. 42.
14. "Journal of Visitors Who Stayed Overnight at Union Village, Ohio," DLC, Shaker Collection, 239.
15. "Letter to David Darrow, Elder John Meacham, and Eldress Ruth Farrington at Union Village, Ohio," from "Ministry, New Lebanon, [N.Y.]," OClWHi, Shaker Collection, IV A 31.
16. Andrews and Andrews, *Shaker Furniture,* p. 45.
17. Isaac Youngs went to live with his Uncle Benjamin at the age of six months and remained with him until the age of nine years. Although his uncle was much involved with the Shakers during this period, Isaac did not actually live with the Shakers during his early years.
18. Edward Deming Andrews, "Millennial Laws, Miscellaneous Rules and Counsels—28," *The People Called Shakers: A Search for a Perfect Society* (New York: Oxford University Press, 1953), p. 287.
19. "Journal of Events, 1806–13, kept by Elder Peter Pease, Union Village, Ohio," DLC, Shaker Collection, 232.
20. "A Domestic Journal of Domestic Occurrences Kept Originally by Joseph Bennet, and then by Isaac Crouch, Nicholas Bennet, Isaac N. Youngs, and John M.

Brown," Church Family, New Lebanon, N.Y., OClWHi, Shaker Collection, V B 68.

21. References to the Bowmans appear throughout several New Lebanon Church Family account books. References to the purchases of tools and the selling of furniture are overshadowed by the Bowmans' sale of hides and skins to the Shakers' tannery.

22. "Journal of a Shaker Community at Canaan, 1813–43," Upper Canaan Family, New Lebanon, N.Y., DLC, Shaker Collection, 43.

23. "A Domestic Journal of Domestic Occurrences Kept Originally by Joseph Bennet," OClWHi, Shaker Collection, V B 70.

24. "A History of the Lower [Canaan] Family Commenced in 1869 and Continued Annually Thereafter," New Lebanon, N.Y., OClWHi, Shaker Collection, V B 84.

25. "Lebanon Springs," *Berkshire County Eagle* 46 (March 4, 1875) p. 3.

26. "Daily Journal Kept by Mary Dryer," Groveland, N.Y., OClWHi, Shaker Collection, V B 24. Some of these purchases are substantiated by the following entries in a Groveland Church Family account book (OClWHi, Shaker Collection, II B 13): "Bot 1 Doz Chairs 12.00" (December 11, 1839), and "Bot 1 Table 5.00" (October 10, 1840). Other purchases included chairs—one dozen on January 23, 1840—and tables—one on July 20, 1840 for $3.75, and two on December 1, 1840, for $4.00 each.

27. "Journal Containing a Sketch of the Origin of the 'Second Family' of the Church at Union Village, Ohio, 1836–1856," DLC, Shaker Collection, 234.

28. Ibid.

29. Journals recording the purchase of furniture for the new Church Family Dwelling House at Mount Lebanon include: OClWHi, Shaker Collection, V B 71, V B 123, and V B 124, and NOC, Accession Number 10,343.

30. "Historical Record of the Church Family, East Canterbury, N.H., 1890–1930," Canterbury Shaker Village Library.

31. Giles Avery, "[Pocket Diary for 1873]," Church Family, New Lebanon, N.Y., OClWHi, Shaker Collection, V B 119.

32. "Historical Record of the Church Family, East Canterbury, N.H., 1890–1930," p. 351.

33. "A Domestic Journal of Domestic Occurrences Kept Originally by Joseph Bennet," OClWHi, Shaker Collection, V B 71.

34. Ibid.

35. "Journal, 1862–1864," DLC, Shaker Collection, 240. The sister who kept this journal either mistakenly used the word "high" instead of "wide" or she was using the word "high" as a generic term to describe the old beds that they had used, which were high and wide enough to accommodate a trundle bed.

36. "Journal of the South Family Consisting of Brief Descriptions of Daily Activities," New Lebanon, N.Y., OClWHi, Shaker Collection, V B 167 and V B 168.

37. "Historical Record of the Church Family, East Canterbury, N.H., 1890–1930."

38. Ibid.

39. Conversation with Olive Hayden Austin in the winter of 1983. Mrs. Austin was a member of the Church Family, Hancock, Mass., from 1905 until 1935.

40. "Historical Record of the Church Family, East Canterbury, N.H., 1890–1930."

41. "Down in Tyringham. As a New York Correspondent Saw Things," *The Pittsfield Sun* 88 (September 15, 1887) p. 6. Reprinted from the *New York Evening Post*.

42. *Enfield Advocate* (September 6, 1918); information courtesy of Robert P. Emlen.

43. Sadie Neale, "Diary for 1929," MPH, Accession Number 1113.

44. Edward Deming Andrews and Faith Andrews, *Fruits of the Shaker Tree of Life: Memoirs of Fifty Years of Collecting and Research* (Stockbridge, Mass.: Berkshire Traveller Press, 1975), pp. 85–92.

45. Sidney Alberts to John Harlow Ott (letter, September 16, 1978), Hancock Shaker Village, Curatorial Records.

46. Berton Roueche, "A Small Family of Seven," *The New Yorker* 23 (August 23, 1947) 46–57.

David Rowley

1. "Religious Experience of David Rowley," Church Family, New Lebanon, N.Y., OClWHi, Shaker Collection, VI B 22. Unless otherwise noted, information concerning David Rowley's early life and religious conversion is from this source.

2. "A Domestic Journal of Domestic Occurrences Kept Originally by Joseph Bennet, and then by Isaac Crouch, Nicholas Bennet, Isaac N. Youngs, and John M. Brown," Church Family, New Lebanon, N.Y., OClWHi, Shaker Collection, V B 67.

3. Isaac Youngs, "A Domestic Journal of Daily Occurrences," Church Family, New Lebanon, N.Y., N, Shaker Collection, Accession Number 13500.

4. Freegift Wells, "Memorandum of Events," Church Family, Watervliet, N.Y., OClWHi, Shaker Collection, V B 285.

5. Isaac Youngs, "A Domestic Journal."

6. Ibid.

7. "Domestic Journal of Important Occurrences Kept for the Elder Sisters at New Lebanon, [N.Y.]," OClWHi, Shaker Collection, V B 60.

8. "A Domestic Journal of Domestic Occurrences Kept Originally by Joseph Bennet," OClWHi, Shaker Collection, V B 70.

9. Ibid.

10. Ibid.

11. Issac Youngs, "A Domestic Journal of Daily Occurrences."

12. Henry DeWitt, "Journal," Church Family, New Lebanon, N.Y., OClWHi, Shaker Collection, V B 97.

13. Issac Youngs, "A Domestic Journal of Daily Occurrences."

14. "Book of Visions," Church Family, New Lebanon, N.Y., NNASPR.

Freegift Wells

1. Freegift Wells, "Miscellaneous Writings Including Diary Entries for 1870," Church Family, Watervliet, N.Y., OClWHi, Shaker Collection, VII B 276.

2. His name is also spelled "Fregift."

3. Family genealogy.

4. Nathaniel S. Prime, *A History of Long Island from its First Settlement by Europeans to the Year 1846* (New York: Robert Carter, 1845), p. 142.

5. "Longevity among the Shakers," *Berkshire County Eagle* 34 (June 4, 1863), p. 1.

6. Freegift Wells, "Miscellaneous Writings."

7. A full treatment of Br. Freegift's work as a chairmaker can be found in Charles R. Muller and Timothy D. Rieman, "Freegift Wells, Chairmaker," in *The Shaker Chair* (Canal Winchester, Ohio: Canal Press, 1984), pp. 6–27.

8. Freegift Wells, "Memorandum of Events," Church Family, Watervliet, N.Y., OClWHi, Shaker Collection, V B 289. Br. Freegift's diaries for the years 1812 to 1840 and 1857 to 1865 (OClWHi, Shaker Collection, V B 285–296) are extant.

9. Freegift Wells, "Memorandum of Events," V B 293.

10. Ibid.

11. "Daily record of events of the Church Family," Union Village, Ohio, OClWHi, Shaker Collection, V B 230.

12. Daniel Miller, "Journal of Passing and Important Events at Union Village Ohio," OClWHi, Shaker Collection, V B 237.

13. Freegift Wells,"Memorandum of Events," V B 296. Unless otherwise noted, information about Br. Freegift's cabinetmaking activities between 1857 and his death are from this source.

14. Freegift Wells, "Memorandum of Events," V B 296.

15. Ibid.

16. "Records of the Church at Watervliet, N.Y.," OClWHi, Shaker Collection, V B 281.

17. "Bodock" probably refers to "Bois d'arc" or properly Osage Orange (*Maclura pomifera*).

18. Ann Buckingham, "Diary for 1871," Church Family, Watervliet, N.Y., N, Shaker Collection, CM16877.

19. Freegift Wells, "Copies of Testimonies, Letters, Remarks and Other Writings," OClWHi, Shaker Collection, VI B 51.

20. Ann Buckingham, "Diary for 1871."

Samuel Calvin Ely

1. "Diary Kept by Calvin Ely, 1780–1816," OClWHi, Shaker Collection, V B 11.

2. Ibid.

3. "Record of Calvin Ely's Death, 1816, Written by His Mother, Beulah Ely," OClWHi, Shaker Collection, VI A 2.

Isaac Newton Youngs

1. Elisha D. Blakeman, "Eulogical, to Brother Isaac N. Youngs Written September 1866," OClWHi, Shaker Collection, VI B 21.

2. Isaac Youngs had an intense interest in music and the use of music in worship. His determined efforts helped bring about a unification of the Shakers' system for writing music. He wrote to Rubin Dickey and Abraham Perkins when he despaired of success: "Concerning our music affair I see no prospect of there being much gained in that matter. . . . Believers are all so rivitted to habit that they are unwilling to alter. Some use the round notes, & some hug tight to the patent notes:—scarcely anyone seems willing to adopt any thing unless to make some alteration themselves, as in the case of altering the patent notes at Watervliet" (August 11, 1839, OClWHi, Shaker Collection, IV A 37). Three years later the situation had changed greatly, due in large part to his efforts. He wrote to David Buckingham on November 16, 1842, "Believers are now approximating so near uniformity in writing music, that it seems encouraging; and if we can get something printed, it will seem to fasten it, so that it will 'stay put' " (OClWHi, Shaker Collection, IV A 38). The next year, in order to "fasten it," Br. Isaac printed one hundred copies of his pamphlet, *A Short Abridgement of the Rules of Music. With Exercise, and a Few Observations, for New Beginners.*

3. "A Domestic Journal of Domestic Occurrences Kept Originally by Joseph Bennet, and then by Isaac Crouch, Nicholas Bennet, Isaac N. Youngs, and John M. Brown," Church Family, New Lebanon, N.Y., OClWHi, Shaker Collection, V B 70–71.

4. Isaac's grandfather, Seth Youngs, Sr., was a well-known eighteenth-century Connecticut clockmaker. His son Benjamin, Isaac's uncle, also became a clockmaker, who moved to Schenectady, New York, in 1766. Benjamin Youngs and his wife lived

in Schenectady until 1806, but in 1792 they purchased four hundred acres of land in Watervliet, forty of which they sold to the Shakers in 1794. In 1799, Benjamin and his wife donated one hundred acres to the Shakers, and this property became the site of the South Family. In 1806 they moved to Watervliet, and while a Shaker there, Benjamin made several clocks that are dated and inscribed with his name.

5. Isaac Youngs, "Clock Maker's Journal with Remarks & Observations. Experiments &c. Beginning in 1815," OClWHi, Shaker Collection, V B 86.

6. Seth Youngs Wells, Br. Isaac's mentor during his early years at Watervliet and later for nearly twenty years at New Lebanon, died in 1847. On the day of Br. Seth's death Br. Isaac wrote, "Brother Seth came into the faith in the year 1798, was gathered to Watervliet. In a short time he was appointed as a lead among the Young Believers, and stood as an elder till the year 1821—when he was released from the Eldership for the purpose of being devoted to writing, preparing Mss. for the Press; and to superintend school affairs as occasion might require. After this he resided mostly at the Church at Watervliet, until the year 1828, when he took up his residence here at New Lebanon: where he has continued in his occupation of writing" (Alonzo G. Hollister, compiler, "Book of Spirit Voices of Communication from Departed Spirits," Mount Lebanon, N.Y., 1873, NNASPR). It seems fitting that after Br. Seth's death, Br. Isaac took over the task of being clerk and scribe for the Church Family.

7. In 1787, Amos Jewett (1753–1834) was among the first to be "gathered" into the Shaker community of New Lebanon, N.Y. He remained there until his death. One known example of his work, now in a private collection, is a clock in a tall pine case signed, "*1796 Amos Jewett Canaan No. 38.*" Another example is a clock dial in the collection of the Shaker Museum in Old Chatham, New York, inscribed in ink: "*1789 Amos Jewett New Lebanon No. 12.*" Br. Amos made clock No. 38 in 1796, which leaves one wondering how many he had made by the time Isaac Youngs came to learn clockmaking from him nineteen years later—or how many he may have made during the rest of his lifetime. Br. Isaac later recalled that in 1815, "I got in to have some privilege in the shop with Amos Jewett who had made wooden clocks, he was very clever to me" (Isaac Youngs, "Clock Maker's Journal," OClWHi, Shaker Collection, V B 86). Upon Br. Amos's death a Shaker brother wrote: "Our worthy and faithful brother Amos Jewett, who continued as peaceable and clever, as ever, and as steady as a clock until he drew his last breath . . . left neither blot nor stain behind him (Isaac Youngs, "A Domestic Journal of Daily Occurrences," Church Family, New Lebanon, N.Y., N, Shaker Collection, Accession Number 13500).

8. Isaac Youngs, "A Clock Maker's Journal," OClWHi, Shaker Collection, V B 86." This manuscript is reproduced in Andrews and Andrews, *Shaker Furniture*, pp. 112–14, and in James V. Gibbs and Robert F. W. Meader, "Shaker Clock Makers," *National Association of Watch and Clock Collectors, Bulletin, Supplement*, No. 7 (Summer 1972), pp. 12–22. Br. Isaac's importance as a clockmaker exceeds his out-put. For many years the repair and maintenance of the community's clocks and those of other Shaker communities as well as neighbors' clocks was his responsibility. In a letter to Amos Stewart, Giles Avery noted: "The old clock in the house hall, the old standby, is in want of the doctor and loudly calls for br[other] Isaac to come home again, notwithstand[ing] our mortification being so illeritate in clockquackery" (OClWHi, Shaker Collection, IV A 37).

9. "Benjamin Lyons's Journal," DLC, Shaker Collection, 45.

10. Isaac Youngs, New Lebanon, N.Y., to Elder Benjamin Seth Youngs, South Union, Ky. (letter, December, 1833), OClWHi, Shaker Collection, IV A 36.

11. Ibid.

12. [Seth Wells?], New Lebanon, N.Y., to Benjamin Seth Youngs, South Union, Ky. (letter, circa 1833), OClWHi, Shaker Collection, IV A 36.

13. "Journal Kept by Isaac N. Youngs," Church Family, New Lebanon, N.Y., OClWHi, Shaker Collection, V B 134.

14. Isaac Youngs, "A Domestic Journal of Daily Occurrences," Church Family, New Lebanon, N.Y., N, Shaker Collection, Accession Number 13500.

15. Ibid.

16. Ibid.

17. Ibid.

18. "Journal Kept by Isaac N. Youngs."

19. Ibid.

20. Isaac Youngs, "A Domestic Journal of Daily Occurences."

21. Isaac Youngs, "A Concise View of the Church of God and of Christ on Earth: Having its Foundation in the Faith of Christ's First and Second Appearing," Church Family, New Lebanon, N.Y. (1856), DWint, Andrews Collection, McKinstry 861.

22. Isaac Youngs, New Lebanon, N.Y., to Andrew Houston, Union Village, Ohio (letter, August 6, 1830), OClWHi, Shaker Collection, IV A 36.

23. Isaac Youngs, "Biography in Verse," Church Family, New Lebanon, N.Y., DWint, Andrews Collection, McKinstry 1010. Reprinted in Andrew Deming Andrews and Faith Andrews, *Fruits of the Shaker Tree of Life: Memoirs of Fifty Years of Collecting and Research* (Stockbridge, Mass: Berkshire Traveller Press, 1975), pp 129–34.

24. "Journal Kept by Isaac Youngs."

25. Ibid.

26. Ibid.

27. Daniel Crosman, New Lebanon, N.Y., to the Ministry at Harvard and Shirley, Mass. (letter, May 12, 1860), OClWHi, Shaker Collection, IV A 43.

28. "A Domestic Journal of Domestic Occurrences Kept Originally by Joseph Bennet," OClWHi, Shaker Collection, V B 71.

29. Ibid.

30. Ibid.

31. Ibid. There are several versions of the cause of Br. Isaac's death, one of which is that he jumped from the window because he thought the building was burning.

32. Alonzo G. Hollister, compiler, "Book of Spirit Voices of Communication from Departed Spirits," New Lebanon, N.Y., 1873, NNASPR.

Benjamin Lyon

1. "Journal of Benjamin Lyon, June 12, 1816—February 8, 1818," DLC, Shaker Collection, 43.

2. Ibid. In *Shaker Furniture* (p. 45), the Andrewses record an inscription on a pine case of drawers with cupboard made at New Lebanon, which read "Aug. 29, 1817. J[?]B & G.L." Although they propose that John or Job Bishop and Garret Lawrence were the makers of this piece, the uncertainty of the reading of the letter "J" in this inscription and the lack of evidence that Garret Lawrence was a cabinetmaker open the possibility that the piece was the work of Anthony Brewster and Benjamin Lyon, with the inscription reading instead, "A B & B. L." This piece of furniture would fit neatly into the sort of work that these two cabinetmakers were doing at about this time. For example, on November 19, 1816, "Benjamin & Anthony finished a case of drawers for the brethrens chamber"; and on January 15 and 20, 1817, Br. Benjamin records that "Anthony and I work at a case of drawers" and "Anthony and I tacles the drawers with considerable zeal" ("Journal of Benjamin Lyon," DLC, Shaker Collection, 43).

3. "Journal of Benjamin Lyon, February 1818—March 1820," DLC, Shaker Collection, 44.

4. Ibid.

5. Ibid.

6. "Farm Journal 1858–1867 [Church Family, Second Order, New Lebanon, N.Y.]," MPH, Accession Number 401. Hannah Train, Jr., was a sister in the Second Order of the Church Family at New Lebanon. She was born on December 30, 1783; was admitted to the Shakers August 18, 1810; and died in July 1864.

7. "A Journal of Domestic Events Kept by Benjamin Lyon. 1839–1847," DeWint, Andrews Collection, McKinstry 834.

Anthony Brewster

1. Benjamin Lyon, "Journal of Benjamin Lyon June 12, 1816–February 8, 1818, Concerning Events in the Family of the Second Order, [New Lebanon, NY]," DLC, Shaker Collection, 43.

2. Isaac Youngs, "Clock Maker's Journal with Remarks & Observations. Experiments &c. Beginning in 1815," OClWHi, Shaker Collection, V B 86.

3. Benjamin Lyon, "Journal."

4. Ibid.

5. Ibid. See also comments on Anthony Brewster and Benjamin Lyon working together on furniture in note 2 of the chapter on Benjamin Lyon.

6. Edward Deming Andrews and Faith Andrews, *Shaker Furniture: the Craftsmanship of an American Communal Sect* (New Haven: Yale University Press), p. 45.

7. The collection at the Shaker Museum in Old Chatham, New York, contains several woodworking planes with the initials "A.B." stamped into them. These planes came from the Church Family workshops at New Lebanon, and it is likely that they were once used by Anthony.

8. Isaac Newton Youngs, "Narrative of Various Events," DLC, Shaker Collection, 42.

9. Isaac Youngs, "A Domestic Journal of Daily Occurrences," Church Family, New Lebanon, N.Y., N, Shaker Collection, Accession Number 13500.

10. Ibid.

Amos Stewart

1. "A Domestic Journal of Domestic Occurrences Kept Originally by Joseph Bennet, and then by Isaac Crouch, Nicholas Bennet, Isaac N. Youngs, and John M. Brown," Church Family, New Lebanon, N.Y., OClWHi, Shaker Collection, V B 67.

2. Benjamin Lyon, "Journal of Benjamin Lyon. June 12, 1816–February 8, 1818, Concerning Events in the Family of the Second Order, [New Lebanon, NY]," DLC, Shaker Collection, 43.

3. "Western Letters, Manuscript III [1809–1911]," Union Village, Ohio, and Pleasant Hill, Ky., DLC, Shaker Collection, 248.

4. Giles B. Avery, "Diary, 1838–1847," Church Family, First and Second Order, New Lebanon, N.Y., OClWHi, Shaker Collection, V B 107. This diary was kept in part by Br. Aaron Bill.

5. "A Domestic Journal of Domestic Occurrences Kept Originally by Joseph Bennet," OClWHi, Shaker Collection, V B 70–71.

6. Several planing machines were made either to be used at New Lebanon or to be sold to other Shaker communities. In 1836, Amos Stewart directed the building of a machine that was sold to the Enfield, New Hampshire, brethren for $400. Isaac Youngs described in his journal the work done on the machine: "On the said machine Amos S[tewart] worked about 775 hours and Hiram R[ude] 816 or about 160 days work at 10 hours pr. day. The iron turning lathe was used 30 days—the cast

iron amounted to $72.54 iron and steel $41.10. . . . It was a good piece of work"
(N, Shaker Collection, Accession Number 13500). The machine weighed 2,800
pounds.

7. Amos Stewart received a patent on November 22, 1864 (Patent Number
45,191) for his "Improvement in Water-Wheels." According to the patent document,
"This invention relates to the peculiar form or shape of the buckets, and to a
particular manner of applying the water to the wheel, whereby the journals [bear-
ings] of the wheel-shaft are not subjected to any lateral pressure, and much friction
thereby avoided."

8. "A Domestic Journal of Domestic Occurrences Kept Originally by Joseph
Bennet," OClWHi, Shaker Collection, V B 70–71.

9. Ibid.

10. From the Ministry, New Lebanon, N.Y., to Elder Peter Long, Groveland,
N.Y. (letter, December 19, 1865), OClWHi, Shaker Collection, IV A 25.

11. "Farm Journal 1858–1867 [Church Family, Second Order, New Lebanon,
NY]," MPH, Accession Number 401.

12. Giles Avery, "Pocket Diary for 1866," Church Family, New Lebanon, N.Y.,
OClWHi, Shaker Collection, V B 112.

13. Ibid.

14. "A Domestic Journal of Domestic Occurrences Kept Originally by Joseph
Bennet," OClWHi, Shaker Collection, V B 71.

15. Ibid.

Robert Johns

1. "Journal A [typescript copy]," South Union, Ky., KyBgW, Shaker Collection. Additional information about Robert Johns was supplied by Julia Neal.

Thomas Hammond, Jr.

1. Thomas Hammond, "Journal [copy]," Church Family, Harvard, Mass.,
OClWHi, Shaker Collection, V B 40.

2. Grove Blanchard, "Journal," Church Family, Harvard, Mass., OClWHi,
Shaker Collection, V B 46.

3. Clara Endicott Sears, *Gleanings from Old Shaker Journals* (Harvard, Mass.:
Fruitlands Museum, 1916), p. 232.

4. "Daily records of activities at both Harvard and Shirley, Massachusetts,"
OClWHi, Shaker Collection, V B 54.

Daniel Sering

1. "Church Journals of Current Events at Union Village [Ohio] Kept by
William Reynolds [1862–1877]," OClWHi, Shaker Collection, V B 255–259.

2. "Church Journals," V B 257.

3. "Church Journals," V B 259.

4. "Church Journals," V B 257.

Richard McNemar

1. Hazel Spencer Phillips, *Richard the Shaker* (Oxford, Ohio: Oxford Press,
1948), p. 73.

2. Ibid., p. 75.

Henry DeWitt

1. Henry DeWitt, "Journal," Church Family, New Lebanon, N.Y., OClWHi,
Shaker Collection, V B 97.

2. Ibid.

3. The term "close [i.e., clothes] pins" as used here refers to the pins or pegs that
were either tenoned or threaded into railings surrounding most Shaker rooms.
Clothes and other items were hung on these pegs.

4. Henry DeWitt, "Journal."

5. Isaac Youngs, "A Domestic Journal of Daily Occurrences," Church Family,
New Lebanon, N.Y., N, Shaker Collection, Accession Number 13500.

6. Henry DeWitt, "Journal."

7. Ibid.   8. Ibid.   9. Ibid.   10. Ibid.

11. "A Domestic Journal of Domestic Occurrences Kept Originally by Joseph
Bennet, and then by Isaac Crouch, Nicholas Bennet, Isaac N. Youngs, and John M.
Brown," Church Family, New Lebanon, N.Y., OClWHi, Shaker Collection,
V B 70.

12. Ibid.

Grove Wright and Abner Allen

1. From the Ministry, Enfield, Conn., to Elder Grove Blanchard, Harvard, Mass.
(letter, December 20, 1852), OClWHi, Shaker Collection, IV A 10.

2. This piece is illustrated in *The Shakers: An Exhibition Concerning Their Fur-*

niture, *Artifacts and Religion with Emphasis on Enfield, Connecticut* [Exhibition Catalogue] (Hartford, Conn.: The Women's Auxiliary of the United Cerebral Palsy Association of Greater Hartford, 1975), p 7.

3. Alonzo G. Hollister, "Autobiography of the Saints, or Stray Leaves from the Book of Life—Grove Wright," OClWHi, Shaker Collection, VI B 37.

4. "History of the Enfield Community with References to Some of the Changes in the Ministry," OClWHi, Shaker Collection, V B 8.

5. Thomas Damon, "Memoranda, &c, Mostly of Events and Things which Have Transpired Since the First of January, 1846," NOC, Accession Number 13,357.

6. Ibid.

7. Grove Wright, Hancock, Mass., to Grove Blanchard, Harvard, Mass. (letter, February 10, 1854), OClWHi, Shaker Collection, IV A 20.

8. Thomas Damon, "Memoranda, &c."

9. Ibid.

10. Ibid.

11. "Daily Memorandum Book of the Center Family [Enfield, Conn.]," OClWHi, Shaker Collection, V B 18.

12. [Grove Wright, "Diary,] 1860," DWint, Andrews Collection, McKinstry 822.

13. Ibid.

14. Thomas Damon, Hancock, Mass., to the Ministry, New Lebanon, N.Y., (letter, May 2, 1861), OClWHi, Shaker Collection, IV A 20.

Orren N. Haskins

1. Orren N. Haskins, "Reflections, 1887," OClWHi, Shaker Collection, VII A 8.

2. Orren Haskins's father, Nathan, took with him to the Shakers a "Set of joiners tools" (OClWHi, Shaker Collection, II A 8).

3. Edward Deming Andrews and Faith Andrews, *Shaker Furniture: The Craftsmanship of an American Sect* (New Haven: Yale University Press, 1937), p. 46.

4. Ibid.

5. "A Domestic Journal of Domestic Occurrences Kept Originally by Joseph Bennet, and then by Isaac Crouch, Nicholas Bennet, Isaac N. Youngs, and John M. Brown," Church Family, New Lebanon, N.Y., OClWHi, Shaker Collection, V B 70–71.

6. "Series of Journals and Diaries Kept by Giles B. Avery," OClWHi, Shaker Collection, V B 104–107, 109–15, 117–26.

7. "A Domestic Journal of Domestic Occurrences Kept Originally by Joseph Bennet."

8. Ibid.

9. Ibid.

10. Ibid.

11. "Journal of the South Family, [New Lebanon, N.Y.]," OClWHi, Shaker Collection, V B 167.

Elisha D'Alembert Blakeman

1. Elisha D. Blakeman, "Journal of Daily Occurrences," OClWHi, Shaker Collection, V B 131.

2. Ibid.

3. Ibid.

4. Stephen Munson, New Lebanon, N.Y., from the Elders at Groveland, N.Y. (letter, October 11, 1838), OClWHi, Shaker Collection, IV A 36.

5. Ibid.   6. Ibid.   7. Ibid.   8. Ibid.

9. Henry DeWitt, "Journal," OClWHi, Shaker Collection, V B 97.

10. Isaac Youngs, "A Domestic Journal of Daily Occurrences," Church Family, New Lebanon, N.Y., N, Shaker Collection, Accession Number 13500.

11. "The Boys Journal of Work," Church Family, New Lebanon, N.,Y., OClWHi, Shaker Collection, V B 137.

12. Ibid.

13. Stooking means gathering and piling sheaves of grain in shocks to cure and dry. The term, used by Br. Elisha, is a British variant of the verb "to shock."

14. "A Domestic Journal of Domestic Occurrences Kept Originally by Joseph Bennet, and then by Isaac Crouch, Nicholas Bennet, Isaac N. Youngs, and John M. Brown," Church Family, New Lebanon, N.Y., OClWHi, Shaker Collection, V B 70–71.

15. "The Boys Journal of Work."

16. Ibid.

17. Isaac Youngs, "A Domestic Journal of Daily Occurrences."

18. [Elisha D. Blakeman], "Statistics Relating to Printing Herb Labels and Packages," OClWHi, Shaker Collection, III A 23.

19. Isaac Youngs, "A Domestic Journal of Daily Occurrences."

20. Isaac Youngs, "A Domestic Journal of Daily Occurrences."

21. Elisha D. Blakeman and James S. Glass, "A Daily Journal or Diary, of Work &c. Performed by the Boys and Their Caretaker, in the First Order, New Lebanon, Columbia Co., N.Y.," NOC, Accession Number 7212.

22. Ibid.   23. Ibid.   24. Ibid.   25. Ibid.

26. "A Domestic Journal of Domestic Occurrences Kept Originally by Joseph Bennet."

27. Ibid.

28. Ibid.

29. "A Daily Journal or Diary, of Work &c. Performed by the Boys and Their Caretaker."

30. Philemon Stewart, New Lebanon, N.Y., to the Beloved Ministry at New Lebanon, N.Y. (letter, March, 1872), OClWHi, Shaker Collection, IV A 44.

31. Polly Ann Reed, "Daily Pocket Diary for 1872," OClWHi, Shaker Collection, V B 165.

32. After Derobigne Mortimer Bennett left his Shaker home, he eventually married and became a successful publisher of the *Truthseeker,* a weekly newspaper dedicated to liberalism in religion. He became nationally prominent when he was imprisoned as a result of charges brought against him for sending indecent materials through the mails. The Shakers defended him in print against the unfair charges of his accuser, Anthony Comstock.

33. Elisha D. Blakeman, *Two Hundred Poetical Riddles. For the Instruction and Amusement of Children and Youth* (New York: D. M. Bennett, 1875).

Samuel Humphrey Turner

1. Isaac Youngs, "A Domestic Journal of Daily Occurrences, Church Family, New Lebanon, N.Y., N, Shaker Collection, Accession Number 13500.

2. Samuel Turner, Pleasant Hill, Ky., to Calvin Green, New Lebanon, N.Y. (letter, April 26, 1827), DLC, Shaker Collection, 245.

3. Isaac Youngs, "A Domestic Journal of Daily Occurrences."

4. The hat form marked with Calvin Reed's name is illustrated in June Sprigg's catalogue *Shaker: Masterworks of Utilitarian Design Created between 1800 and 1875 by the Master Craftsmen and Craftswomen of America's Foremost Communal Religious Sect* (Katonah, N.Y.: Katonah Gallery, 1983), p. 26, without attribution to Samuel Turner. Both hat forms are illustrated in her catalogue *Shaker Design* (New York: Whitney Museum of American Art, 1986), pp. 176–77, in which Sprigg speculates about the possibility of this form having been made by Samuel Turner.

5. Isaac Youngs, "A Domestic Journal of Daily Occurrences."

Giles Bushnell Avery

1. Giles Avery kept personal diaries over the years, and a good many of these still exist. A relatively complete collection of his diaries, covering the periods 1832–47, 1859–69, and 1871–81, is in the Western Reserve Historical Society Library, OClWHi, Shaker Collection, V B 104–107, 109–15, 117–26.

2. Giles Bushnell Avery, *Autobiography by Elder Giles B. Avery, of Mount Lebanon, N.Y.* (East Canterbury, N.H.: United Society of Shakers, 1891).

3. Giles Avery, "Pocket Diary for 1880," OClWHi, Shaker Collection, V B 125.

4. Ibid.

5. Giles Bushnell Avery, *Autobiography by Elder Giles B. Avery.*

6. Ibid.

George M. Wickersham

1. "A Domestic Journal of Domestic Occurrences Kept Originally by Joseph Bennet, and then by Isaac Crouch, Nicholas Bennet, Isaac N. Youngs, and John M. Brown," Church Family, New Lebanon, N.Y., OClWHi, Shaker Collection, V B 70. Shumway was the surname of a family living in the towns of New Lebanon and Lebanon Springs. Members of this family frequently worked for the Shakers as carpenters and cabinetmakers. Either William, John, or Charles may have been employed to build this piece of furniture. Wickersham designed the Great Stone Barn, of which only the shell still stands at the North Family site following a fire in 1972. George Wickersham's plans for this barn are in the collection of the New York State Museum.

2. John B. Wickersham of Philadelphia, who died on March 25, 1892, was a manufacturer of ornamental iron furniture and iron railings and fences. He worked in New York and Washington, D.C., as well as in Philadelphia. In his obituary in the *Philadelphia Public Ledger,* he was credited with conceiving the idea for and publishing illustrations of an elevated railway to relieve crowded conditions along Broadway in New York City. He was also credited with designing fire escapes that were, according to the *Ledger,* copied throughout the country.

3. A photograph of this lap desk was published as illustration number 38 in *The Shakers: An Exhibition Concerning Their Furniture, Artifacts and Religion with Emphasis on Enfield, Connecticut* [Exhibition Catalogue] (Hartford, Conn: The Women's Auxiliary of the United Cerebral Palsy Association of Greater Hartford, 1975).

4. George M. Wickersham, *How I Came to Be a Shaker* (Mount Lebanon, N.Y.: 1891).

5. "Diary Kept by an Unidentified Sister," New Lebanon, N.Y., OClWHi, Shaker Collection, V B 173.

Alfred Merrick Collier

1. Arthur Lake Collier, *A Family Sketch* (Salem, Mass.: privately printed by Lavender Printing Co., 1951), pp. 22–29.

2. Thomas Hammond, "Journal," Church Family, Harvard, Mass., OClWHi, Shaker Collection, V B 40.

3. Grove B. Blanchard, "Journal," Church Family, Harvard, Mass., OClWHi, Shaker Collection, V B 45.

4. Grove B. Blanchard, "Journal," Church Family, Harvard, Mass., OClWHi, Shaker Collection, V B 46.

5. "Physicians' Journal . . . Collected by Susan H. Myrick in 1843," Harvard, Mass., OClWHi, Shaker Collection, V B 41.

6. "Daily Journal Containing Brief Comments on Weather, Farming, Meetings, and Visitors," Harvard, Mass., OClWHi, Shaker Collection, V B 53.

7. "A Journal Kept by Alfred Collier for His Own Benefit. Continued from Book No. 2. Commenced Feb. 1859," Church Family, Harvard, Mass., MHarF.

8. Daily Record of activities both at Harvard and Shirley, OClWHi, Shaker Collection, V B 55.

9. [Alfred Collier], "Journal Kept by an Unidentified Resident," OClWHi, Shaker Collection, V B 219. This section draws heavily from the "Journal."

10. "A Journal Kept by Alfred Collier for His Own Benefit."

11. [Alfred Collier], "Journal Kept by an Unidentified Resident."

12. Grove B. Blanchard, "Journal for the Year 1864," MPH, Accession Number 327.

13. Ibid.

14. Arthur Lake Collier, *A Family Sketch: Supplement* (privately printed, 1958), pp. 528–32.

15. Collier, *A Family Sketch,* pp. 82, 263–64.

Elijah Myrick

1. "Harvard Church Family Records, November 1840 to June 1843," MHarF.

2. "Journal Containing Some of the Most Important Transactions of the Church at Harvard, [Mass.]," OClWHi, Shaker Collection, V B 50.

3. Ibid.

4. Grove B. Blanchard, "Journal," Church Family, Harvard, Mass., OClWHi, Shaker Collection, V B 46.

5. Patent Number 90380, was granted to Elijah Myrick on May 25, 1869.

6. Polly Ann Reed, "Pocket Diary for 1873," Mount Lebanon, N.Y., OClWHi, Shaker Collection, V B 166.

Thomas Damon

1. "Testimony of Olive Damon," DLC, Shaker Collection, 2.

2. Thomas Hammond, "Journal," Church Family, Harvard, Mass., OClWHi, Shaker Collection, V B 36.

3. Thomas Damon, Hancock, Mass., to George Willcox, Enfield, Conn. (letter, December 23, 1846), OClWHi, Shaker Collection, IV A 19.

4. John Harlow Ott, *Hancock Shaker Village: A Guidebook and History* (Pittsfield, Mass.: Shaker Community, Inc., 1976), second ed., pp. 116–17.

5. This accounting of pails and swifts made at Hancock from 1854 through 1860 is from "[Grove Wright, Diary,] Hancock, Mass. 1860," DWint, Andrews Collection, McKinstry 822.

Year	Pails	Swifts	No. 1	No. 2	No. 3
1854	154	910			
1855	201	801			
1856	200	1152	492	465	266
1857	292	925	398	327	200
1858	197	416	179	110	127
1859	133	1211	294	294	235
1860	105	1028	349	406	273

6. Thomas Damon, "Memoranda, &c., Mostly of Events and Things which Have Transpired Since the First of January, 1846," NOC, Accession Number, 13,357.

7. "Daily Memorandum Book of the Center Family, [Enfield, Connecticut]," OClWHi, Shaker Collection, V B 18.

Emmory Brooks

1. Jennie Wells, Watervliet, N.Y., to Dr. Charles Adams, Director, New York State Museum, Albany, N.Y. (letter), N, Shaker Collection.

2. Genevieve DeGraw, "Home Notes," *Shaker Manifesto* 22 (February 1892), p. 44.

Eli Kidder

1. Until the early part of the nineteenth century, when a person's name began with "J," it was often printed as "I," as it is in this instance.

2. "Domestic Journal of Important Occurrences Kept by the Elder Sisters at

New Lebanon," OClWHi, Shaker Collection, V B 60. Br. Eli's illness is also mentioned in a letter dated February 17, 1845, from the Ministry at Enfield, N.H., to Elder Rufus Bishop at New Lebanon, N.Y. (OClWHi, Shaker Collection, IV A 13): Br. Eli Kidder "has been confined to his room all winter; and it is expected that he cannot be restored to health. He is troubled with an affection of the liver, combined with dropsy."

3. Henry C. Blinn, "A Historical Record of the Society of Believers in Canterbury, N.H., East Canterbury, 1892," volume I, p. 211, Shaker Library, Canterbury, N.H.

Henry Clay Blinn

1. *In Memoriam: Elder Henry C. Blinn 1824–1902* (Concord, N.H.: Rumford Printing Co., 1905). This memorial, which includes Henry's autobiographical notes, is the source for much of the quoted information in this portrait.

2. Blinn's maps are discussed in Robert P. Emlen, *Shaker Village Views* (Hanover, N.H.: University Press of New England, 1987), pp. 103–13.

3. "Journal of Trips Made by the Harvard Ministry to Other Shaker Communities," OClWHi, Shaker Collection, V B 36.

4. *In Memoriam*.

5. Polly Ann Reed, "Pocket Diary for 1873," OClWHi, Shaker Collection, V B 166.

6. *In Memoriam*.

7. Ibid.

Henry Green

1. Mary Grace and Charles H. Carpenter, "The Shaker Furniture of Elder Henry Green," *Antiques* 105 (May 1974) 119–25.

Thomas Fisher

1. Edward Deming Andrews and Faith Andrews, *Shaker Furniture: The Craftsmanship of an American Communal Sect* (New Haven: Yale University Press, 1937), p. 62.

Delmer Charles Wilson

1. A carrier is an oval box with an attached handle. Br. Delmer made the carriers, and the Shaker sisters lined them with cloth and added the fittings needed to make them into fancy sewing baskets. "In Memoriam: Delmer Charles Wilson, 1873–1961," *The Shaker Quarterly* 1 (Winter 1961) 135–37.

2. Theodore E. Johnson, *Hands to Work and Hearts to God: The Shaker Tradition in Maine* (Brunswick, Maine: Bowdoin College, 1969).

Selected Bibliography

Andrews, Edward Deming. *The Community Industries of the Shakers.* New York State Museum Handbook, no. 15. Albany: University of the State of New York, 1932.

———. "Designed for Use—The Nature and Function in Shaker Craftsmanship." *New York History* 31 (July 1950):331–41. Also issued separately under the title *Shaker Furniture,* Cooperstown, N.Y.: New York Historical Association, 1950.

———. [Exhibition Catalogue]. Whitney Museum of American Art, New York, N.Y., November 12–December 12, 1935. New York: Whitney Museum of American Art, 1935.

———. *The Furnishings of Shaker Dwellings and Shops* [Exhibition Catalogue]. Berkshire Museum, Pittsfield, Mass., October 10–30, 1932. Pittsfield: Berkshire Museum, 1932.

———. "Kentucky Shakers." *Antiques* 52 (November 1947):356–57.

———. "Living with Antiques." *Antiques* 81 (April 1962):408–11.

———. "The New York Shakers and Their Industries." *Circular 2.* Albany: New York State Museum, October 1930.

———. *Shaker Craftsmanship and Art* [Exhibition Catalogue]. Berkshire Museum, Pittsfield, Mass., July 1940. Pittsfield: Berkshire Museum, 1940.

———. "Shaker Design." *Art in America* 46 (September 1958):45–49.

———. *Shaker Furniture* [Exhibition Program]. Lenox Library Association, Lenox, Mass., August 23–September 8, 1934. Lenox: Lenox Library Association, 1934.

———. "Shaker Furniture." *Interior Design* 25 (May 1954):60–66.

———. "A Shaker House in Canaan, New York." *Antiques* 82 (April 1962): 408–11.

Andrews, Edward Deming, and Faith Andrews. "Craftsmanship of an American Religious Sect." *Antiques* 14 (August 1928):132–36.

———. "The Furniture of an American Religious Sect." *Antiques* 15 :191–96.

———. "An Interpretation of Shaker Furniture." *Antiques* 23 (January 1933): 6–9.

———. *Religion in Wood: A Book of Shaker Furniture.* Bloomington: Indiana University Press, 1966.

———. *Shaker Furniture: The Craftsmanship of An American Communal Sect.* New Haven: Yale University Press, 1937.

———. *Work and Worship: The Economic Order of the Shakers.* Greenwich, Conn.: New York Graphic Society, 1974.

"Antiques in Domestic Settings. [No.] XII. Shaker Home of Mr. and Mrs. E. D. Andrews in Pittsfield, Mass."*Antiques* 30 (October 1936):162–63.

"Antiques in Domestic Settings. [No.] XXIX. Summer Home of Mr. and Mrs. E. D. Andrews." *Antiques* 35 (January 1939):10, 30–32.

Blatchford, Isabel. "The Shakers and Their Achievement." *Arts and Antiques* 1 (May 1965):25–31.

Butler, J. T. "Shaker Arts and Crafts." (London) *Connoisseur* 177 (June 1971): 130–32.

Carpenter, Mary Grace, and Charles H. Carpenter. "The Shaker Furniture of Elder Henry Green." *Antiques* 105 (May 1974):119–25.

"Children's Furniture." *Design Quarterly,* no. 57 (1963): 46–48.

Coomaraswamy, A. K. "Shaker Furniture." *Good Work* 28 (Summer 1965): 69–71.

Day, Cyrus L. "Late Shaker Chairs." *Antiques* 64 (November 1953):396.

Dodd, Eugene Merrick. "Functionalism in Shaker Crafts." *Antiques* 98 (October 1970):588–92.

Drew, M. "Native American Furniture." *Hobbies* 55 (February 1951):65–66.

Dyer, Walter A. "The Furniture of the Shakers: A Plea for its Preservation as Part of our National Inheritance." *House Beautiful* 65 (May 1929):650, 669–73.

Dyer, Walter, and Ester Stevens Fraser. *The Rocking Chair: An American Institution.* New York, 1928, pp. 36–41.

Emerich, A. D., and A. H. Benning, eds. *Community Industries of the Shakers: A New Look. A Catalog of Highlights of an Exhibition at the New York State Museum 1983–84.* Albany: Shaker Heritage Society, 1983.

Filley, Dorothy M. *Recapturing Wisdom's Valley: The Watervliet Shaker Heritage, 1775–1975.* Colonie, N.Y.: Town of Colonie and Albany Institute of History and Art, 1975.

Flint, Charles L. *Mount Lebanon Shaker Collection.* New Lebanon, N.Y.: Mount Lebanon Shaker Village, 1988.

Gibbs, James V., and Robert F. W. Meader. "Shaker Clock Makers." *National Association of Watch and Clock Collectors, Bulletin, Supplement,* no. 7 (Summer 1972).

Handberg, Ejner. *Shop Drawings of Shaker Furniture and Woodenware.* Stockbridge, Mass.: Berkshire Traveller Press, [1973].

———. *Shop Drawings of Shaker Furniture and Woodenware.* Stockbridge, Mass.: Berkshire Traveller Press, 1980.

———. *Shop Drawings of Shaker Furniture and Woodenware—Book II.* Stockbridge, Mass.: Berkshire Traveller Press, [1975].

———. *Shop Drawings of Shaker Furniture and Woodenware—Volume III.* Stockbridge, Mass.: Berkshire Traveller Press, 1977.

Kassay, John. *The Book of Shaker Furniture.* Amherst, Mass.: University of Massachusetts, 1980.

Knotts, Benjamin. "Hands to Work and Hearts to God." *Metropolitan Museum of Art Bulletin,* n.s 1 (March 1943):231–36.

Lassiter, William. "The Shakers and Their Furniture." *New York History* 44 (July 1946):369–71.

Malcolm, Janet. "The Modern Spirit in Shaker Design." *Early American Antiques* 2 (April 1974):8–13. Previously published in *Shaker: Furniture and Objects from the Faith and Edward Deming Andrews Collections.* 1973. pp. 18–22.

Meader, Robert F. W. *Illustrated Guide to Shaker Furniture.* New York: Dover Publications, 1972.

Muller, Charles R. *The Shaker Way.* Worthington, Ohio: Ohio Antiques Review, 1979.

Ray, Mary Lyn. "A Reappraisal of Shaker Furniture." In *Winterthur Portfolio 8,* ed. by Ian M. G. Quimby. Charlottesville: Pub. for Henry Francis Du Pont Winterthur Museum by University Press of Virginia, 1973.

———. Introduction to True Gospel Simplicity: Shaker Furniture in New Hampshire. Concord, N.H.: New Hampshire Historical Society, 1974.

Renwick Gallery. *Shaker: Furniture and Objects from the Faith and Edward Deming Andrews Collections Commemorating the Bicentenary of the American Shakers.* Washington, D.C.: Smithsonian Institution Press, 1973.

Rieman, Timothy D., and Charles R. Muller. *The Shaker Chair.* Canal Winchester, Ohio: Canal Press, 1984.

The Shaker Chair: Strength, Spriteliness & Modest Beauty [Exhibition Catalogue]. The Shaker Museum, Old Chatham, N.Y., June 26–October 15, 1982. Old Chatham, N.Y.: Shaker Museum, 1982.

The Shakers: An Exhibition Concerning Their Furniture, Artifacts and Religion with Emphasis on Enfield, Connecticut [Exhibition Catalogue]. The Women's Auxiliary of the United Cerebral Palsy Association of Greater Hartford, Conn., November 7–11, 1975. Hartford, Conn.: The Women's Auxiliary of the United Cerebral Palsy Association of Greater Hartford, 1975.

The Shakers: Pure of Spirit, Pure of Mind [Catalogue]. Duxbury, Mass.: Art Complex Museum, 1983.

The Shakers: Their Arts and Crafts [Exhibition Catalogue]. Philadelphia Museum of Art, April 19–May 20, 1962. *Philadelphia Museum Bulletin* 57 (Spring 1962):67–114.

Shea, John. *The American Shakers and Their Furniture, with Measured Drawings of Museum Classics.* New York: Van Nostrand and Reinhold, 1971.

Sprigg, June. *By Shaker Hands*. New York: Alfred A. Knopf, 1975.

————. *Shaker: Masterworks of Utilitarian Design Created between 1800 and 1875 by the Master Craftsmen and Craftswomen of America's Foremost Communal Religious Sect* [Exhibition Catalogue]. The Katonah Gallery, Katonah, N.Y., November 20, 1983–January 8, 1984. Katonah, N.Y.: Katonah Gallery, 1983.

————. *Shaker: Original Paints & Patinas*. Catalogue of an exhibition held at the Muhlenberg College for the Arts, Allentown, Penn., November 17, 1987–January 10, 1988. 1987.

————. *Shaker Design*. Catalogue of an exhibition held at the Whitney Museum of American Art, New York, May 29–August 31, 1986; and at the Corcoran Gallery of Art, Washington, D.C., October 4, 1986–January 4, 1987. New York: Whitney Museum of American Art, 1986.

True Gospel Simplicity: Shaker Furniture in New Hampshire [Exhibition Catalogue]. New Hampshire Historical Society, Concord, N.H., July 3–September 30, 1974. Concord, N.H.: New Hampshire Historical Society, 1974.

Upton, Charles W., and Helen Upton. "Living with Antiques: Shaker Adventure." *Antiques* 90 (July 1966):84–89.

Photo Credits

Ill. 1, 2, 3, 6, 11, 12, 13, 17, 18, 19, 23, 29, 32, 41, 42, 46, 47, 48, 49, 52, 53, 55, 56, 57, 58, 59, 60, 61, 62, 64, 69, 74, 84, 85, 92, 93, 95, 100, 104, 105, 113, 118, 119, 123, 124, 131, 133, and frontispiece: Paul J. Rocheleau

Ill. 20, 54, 63, 65, 66, 70, 71, 72, 73, 77, 79, 80, 102, and 103: Timothy D. Rieman

Ill. 21: Jerry V. Grant

Ill. 25: Mary Rezny

Ill. 33: Elmer Ray Pearson

Ill. 34 and 107: Lees Studio

Ill. 38: Robert F. Kent

Ill. 40: David Hildebrand

Ill. 43, 44, and 45: Joseph E. Worley

Ill. 50: Daniel Farber

Ill. 67 and 68: John Kassay

Ill. 81: June Sprigg

Ill. 86 and 87: Greg Heisey

Ill. 90, 106, and 111: William F. Winter

Ill. 99: Richard Lewis

Ill. 108, 109, 110, and 112: Harry Bigelman

Ill. 116 and 117: Eric Mitchell

Ill. 125: Perron Studio

Ill. 132: Bill Finney

Ill. 135: Ann Chwatsky

Index